AI Fro...
Navigating the Cutting Edge

Book Three of the NewBits AI Trilogy

Our Journey Reaches New Heights as We Explore the Latest Frontiers of Artificial Intelligence.

Through Breakthrough Technologies and Innovation, We Will Be Discovering How Advanced AI Systems are Transforming Our World and Shaping Our Future.

"It's all about the bits...especially the new bits."

GIL OREN

GIL OREN

AI FRONTIER: NAVIGATING THE CUTTING EDGE

AI Frontier: Navigating the Cutting Edge
Book Three of the NewBits AI Trilogy
by Gil Oren

Published by NewBits Media
A Division of NewBits, LLC
newbits.ai
First Edition: 2024
Printed in the United States of America

ISBN: 9798301297458

This is a work of non-fiction. All information presented is believed to be accurate at the time of publication. The author and publisher disclaim any liability in connection with the use of this information.

AI DISCLOSURE
This book was created in collaboration with artificial intelligence. Content was partially generated, edited, and refined using leading AI language models. The author has carefully reviewed, verified, and takes full responsibility for all content. This approach aligns with our mission at NewBits Media, a division of NewBits, LLC, to demonstrate practical applications of AI technology while maintaining high standards of quality and accuracy.

Cover design created with AI assistance.

Some names and identifying details may have been changed to protect the privacy of individuals.

GIL OREN

To My Friends, My Chosen Family

- whose friendship is a treasured gift,
illuminating my path and enriching my journey.

GIL OREN

TABLE OF CONTENTS

GIL OREN

WELCOME TO THE NEWBITS AI TRILOGY:
BOOK THREE

Our journey through the world of Artificial Intelligence has been transformative. Book One established the fundamental principles that form the bedrock of AI understanding, while Book Two equipped us with practical tools and applications. Now, we stand at the forefront of innovation, ready to explore the cutting edge of AI technology. As breakthrough developments emerge at an unprecedented pace, understanding these advancements and their implications has become essential for anyone seeking to remain at the vanguard of technological progress.

AI Frontier: Navigating the Cutting Edge charts our course through the latest developments shaping the future of artificial intelligence. Where Book One illuminated AI's foundations and Book Two revealed its practical applications, this final volume of our trilogy explores the breakthrough technologies and innovations driving AI's evolution. We'll examine revolutionary advances across the entire AI landscape, from groundbreaking research and model architectures to emerging tools, platforms, and development frameworks. Our journey continues through sophisticated language models, data analytics tools, audio and visual processing platforms, healthcare applications, robotics systems, gaming innovations, and emerging cross domain integrations. As these technologies advance, we'll explore the heightened importance of ethical considerations and responsible development practices at the cutting edge. This knowledge is crucial not only for technologists but for decision makers and innovators across all sectors seeking to understand and leverage emerging AI capabilities.

Our exploration now takes us into the heart of AI innovation, examining transformative developments in core technologies and their applications. You'll discover how cutting edge AI systems, tools, and platforms are reshaping our understanding of what's possible, learn to evaluate emerging technologies, and understand their potential impact across various domains. Whether you're a professional tracking technological progress or an enthusiast eager to glimpse the future of AI, this book provides the insights needed to navigate this rapidly evolving landscape.

The timing of this volume is particularly significant. As AI capabilities expand exponentially, the gap between breakthrough developments and their practical understanding grows wider. Organizations and individuals often struggle to grasp the implications of emerging AI technologies, tools, and platforms and their potential impact on various sectors. This book bridges that gap, providing clear insight into the latest developments shaping the AI landscape.

This exploration of cutting edge developments represents the culmination of our trilogy. Building on the fundamentals from Book One and the practical applications from Book Two, it reveals how current innovations are reshaping our world and defining our future. Each chapter unveils another facet of AI's evolving capabilities, empowering you to understand and evaluate emerging technologies. The knowledge gained here will prove invaluable in anticipating and adapting to future developments in AI technology.

Throughout this book, we maintain our commitment to clarity and comprehensive coverage. Complex innovations are examined thoughtfully, with real world examples illustrating their potential impact and applications. You'll gain not just awareness of cutting edge developments, but the understanding needed to evaluate their significance and potential implications for various domains.

The insights developed through this volume will prove crucial in a world increasingly shaped by artificial intelligence. As breakthrough technologies continue to emerge and evolve, the ability to understand and evaluate these developments becomes essential. Whether you're looking to anticipate technological trends, guide strategic decisions, or ensure responsible implementation of advanced AI capabilities, this book provides the foundation you need.

The path ahead is both enlightening and transformative. Through detailed examination and clear explanations, we'll explore the innovations driving AI's evolution, the ethical considerations they raise, and the responsible practices they demand. We'll discover how different sectors are being reshaped by breakthrough technologies, and how these advances are creating new possibilities across domains.

Let's continue our journey together, exploring the frontiers of artificial intelligence and understanding the developments shaping our future. Welcome to the final phase of your AI journey, where innovation meets understanding, and potential transforms into reality.

GIL OREN

CHAPTER 1: INTRODUCTION TO AI FRONTIER

The landscape of artificial intelligence has transformed dramatically since our exploration began. From foundational concepts to practical applications, we have witnessed an unprecedented acceleration in AI capabilities, accessibility, and impact. As we embark on this final volume of our trilogy, we stand at a remarkable threshold where breakthrough technologies are reshaping our understanding of what's possible with AI while demanding increased attention to responsible advancement.

The evolution of AI development tells a compelling story of innovation and transformation. Where once AI implementation required extensive expertise and substantial resources, we now see the emergence of sophisticated systems that push the boundaries of capability while becoming increasingly accessible. This progression from complex, specialized systems to more advanced yet implementable solutions marks a fundamental shift in how we approach artificial intelligence.

The current state of AI innovation reflects both the

maturation of established approaches and the emergence of groundbreaking new paradigms. We see this in the convergence of research and practical application, where theoretical advances rapidly translate into real-world capabilities. The scale of modern AI systems has grown exponentially, enabling capabilities that were once thought beyond reach while presenting new challenges and opportunities for implementation and responsible development.

Understanding these cutting-edge developments requires a sophisticated perspective that builds upon our previous exploration. The fundamental concepts we examined in Book One and the practical applications we explored in Book Two now serve as the foundation for comprehending more advanced innovations. This progression allows us to delve deeper into the technological breakthroughs shaping AI's evolution while maintaining clear connections to established principles.

Our journey through this book will explore the frontiers of AI advancement across multiple dimensions. From revolutionary research breakthroughs to innovative application domains, we will examine how cutting-edge developments are transforming the possibilities of artificial intelligence. This exploration encompasses the full spectrum of modern AI innovation, providing comprehensive insight into the technologies shaping our future and the principles guiding their responsible development.

The importance of advanced understanding becomes particularly crucial as AI capabilities continue to expand. Organizations and individuals must now grasp not only the fundamentals of AI but also the implications and applications of breakthrough technologies. This deeper comprehension enables more effective evaluation, implementation, and optimization of advanced AI solutions while supporting informed decision-making about emerging capabilities.

As we begin this exploration of AI's cutting edge, we find

ourselves at a unique moment in technological evolution. The convergence of increased computational power, sophisticated algorithms, and innovative approaches has created unprecedented opportunities for advancement. Understanding these developments, their implications, and their potential applications becomes essential for anyone seeking to remain at the forefront of AI innovation while ensuring its responsible progression.

The modern AI landscape represents an intricate ecosystem where academic research, open source initiatives, and proprietary development converge to drive innovation forward. Research institutions worldwide contribute groundbreaking discoveries that expand our theoretical understanding and practical capabilities. These academic advances often begin as published papers and prototype implementations before evolving into practical applications that reshape the field, with leading institutions establishing frameworks for evaluating both capabilities and implications.

The research community continues to push boundaries in fundamental areas of AI development. Universities, research laboratories, and dedicated AI institutes collaborate across borders, sharing knowledge and building upon each other's discoveries. This collaborative approach accelerates the pace of innovation while ensuring rigorous validation of new approaches and methodologies. The peer review process and academic discourse provide crucial verification of emerging technologies while identifying potential limitations and areas for improvement.

Open source development has emerged as a powerful force in the AI landscape. Community driven initiatives enable widespread collaboration, allowing developers and researchers worldwide to contribute to advancing AI capabilities. This democratization of AI development has led to the creation of sophisticated frameworks and models that rival proprietary solutions in capability while maintaining transparency and accessibility. The open source movement continues to accelerate innovation through shared knowledge and collaborative improvement.

Proprietary AI development brings another crucial dimension to the landscape. Commercial organizations invest substantial resources in pushing technological boundaries while focusing on practical applications and scalable solutions. These efforts often result in breakthrough capabilities that demonstrate the commercial viability of advanced AI technologies. The interaction between proprietary development and open source initiatives creates a dynamic environment that drives progress across the field.

The convergence of these different approaches has become a defining characteristic of modern AI development. Research breakthroughs inform both open source and proprietary development, while practical implementations provide valuable feedback that guides further research. This symbiotic relationship creates a virtuous cycle of innovation, where advances in one area catalyze progress in others.

The impact of scale in modern AI development cannot be overstated. The ability to deploy increasingly large models and process massive datasets has revealed new capabilities while challenging traditional assumptions about AI limitations. This scaling effect manifests across all areas of AI development, from research experiments to production systems, creating opportunities for innovation while demanding new approaches to implementation and optimization.

The future directions of AI research appear both promising and challenging. As our understanding of AI capabilities grows, new questions and opportunities emerge. The research community continues to explore fundamental questions about AI architecture, training methodologies, and implementation approaches. These investigations promise to yield new insights while opening fresh avenues for practical application.

The sophistication of modern AI systems emerges from the intricate interplay of advanced components working in concert. Next-generation models represent significant advances in architectural design and processing capability, moving beyond traditional approaches to achieve new levels of performance and efficiency. These advances in model architecture establish the foundation for more sophisticated AI applications while demanding equally advanced supporting infrastructure.

Development tools have evolved in parallel with model capabilities, providing the sophisticated frameworks and utilities necessary for working with advanced AI systems. Modern development environments support the entire AI lifecycle, from initial experimentation through deployment and monitoring. This evolution in tooling reflects the increasing complexity of AI systems while making advanced capabilities more accessible to practitioners with varying levels of expertise.

Emerging platforms provide the sophisticated infrastructure required to support advanced AI operations. These platforms handle increasingly complex requirements for computation, data management, and system optimization. The evolution of AI platforms demonstrates how infrastructure must advance alongside AI capabilities, creating environments capable of supporting next-generation applications while maintaining operational efficiency and incorporating built-in safeguards.

Integration technologies have become increasingly crucial as AI systems grow more complex. Modern AI implementations often require sophisticated approaches to combining multiple components and capabilities. The ability to effectively integrate diverse AI components while maintaining system performance, reliability, and appropriate controls represents a key consideration in advanced implementations. This integration challenge drives innovation in system architecture and implementation methodology.

Performance breakthroughs emerge from the combined advancement of these components. Improvements in model architecture complement advances in development tools and platforms, creating opportunities for enhanced capability and efficiency. Understanding how these components work together becomes essential for evaluating and implementing advanced AI solutions. The interrelationship between components often determines both the possibilities and limitations of AI implementations.

Implementation considerations take on new dimensions at the cutting edge of AI development. Advanced systems require sophisticated approaches to deployment, optimization, and maintenance. The complexity of modern AI components demands careful attention to system architecture and operational requirements. Successfully navigating these considerations requires deep understanding of component capabilities, interactions, and governance mechanisms.

The contemporary AI ecosystem represents an intricate network of specialized capabilities that together form a comprehensive landscape of technological advancement. This ecosystem has evolved to address increasingly sophisticated challenges across multiple domains, with each area developing unique approaches while benefiting from shared technological progress. The interaction between different domains creates a rich environment for innovation and practical advancement, guided by established development principles.

Language processing stands as one of the most rapidly evolving areas within the AI ecosystem. The ability to understand and generate human language has progressed significantly, enabling more sophisticated interactions between humans and machines. This evolution in language capabilities influences developments across the entire AI landscape, demonstrating how advances in one domain can catalyze progress in others while raising new considerations for implementation.

Data analysis capabilities have similarly transformed, moving beyond traditional statistical approaches to more sophisticated forms of insight generation. The ability to process and understand complex data patterns continues to evolve, enabling more nuanced analysis and prediction. This progression in data processing capability underpins advances across the broader AI ecosystem while incorporating mechanisms for data governance.

Audio and visual processing systems have achieved new levels of sophistication, enabling more advanced interpretation and generation of rich media content. These capabilities increasingly mirror human perceptual abilities while offering unique advantages in processing speed and scale. The evolution of these systems demonstrates the expanding boundaries of AI capability while highlighting the importance of domain-specific innovation and appropriate safeguards.

Healthcare applications of AI represent a crucial area of development where technological capability meets practical necessity. The integration of AI systems into healthcare contexts continues to evolve, demanding both technical sophistication and careful attention to practical requirements. This domain exemplifies how AI capabilities must adapt to specific operational contexts while maintaining reliability, effectiveness, and appropriate protocols.

Robotics applications demonstrate the physical embodiment of AI advancement, where software capabilities meet real-world interaction requirements. The evolution of robotic systems shows how AI can extend beyond pure computation to influence physical world operations. This integration of AI with physical systems creates unique challenges while opening new possibilities for practical application and safety considerations.

Gaming systems showcase the potential for AI to create interactive and adaptive experiences. The evolution of AI in gaming contexts demonstrates how technological capabilities can enhance human experience and engagement. This domain continues to push boundaries in real-time decision making and dynamic response generation while developing frameworks for user interaction.

Cross-domain integration represents an emerging frontier where capabilities from different areas combine to create new possibilities. The ability to effectively combine specialized capabilities enables more sophisticated applications while presenting unique implementation challenges. This integration trend suggests future directions for AI development while highlighting the importance of comprehensive understanding and coordinated advancement.

The ecosystem's continuous evolution demands careful attention to both specialized capabilities and their potential combinations. Understanding these relationships helps guide effective implementation while suggesting possibilities for future development. The interaction between different domains creates a dynamic environment where innovation in one area often enables advances in others, requiring balanced consideration of capabilities and implications.

Navigating the complexity of cutting-edge AI technologies requires sophisticated approaches to evaluation and implementation. Organizations must develop comprehensive frameworks for assessing both the potential and limitations of advanced AI capabilities. These evaluation approaches need to consider not only technical performance but also practical applicability and operational implications. The ability to effectively evaluate emerging technologies becomes increasingly crucial as AI capabilities expand and diversify.

Technical requirements at the cutting edge of AI implementation often extend beyond traditional infrastructure considerations. Advanced AI systems demand careful attention to computational resources, data management capabilities, and system architecture. Understanding these requirements becomes essential for successful implementation while helping guide resource allocation and planning decisions. The sophisticated nature of modern AI systems requires equally sophisticated approaches to technical evaluation and preparation.

Implementation challenges take on new dimensions when working with advanced AI technologies. Organizations must consider not only technical integration requirements but also operational impacts and organizational readiness. The complexity of modern AI systems demands careful attention to implementation strategy and execution. Successfully addressing these challenges requires comprehensive understanding of both technological capabilities and practical constraints.

Resource considerations extend beyond immediate implementation needs to encompass ongoing operational requirements and future scaling capabilities. Organizations must evaluate both current needs and potential future demands while planning for sustainable operation. The sophisticated nature of advanced AI systems often requires careful balance between capability requirements and resource constraints. Understanding these relationships helps guide effective resource planning and allocation.

Risk assessment becomes particularly crucial when implementing cutting-edge technologies. Organizations must evaluate both technical and operational risks while developing appropriate mitigation strategies. The complexity of advanced AI systems introduces new categories of risk that require careful consideration. Effective risk assessment helps guide implementation decisions while supporting sustainable operation and appropriate governance.

Success metrics for advanced AI implementations must encompass both technical performance and practical impact. Organizations need sophisticated approaches to measuring and evaluating system effectiveness. These metrics must consider not only immediate operational impacts but also longer-term strategic implications. The ability to effectively measure and evaluate success becomes crucial for guiding ongoing development and optimization.

The interplay between these various aspects of complexity creates both challenges and opportunities for organizations implementing advanced AI systems. Success requires careful attention to multiple dimensions of implementation while maintaining focus on practical objectives. Understanding these relationships helps guide effective navigation of the complex landscape of cutting-edge AI technology while ensuring appropriate oversight and control mechanisms.

Building effective strategies for advanced AI implementation requires sophisticated approaches that account for both current capabilities and future developments. Planning for innovation demands careful consideration of technological trajectories while maintaining practical focus on organizational objectives. Strategic planning must balance ambitious goals with realistic assessment of capabilities and constraints. This balance becomes particularly crucial when working with cutting-edge technologies that continue to evolve rapidly.

Infrastructure requirements for advanced AI implementation extend beyond traditional technology considerations. Organizations must plan for sophisticated computational needs while ensuring scalability and operational efficiency. Strategic infrastructure planning needs to account for both immediate requirements and potential future demands. The evolving nature of AI technology requires flexible approaches to infrastructure development that can adapt to emerging capabilities and requirements while maintaining appropriate controls.

Expertise development takes on particular importance in advanced AI implementation. Organizations must cultivate sophisticated understanding across multiple domains while maintaining currency with evolving technologies. The development of internal expertise requires careful attention to both technical depth and practical application capability. Strategic approaches to expertise development help ensure sustainable implementation while supporting ongoing innovation and responsible development practices.

Timeline considerations for advanced AI initiatives must

account for both technological maturity and organizational readiness. Strategic planning needs to establish realistic timeframes while maintaining flexibility for emerging opportunities. The rapid evolution of AI capabilities requires careful attention to implementation timing and sequencing. Understanding these temporal aspects helps guide effective strategic planning while supporting successful implementation.

Adaptation strategies become crucial elements of advanced AI planning. Organizations must develop approaches for responding to technological evolution while maintaining operational stability. Strategic planning needs to incorporate mechanisms for evaluating and adopting emerging capabilities. The ability to effectively adapt to changing technological landscapes helps ensure long-term success while maximizing value from AI investments.

Performance optimization represents a continuing focus of advanced AI strategy. Organizations must develop sophisticated approaches to monitoring and improving system effectiveness. Strategic planning needs to incorporate mechanisms for ongoing evaluation and enhancement. The complex nature of advanced AI systems requires careful attention to optimization opportunities across multiple dimensions of operation while maintaining appropriate safeguards.

The integration of these strategic elements creates the foundation for successful advanced AI implementation. Organizations must maintain comprehensive perspective while focusing on specific objectives and requirements. Strategic planning helps guide effective resource allocation while supporting sustainable development. Understanding these relationships becomes crucial for building effective approaches to advanced AI implementation that balance innovation with responsibility.

As we stand at the frontier of artificial intelligence, the path ahead presents unprecedented opportunities for advancement and innovation. Research trajectories continue to expand our understanding of what's possible, pushing the boundaries of AI capabilities while revealing new areas for exploration. The convergence of theoretical advancement and practical implementation creates an environment rich with potential for meaningful progress. This dynamic landscape demands both vision and pragmatism as we navigate the evolving world of AI technology.

Technology evolution proceeds at an accelerating pace, driven by breakthroughs across multiple domains. The interaction between different areas of advancement creates opportunities for innovation while demanding sophisticated approaches to implementation and integration. Understanding these evolutionary patterns helps guide preparation for emerging capabilities while supporting effective decision making about current implementations. The continuing maturation of AI technology suggests both exciting possibilities and important considerations for future development.

Integration trends point toward increasingly sophisticated combinations of AI capabilities. The ability to effectively combine different aspects of AI technology creates new possibilities for practical application. These integration patterns suggest important directions for future development while highlighting the need for comprehensive understanding of AI capabilities. The evolution of integration approaches provides crucial context for planning and implementation decisions.

Preparation strategies for future developments must account for both technological advancement and practical implementation requirements. Organizations need sophisticated approaches to evaluating and adopting emerging capabilities while maintaining operational stability. Understanding potential development paths helps guide effective preparation while supporting sustainable implementation. The ability to effectively prepare for future developments becomes increasingly crucial as AI technology continues to evolve.

Continuous learning remains essential for maintaining effectiveness in this dynamic environment. The rapid evolution of AI capabilities demands ongoing attention to emerging developments and their practical implications. Understanding these learning requirements helps guide professional development while supporting organizational capability building. The commitment to continuous learning provides crucial foundation for long-term success in AI implementation.

Our journey through the cutting edge of AI technology promises both excitement and challenge. The chapters ahead will explore specific aspects of this landscape in detail, providing comprehensive understanding of current capabilities while suggesting future directions. This exploration will maintain focus on practical application while examining the sophisticated technologies shaping the future of artificial intelligence. Together we will navigate this complex landscape, building understanding that supports effective and responsible implementation of advanced AI capabilities.

GIL OREN

CHAPTER 2: RESEARCH BREAKTHROUGHS

Our exploration of AI's cutting edge begins with the foundational breakthroughs driving innovation across the field. The research landscape has evolved dramatically, transforming how we approach artificial intelligence development and implementation. The emergence of large language models like GPT-4, PaLM, and Claude, alongside breakthroughs in multimodal systems like GPT-4V and Gemini, demonstrates the accelerating pace of innovation. Major research institutions including Google DeepMind, Google Research, and Stanford's AI Lab, alongside industrial laboratories like OpenAI and Anthropic, have established new paradigms for how breakthrough discoveries emerge and propagate.

The velocity of research advancement continues to increase, powered by unprecedented computational capabilities exemplified by systems like NVIDIA's H100 GPUs and Google's TPU v4 clusters, alongside sophisticated methodological approaches. Researchers now tackle challenges that seemed insurmountable just years ago, as demonstrated by achievements in protein structure prediction through Google DeepMind's AlphaFold 2, and advances in reasoning capabilities through chain-of-thought prompting. This acceleration of discovery has created a dynamic environment where breakthrough innovations emerge with increasing frequency.

The research landscape itself has undergone fundamental transformation. Traditional boundaries between academic and industrial research have blurred, exemplified by collaborations like the Stanford Institute for Human-Centered AI's partnerships with industry leaders, and Berkeley AI Research's joint projects with major technology companies. Major technology companies now maintain research divisions that rival academic institutions, as demonstrated by Microsoft Research's worldwide laboratories and Google DeepMind's extensive research operations.

Understanding these research breakthroughs becomes essential for anyone working at the forefront of AI technology. From foundation models achieving human-level performance on professional examinations to breakthrough capabilities in multimodal understanding, these advances shape both theoretical understanding and practical application. The impact extends from fundamental research to immediate practical applications, influencing how organizations approach AI implementation across sectors.

The convergence of multiple research streams has created particularly fertile ground for innovation. Advances in attention mechanisms have catalyzed breakthroughs in language models, while improvements in training methodologies have enabled more efficient resource utilization. This interconnected nature of modern AI research demonstrates the importance of maintaining broad awareness across the field.

Validation and verification of research breakthroughs have taken on increased importance, with organizations like Papers with Code and Hugging Face establishing new standards for reproducibility and verification. The research community has developed sophisticated approaches to ensuring reliability and reproducibility of new discoveries, exemplified by initiatives like MLFlow and Weights & Biases for experiment tracking.

In this chapter, we examine the critical research developments transforming our understanding of artificial intelligence. From evolutionary improvements to revolutionary discoveries, we will explore how research breakthroughs are reshaping the AI landscape, while maintaining focus on verified achievements rather than speculative possibilities.

The evolution of artificial intelligence research represents a remarkable journey of scientific discovery and technological advancement. From the foundational breakthroughs of deep learning pioneers like Geoffrey Hinton, Yoshua Bengio, and Yann LeCun to contemporary achievements, research paradigms have transformed dramatically. The progression from AlexNet's 2012 ImageNet victory to modern systems like GPT-4 demonstrates both the acceleration of capability advancement and the sophistication of current research approaches.

Research paradigms have transformed dramatically with the emergence of new computational capabilities and methodological approaches. The introduction of transformer architectures through the landmark "Attention is All You Need" paper by Vaswani et al. marked a fundamental shift in how researchers approach AI system design. This architectural innovation, combined with scaling studies like those conducted by Google Research and Microsoft Research, has revealed new possibilities for model capability enhancement. The relationship between model scale and performance, documented in papers like "Scaling Laws for Neural Language Models," has established new frameworks for understanding AI system development.

The modern research framework has evolved to accommodate increasing complexity in artificial intelligence investigations. Leading institutions have developed sophisticated research infrastructures, exemplified by Google DeepMind's integrated research environments and OpenAI's massive computational clusters. Stanford's Center for Research on Foundation Models (CRFM) demonstrates how academic institutions are adapting to investigate large-scale AI systems. These frameworks support both theoretical investigation and practical validation, ensuring robust advancement of the field.

The emergence of large-scale research initiatives has transformed how the community approaches complex challenges. Projects like Google's Pathways initiative and Meta AI's open research frameworks demonstrate new models for coordinating sophisticated research efforts. The success of these initiatives has established new paradigms for research collaboration, exemplified by multi-institution efforts like BigScience and LAION.

The research community itself has undergone significant transformation. What began as primarily academic endeavors now includes major industrial laboratories, demonstrated by Microsoft Research's global network of facilities and Google DeepMind's expansion beyond game-playing systems to fundamental scientific challenges. This expansion has accelerated discovery while introducing diverse perspectives, as seen in breakthrough achievements like Google DeepMind's AlphaFold 2 and Google's PaLM model series.

Computational resources have emerged as a crucial factor in research advancement. The development of specialized AI hardware like NVIDIA's H100 GPUs and Google's TPU v4 chips has enabled research at unprecedented scales. This computational capability has revealed new possibilities, as demonstrated by models like Anthropic's Constitutional AI research and Microsoft's development of specialized training infrastructures.

The evolution of research methodology has been particularly significant in recent years. The development of sophisticated training approaches like chain-of-thought prompting, constitutional AI techniques, and advanced few-shot learning methods demonstrates the field's growing methodological sophistication. These advances, combined with improved validation techniques exemplified by tools like Weights & Biases and MLFlow, have created more robust frameworks for research advancement.

The role of theoretical research has evolved alongside practical advancement. Work in areas like mechanistic interpretability, as pioneered by researchers at Anthropic and other institutions, demonstrates the continuing importance of fundamental understanding. The integration of theoretical insight with practical experimentation, seen in developments like sparse mixture of experts models and improved attention mechanisms, continues to drive the field forward.

The landscape of AI research represents a complex network of academic institutions, industry laboratories, and government research programs working in concert to advance artificial intelligence capabilities. Stanford's Institute for Human-Centered AI (HAI), MIT's Computer Science and Artificial Intelligence Laboratory (CSAIL), and Berkeley AI Research (BAIR) exemplify how traditional academic centers have evolved to address modern AI challenges. These institutions combine fundamental research with practical investigation, establishing new models for AI advancement.

Industry research laboratories have emerged as powerful forces in advancing AI capabilities. Google DeepMind's expansion beyond game-playing systems to fundamental scientific research, demonstrated by achievements like AlphaFold 2, exemplifies this evolution. Google Research's contributions through projects like PaLM and LaMDA, Microsoft Research's global network of laboratories, and OpenAI's breakthrough developments with GPT series models showcase how industrial research has transformed the field. The scale of these operations often enables investigation at levels previously unattainable in academic settings.

The interaction between academic and industry research creates productive tensions that drive innovation forward. Collaborations like Stanford's partnership with Microsoft Research on foundation models, and MIT's collaboration with IBM on AI hardware development, demonstrate new models of joint research. Carnegie Mellon University's partnerships with Argo AI and Aurora for autonomous vehicle research exemplify how these relationships accelerate practical applications while maintaining theoretical rigor.

Government research programs contribute another vital dimension to the AI research ecosystem. DARPA's AI Next campaign and the National Science Foundation's National AI Research Institutes program demonstrate sustained commitment to fundamental AI research. The European Union's Horizon Europe program and Japan's RIKEN Center for Advanced Intelligence Project showcase how different nations approach AI research support.

International collaboration has become increasingly central to AI research advancement. The Partnership on AI, involving organizations across continents, demonstrates new models for global cooperation. Major conferences like NeurIPS, ICML, and ICLR have evolved into crucial venues for international knowledge exchange, while initiatives like Papers with Code and arXiv enable rapid global dissemination of research findings.

The research community operates through sophisticated mechanisms for sharing and validating discoveries. Platforms like Hugging Face have transformed how models and code are shared, while tools like Weights & Biases and MLFlow enable detailed experiment tracking and reproduction. These platforms supplement traditional peer review processes with practical validation capabilities.

Peer-reviewed journals and conferences maintain their role as crucial venues for research validation. Top-tier conferences like NeurIPS (with over 13,000 attendees in 2023) and ICML demonstrate the scale of modern AI research discourse. The development of new publication models, like the rapid review processes adopted by venues such as ICLR, shows how the community adapts to accelerating research pace.

Knowledge sharing mechanisms have evolved significantly to support the increasing pace and complexity of AI research. GitHub's integration of AI-specific features, including model cards and sophisticated versioning for large files, demonstrates how sharing platforms adapt to AI development needs. The emergence of specialized platforms like Papers with Code, which links research papers directly to implementations, showcases new approaches to research dissemination.

The landscape of AI research encompasses several crucial areas where breakthrough discoveries continue to advance the field. Model architecture innovations demonstrate this progress, from the fundamental transformer architecture introduced by Google Research to more recent developments like Google DeepMind's Perceiver and Microsoft's DeepSpeed. These architectural breakthroughs arise from deep theoretical work while enabling practical advances in system capability.

The investigation of architectural principles has revealed important insights about system design and capability. Google's development of the Pathways architecture, designed to enable more efficient multi-task learning, exemplifies how architectural research addresses fundamental challenges. Meta AI's advances in sparse expert models and Microsoft's work on efficient attention mechanisms demonstrate continuing innovation in basic system design, while maintaining focus on practical applicability.

Training methodology advances have transformed how artificial intelligence systems develop their capabilities. The emergence of techniques like chain-of-thought prompting, demonstrated in papers from Google Research and Stanford, has opened new possibilities for model instruction. Anthropic's constitutional AI approach and Google DeepMind's reward modeling work show how research continues to uncover more effective training methods. These methodological advances often combine theoretical insights with practical innovations.

Optimization techniques represent another crucial area of research breakthrough. NVIDIA's development of FP8 precision training and Microsoft's DeepSpeed Zero optimization series demonstrate how research continues to improve training efficiency. Google's work on model distillation and Meta AI's advances in efficient training showcase ongoing innovation in optimization approaches, while maintaining practical applicability.

The pursuit of efficiency improvements emerges through focused research into system operation. Advances like Google's PaLM model architecture and OpenAI's innovations in model scaling demonstrate how research continues to enhance performance while managing computational requirements. Google DeepMind's work on more efficient attention mechanisms and Microsoft's advances in model compression show ongoing progress in efficiency enhancement.

Scaling breakthroughs continue to emerge as crucial research achievements. The development of techniques for training increasingly large models, as demonstrated by advances from organizations like Google DeepMind, Anthropic, and Google Research, reveals new insights about AI system behavior. These scaling advances often challenge traditional assumptions about model capability and resource requirements.

Novel applications emerge as another significant research area. Google DeepMind's application of AI to protein structure prediction through AlphaFold 2, and subsequent advances in scientific discovery, demonstrate how research breakthroughs enable new capabilities. Google Research's advances in multimodal understanding and OpenAI's developments in code generation showcase how research continues to expand AI's practical applications.

The synthesis of these various research areas creates opportunities for comprehensive advancement. The combination of architectural innovations with improved training methods, as seen in systems like Anthropic's Claude and Google's PaLM, demonstrates how different research streams contribute to overall progress. This integration of research advances continues to drive the field forward while revealing new possibilities for future investigation.

Research methodology in artificial intelligence has evolved to meet the increasing complexity of breakthrough developments. Stanford's Center for Research on Foundation Models (CRFM) exemplifies this evolution through their comprehensive evaluation frameworks for large language models. The establishment of standardized evaluation suites, such as HELM (Holistic Evaluation of Language Models), demonstrates the field's commitment to rigorous validation methodologies.

The research community has developed sophisticated frameworks for validating new discoveries. Microsoft Research's development of the SuperGLUE benchmark, succeeding the original GLUE benchmark, showcases how evaluation standards evolve with technological advancement. Google Research's Beyond the Imitation Game (BIG-bench) initiative, comprising over 200 tasks, demonstrates the growing sophistication of validation approaches.

Benchmark development has emerged as a crucial aspect of research validation. The emergence of specialized benchmarks like Meta AI's MMLU (Massive Multitask Language Understanding) and Anthropic's constitutional AI evaluation metrics shows how validation requirements evolve with technological capability. The development of adversarial testing frameworks by organizations like OpenAI and Google DeepMind demonstrates growing attention to robust evaluation methodologies.

Performance metrics have grown increasingly sophisticated to address complex AI capabilities. The development of evaluation frameworks like EleutherAI's Language Model Evaluation Harness and HuggingFace's Evaluate library showcases how the community approaches comprehensive assessment. Stanford's Foundational Model Observatory and Berkeley's TAPE benchmark for protein engineering models demonstrate domain-specific evaluation approaches.

Testing frameworks have advanced significantly to support rigorous validation. The adoption of tools like Weights & Biases for experiment tracking and MLflow for model lifecycle management shows how validation infrastructure has matured. Google Research's Model Cards framework and Meta AI's improvements in model documentation demonstrate growing emphasis on comprehensive validation approaches.

Reproducibility approaches have gained increasing importance in artificial intelligence research. Initiatives like Papers with Code, which links research papers directly to implementations, and the adoption of platforms like CodeOcean for computational reproducibility, showcase new standards in research validation. The deployment of sophisticated versioning systems through platforms like DVC (Data Version Control) demonstrates growing attention to reproducibility requirements.

Validation standards continue to evolve alongside technological advancement. The development of specialized testing frameworks like Microsoft's Responsible AI tools and Google's Model Card Toolkit shows how validation incorporates broader considerations beyond pure performance. Intel's Trusted AI framework and IBM's AI Fairness 360 toolkit demonstrate how validation increasingly encompasses ethical and reliability considerations.

Methodological rigor has become increasingly central to artificial intelligence research. The adoption of standardized evaluation protocols, as demonstrated by organizations like Allen AI Institute through their systematic approach to model evaluation, shows growing emphasis on comprehensive validation. Google DeepMind's extensive validation protocols for systems like AlphaFold 2 demonstrate how rigorous validation supports breakthrough achievements.

The transition from theoretical research to practical implementation represents a crucial phase in advancing artificial intelligence capabilities. Google's deployment of BERT into search systems, transforming search results for millions of users, exemplifies successful research implementation at scale. OpenAI's progressive deployment strategy, from GPT-3's initial API release to ChatGPT's widespread availability, demonstrates how organizations navigate the complex journey from research breakthrough to practical application.

Technology transfer methods have evolved substantially to support effective implementation. Microsoft Research's integration of GPT-4 technology across their product suite, from GitHub Copilot to Bing Chat, showcases sophisticated approaches to research deployment. Google DeepMind's careful progression from AlphaFold 2's research success to its widespread availability through the AlphaFold Protein Structure Database, in collaboration with EMBL-EBI, illustrates effective research translation strategies.

The research community has developed comprehensive frameworks for guiding implementation efforts. Meta AI's PyTorch ecosystem, evolving from research tool to production platform, demonstrates successful research-to-implementation transition. Google's TensorFlow Extended (TFX) framework, incorporating lessons from large-scale deployments, showcases how implementation experience influences development tools. NVIDIA's RAPIDS suite exemplifies how hardware innovations support efficient research implementation.

Industry applications of research breakthroughs require careful consideration of practical constraints. Anthropic's deployment of Claude models through carefully managed API access demonstrates balanced implementation approaches. The adoption of transformer-based models in practical applications, from DeepL's translation services to Grammarly's writing assistance, shows how research advances translate into user-facing applications.

Scaling requirements have become increasingly central to implementation planning. Microsoft's Azure AI infrastructure, supporting massive model deployment, showcases sophisticated scaling approaches. Google Cloud's Vertex AI platform and Amazon's SageMaker demonstrate how cloud providers enable research deployment at scale. These implementations often reveal new challenges that drive further research investigation.

Resource planning for research implementation has evolved significantly. NVIDIA's development of specialized AI hardware, from A100 to H100 GPUs, shows how implementation requirements influence technology development. AMD's MI300 series and Google's TPU v4 chips demonstrate continuing evolution in implementation infrastructure. Organizations must carefully consider these hardware developments alongside software and operational requirements.

Adaptation strategies continue to evolve as implementation experience grows. IBM's deployment of Watson technologies across various domains demonstrates how organizations adapt research implementations to specific contexts. Salesforce's Einstein platform shows how research advances can be adapted for enterprise applications. These adaptation approaches often combine multiple strategies to ensure successful implementation.

Implementation validation has emerged as a crucial aspect of research translation. Microsoft's staged deployment approach for GitHub Copilot, progressing from limited preview to general availability, demonstrates careful validation practices. Google's canary deployments for AI features in search and other products show how organizations validate implementations in production environments.

Knowledge transfer during implementation demands sophisticated approaches. NVIDIA's CUDA ecosystem and Intel's OneAPI demonstrate how hardware manufacturers support implementation knowledge transfer. The development of specialized training programs by cloud providers, like AWS's Machine Learning University and Google's ML bootcamps, shows growing attention to implementation expertise development.

The integration of these implementation elements creates comprehensive approaches to research deployment. Organizations like Meta AI demonstrate this through their end-to-end machine learning platforms, supporting everything from research experimentation to production deployment. The success of these integrated approaches often depends on careful attention to multiple factors, from technical infrastructure to operational processes.

The advancement of artificial intelligence research encounters various challenges that demand innovative solutions. The computational requirements of large language models, exemplified by GPT-4's training needs and PaLM's massive computational scale, demonstrate how resource demands drive innovation. Organizations like Google Research and Microsoft Research continue developing novel approaches to address these fundamental challenges while maintaining research momentum.

Computational limitations represent persistent challenges in artificial intelligence research. NVIDIA's development of the H100 GPU architecture, with specialized hardware for transformer operations, demonstrates how hardware evolution addresses computational challenges. Google's TPU v4 chips and custom interconnect technologies show how organizations approach system-level optimization. AMD's MI300 series and Intel's Gaudi2 processors exemplify how competition drives innovation in computational capabilities.

The optimization of computational resource utilization has

emerged as a crucial focus. Microsoft's DeepSpeed Zero series, enabling efficient large model training, demonstrates innovative approaches to resource management. Google's GShard and Switch Transformer architectures show how architectural innovations address computational challenges. Meta AI's advances in sparse computation and mixture of experts models exemplify novel approaches to resource utilization.

Data requirements present another significant dimension of research challenge. The creation of massive datasets like LAION-5B for image-text pairs and The Pile for language models shows how organizations address data needs. Google's C4 dataset and Meta AI's CCMatrix demonstrate sophisticated approaches to data curation. The development of synthetic data generation techniques, as shown by NVIDIA's GAN-based approaches and OpenAI's data augmentation strategies, reveals novel solutions to data challenges.

The evolution of data handling approaches has transformed how researchers address data-related challenges. The development of efficient storage and processing systems, like Google's Cloud Storage for ML and Amazon's SageMaker data handling capabilities, demonstrates infrastructure-level solutions. Microsoft's Azure ML data management and IBM's Watson Data platform show how organizations approach comprehensive data handling requirements.

Architecture constraints continue to influence research direction. Google DeepMind's Perceiver architecture and Google's PaLM demonstrate approaches to handling architectural limitations. Anthropic's constitutional AI research and OpenAI's InstructGPT methodology show how organizations address architectural challenges through novel training approaches. Meta AI's advances in efficient attention mechanisms exemplify architectural innovation addressing specific constraints.

Training challenges persist as systems become more sophisticated. Microsoft's Megatron-Turing NLG training methodology and Google's Pathways system demonstrate approaches to complex training requirements. OpenAI's developments in reinforcement learning from human feedback (RLHF) and Anthropic's constitutional AI training show novel approaches to capability development. Google DeepMind's advances in efficient training methods exemplify continuing innovation in addressing training challenges.

Implementation barriers represent another category of research challenge. NVIDIA's CUDA ecosystem development and Intel's OneAPI initiative demonstrate how organizations address implementation complexity. Google's JAX framework and Meta's PyTorch developments show how software tools evolve to address implementation challenges. The creation of specialized deployment platforms, like Hugging Face's model hub and AWS's SageMaker, exemplifies solutions to deployment barriers.

Emerging solutions continue to advance the field despite persistent challenges. Organizations like Google DeepMind demonstrate this through innovations in protein structure prediction, while Google Research's advances in multimodal understanding show novel approaches to complex problems. OpenAI's developments in code generation and Microsoft's advances in language model capabilities exemplify how research continues to address fundamental challenges while creating new possibilities.

The trajectory of artificial intelligence research continues to evolve as new possibilities emerge and existing directions mature. Stanford's Institute for Human-Centered AI research agenda and MIT's Computer Science and Artificial Intelligence Laboratory's strategic focus areas demonstrate how leading institutions approach research direction setting. These research trajectories build upon current achievements while identifying promising areas for investigation.

Research possibilities continue to expand through technological advancement. Google DeepMind's success with AlphaFold 2 has opened new directions in scientific discovery, while Google Research's advances in multimodal understanding through systems like PaLM demonstrate emerging capabilities. OpenAI's progress in code generation and Microsoft Research's developments in natural language processing showcase how current achievements suggest new research directions.

The assessment of research directions has evolved to incorporate sophisticated consideration of both potential impact and practical feasibility. The Allen Institute for AI's research roadmap and Carnegie Mellon University's AI initiatives demonstrate how organizations evaluate and prioritize research directions. Berkeley AI Research's focus areas and Stanford's AI Index report show how institutions assess and track research progress systematically.

Resource implications for future research directions demand careful consideration. NVIDIA's GPU development roadmap and Google's TPU advancement plans demonstrate how hardware capabilities influence research possibilities. Microsoft's Azure AI infrastructure investments and Amazon's AWS capacity planning show how organizations approach resource provision for future research needs. These resource considerations significantly influence the feasibility and timing of research initiatives.

The evaluation of resource requirements has become increasingly sophisticated. Meta AI's infrastructure planning and IBM Research's quantum computing initiatives demonstrate how organizations assess future resource needs. Intel's AI accelerator development and AMD's processor roadmap show how hardware manufacturers anticipate future research requirements. These evaluations help guide both research direction and infrastructure development.

The research community itself continues to evolve, as demonstrated by the growing collaboration between academic institutions and industry laboratories. Stanford's partnerships with major technology companies and MIT's industry collaboration programs show how research relationships continue to develop. The expansion of research conferences like NeurIPS and ICML demonstrates the community's growing scale and sophistication.

Development trajectories emerge from current achievements while suggesting future directions. Google Research's language model development progression and OpenAI's capability scaling demonstrate how current work influences future directions. Google DeepMind's scientific application focus and Anthropic's emphasis on AI safety show how organizations chart distinct research paths while maintaining connection to broader community advancement.

The integration of research directions has become increasingly important. Microsoft Research's comprehensive AI strategy and Meta AI's interconnected research initiatives demonstrate how organizations approach coordinated advancement. Google's Pathways initiative and Google DeepMind's multifaceted research program show how organizations maintain coherent research direction while pursuing multiple objectives.

Our exploration of research breakthroughs reveals the dynamic nature of artificial intelligence advancement. From Google DeepMind's achievements in protein structure prediction to Google's advances in large language models through PaLM, these fundamental discoveries continue to reshape our understanding of what's possible. Microsoft Research's contributions to efficient model training and Meta AI's advances in scalable architectures demonstrate how research breakthroughs translate into practical capabilities.

The impact of research breakthroughs extends beyond immediate discoveries. OpenAI's progression from GPT-3 to GPT-4 demonstrates how initial breakthroughs lead to cascading advances. Anthropic's developments in constitutional AI and Google's advances in multimodal understanding show how research in one area often enables progress in others. Stanford's foundation model research and MIT's work on robust AI systems exemplify how academic institutions continue to drive fundamental advancement.

The methodological advances emerging from research investigation have particular significance. The development of sophisticated training approaches, exemplified by Microsoft's DeepSpeed innovations and Google's Pathways system, demonstrates how methodology evolves to support increasingly complex research. Google DeepMind's advances in reinforcement learning and Meta AI's progress in self-supervised learning show how methodological innovation enables new research possibilities.

The collaborative nature of modern research, demonstrated through initiatives like the Partnership on AI and the BigScience workshop, has transformed how breakthroughs emerge and propagate. International cooperation, exemplified by collaborations between institutions like Stanford and Oxford, and cross-industry partnerships like those between Microsoft and OpenAI, create powerful mechanisms for advancing artificial intelligence capabilities.

The relationship between research breakthroughs and practical implementation continues to evolve. Google's deployment of BERT in search and Microsoft's integration of GPT-4 across their product suite demonstrate effective pathways from research to application. Google DeepMind's success in deploying AlphaFold 2 through public databases and Meta's open-source releases of large language models show how research advances become accessible to broader communities.

As we move forward to examine the open source AI landscape, we carry forward understanding of how research breakthroughs drive technological advancement. The open source community has emerged as a powerful force in artificial intelligence development, building upon foundational research discoveries while creating new possibilities for innovation. Projects like Hugging Face's model hub and Meta's PyTorch demonstrate how open source initiatives transform research breakthroughs into accessible technologies. Our next chapter explores this vibrant ecosystem, examining how collaborative development advances artificial intelligence while ensuring broad access to cutting-edge capabilities.

GIL OREN

CHAPTER 3: OPEN SOURCE AI EVOLUTION

The research breakthroughs we explored in the previous chapter find remarkable expression through the open source movement in artificial intelligence, where theoretical advances transform into widely accessible technology. This transformation has created a vibrant ecosystem where innovation flows freely between researchers, developers, and practitioners. At the heart of this evolution stands Meta's bold decision to release LLaMA, a moment that marked a significant shift in how major organizations approach sharing cutting-edge AI technology.

The open source landscape has matured into a sophisticated environment where community-driven development rivals proprietary systems in capability and scale. This maturity becomes evident through platforms like Hugging Face, which has evolved from a simple model-sharing site into a comprehensive ecosystem hosting hundreds of thousands of models and datasets. The platform's growth reflects the broader evolution of open source AI, where community collaboration creates powerful alternatives to commercial solutions.

The significance of this movement extends far beyond simple code sharing. When the BigScience initiative launched BLOOM, it demonstrated how international collaboration could create state-of-the-art language models through open development. This achievement, involving hundreds of researchers across multiple continents, challenged traditional assumptions about the necessity of closed development for advanced AI systems. Similarly, Stability AI's release of Stable Diffusion showed how open source projects could rapidly advance emerging fields like image generation, sparking widespread innovation and application.

Major technology organizations have recognized and embraced this shift toward openness. We see this in how PyTorch, originally developed at Facebook (now Meta), has grown into the predominant framework for AI research. Its adoption by researchers and developers worldwide demonstrates how open source tools can become the foundation for advancing the entire field. Google's strategic decision to release frameworks like TensorFlow and JAX further illustrates how industry leaders have come to view open source as crucial for AI advancement.

The impact of open source extends deeply into how developers work and learn. Tools like GitHub's Copilot and GitLab's AI-enhanced development environments, built upon open source foundations, are transforming how developers approach AI implementation. Meanwhile, platforms like MLflow have emerged to address the unique challenges of machine learning operations, showing how the community creates sophisticated solutions for complex problems.

Education and knowledge sharing have flourished in this open environment. The success of initiatives like Fast.ai shows how open source enables innovative approaches to AI education, making advanced concepts accessible to broader audiences. The widespread availability of high-quality, freely accessible resources has democratized AI education, creating new pathways for people to enter the field and contribute to its advancement.

As we explore the open source AI landscape, we'll discover how collaborative development has become a powerful force in advancing artificial intelligence while ensuring broad access to cutting-edge capabilities. This journey reveals both the current state of open source AI and the promising directions emerging from community-driven innovation. The chapters ahead will examine how this vibrant ecosystem continues to shape the future of artificial intelligence, making sophisticated capabilities accessible to developers and organizations worldwide.

The foundation of open source artificial intelligence represents a fascinating journey of community development and technical innovation. At its core lies a complex network of organizations, developers, and institutions working together to advance AI technology. The Linux Foundation AI & Data initiative stands as a testament to this collaboration, bringing together diverse projects under a unified vision for open AI development. Through this foundation, crucial projects like PyTorch and ONNX have found a stable home, enabling their growth while maintaining independence.

The historical evolution of open source AI tells a compelling story of transformation. Consider TensorFlow's journey from its origins as Google Brain's internal DistBelief system to becoming a global open source platform. This evolution demonstrates how proprietary technology can evolve into a community resource that benefits the entire field. Similarly, PyTorch's transformation from Facebook's research tool to the preferred platform for AI research worldwide illustrates how community adoption can drive rapid advancement and innovation.

Community structures have matured alongside technical capabilities, developing sophisticated approaches to organization and governance. The emergence of focused initiatives like NumFOCUS shows how the community has learned to support critical scientific computing projects. Their stewardship of essential tools like NumPy and Pandas demonstrates how structured organization can ensure the stability of fundamental technologies while enabling continuous innovation.

The values and principles guiding open source AI development have evolved through practical experience and community consensus. The widespread adoption of the MIT License in AI projects reflects a careful balance between openness and practical utility. This choice has proven particularly significant for AI development, where research and commercial interests often intersect. Projects like TensorFlow and PyTorch, operating under the Apache 2.0 License, show how licensing choices can foster both academic research and commercial application.

Governance in open source AI has developed unique characteristics that reflect the field's specific needs. The Python Software Foundation's approach to managing AI-related libraries demonstrates how established organizations can adapt to new challenges. Meanwhile, newer initiatives like the Ray project show how governance can evolve to handle the complexity of modern AI systems, balancing academic innovation with industrial application.

Development standards have emerged through a process of community learning and adaptation. Google's contribution guidelines for TensorFlow, refined through years of experience managing thousands of contributors, demonstrate how large projects maintain quality while encouraging participation. The scikit-learn project's documentation standards show how communities can establish and maintain high-quality practices across a large contributor base.

The integration of these foundational elements creates robust frameworks for continued advancement. The Jupyter ecosystem exemplifies this integration, providing a comprehensive environment that supports both development and education. Its evolution from simple notebooks to a complete platform for interactive computing shows how community needs drive technological advancement. The conda package manager's growth into a crucial tool for AI development further demonstrates how infrastructure evolves to support increasingly sophisticated requirements.

These foundations continue to evolve as artificial intelligence technology advances. New challenges in model distribution, computation management, and collaboration constantly emerge, driving innovation in how the community organizes and operates. The success of platforms like Hugging Face shows how new organizational models can arise to meet emerging needs while maintaining the core values of open source development.

The landscape of major open source projects in artificial intelligence tells a remarkable story of community achievement and technological advancement. At the forefront of this evolution stands PyTorch, whose journey from research tool to industry standard illustrates the potential of open source development. Its adoption by the vast majority of researchers at prestigious conferences like NeurIPS and ICML demonstrates how community-driven projects can become the backbone of scientific advancement in AI.

Framework evolution in open source AI reveals the community's ability to address increasingly sophisticated challenges. Google Research's development of JAX represents a new chapter in this evolution, bringing functional programming principles to machine learning. Its broad adoption within Google, including by teams at Google DeepMind, and by external organizations like Cohere shows how innovative approaches can quickly gain traction when openly shared. The emergence of specialized frameworks like PyTorch Lightning demonstrates how the community identifies and addresses specific development needs, making advanced AI techniques more accessible to a broader audience.

The story of open source model development has reached

new heights with projects that rival proprietary systems in scale and capability. The BLOOM initiative stands as a testament to what the community can achieve through collaboration, bringing together researchers and institutions worldwide to create a multilingual language model of unprecedented scale. Similarly, Stability AI's release of Stable Diffusion transformed the landscape of image generation, demonstrating how open source projects can democratize access to cutting-edge AI capabilities.

Tool creation within the open source ecosystem has evolved to support increasingly sophisticated development workflows. The widespread adoption of Weights & Biases illustrates how the community approaches the challenge of experiment tracking and collaboration. Their integration with thousands of organizations' workflows shows how open source tools can become essential components of professional AI development. Similarly, MLflow's evolution from a simple tracking tool to a comprehensive platform for machine learning lifecycle management demonstrates how community projects mature to meet enterprise needs.

Platform advancement through open source has revolutionized how organizations deploy and scale AI systems. Kubeflow's adoption by major organizations like Spotify and Bloomberg shows how community-driven solutions can address complex deployment challenges. The Ray project's success in distributed computing demonstrates how open source platforms can solve sophisticated technical challenges while maintaining accessibility for a broad range of users.

Infrastructure solutions in open source AI have grown to support industrial-scale applications. The ONNX project exemplifies how the community addresses the challenge of model interoperability, creating standards that enable flexibility in model deployment. Apache Arrow's processing of massive datasets across numerous organizations shows how open source infrastructure can meet the demands of production environments while maintaining efficiency and reliability.

Community contributions continue to drive innovation across all aspects of AI development. The Hugging Face Transformers library stands as a prime example of how collaborative development can create comprehensive solutions that benefit the entire field. Its growth from a simple model repository to a crucial platform for AI development demonstrates the power of community-driven innovation. The success of projects like spaCy in natural language processing shows how focused community efforts can create professional-grade tools that advance specific domains within AI.

The integration of these various projects creates a rich ecosystem that continues to evolve and expand. We see this in how the Open Neural Network Exchange (ONNX) has grown beyond simple model exchange to become a comprehensive standard for AI deployment. Similarly, Apache TVM's development shows how the community approaches the challenge of optimizing models for diverse hardware platforms, creating solutions that benefit the entire field.

The evolution of development models and practices in open source AI represents a sophisticated journey of community learning and adaptation. As projects grow in complexity and scale, the community has established robust approaches that balance innovation with stability. This evolution becomes particularly evident in how major projects like PyTorch manage their development processes, combining rigorous quality control with the flexibility needed for rapid advancement.

Collaborative development forms the cornerstone of open source AI advancement, with modern practices emerging from years of community experience. The PyTorch development process exemplifies this maturity, coordinating contributions from over 2,000 active developers while maintaining code quality and project coherence. This sophisticated collaboration extends beyond code contribution to encompass documentation, testing, and community support. The success of such approaches has influenced how other projects structure their development processes, as seen in the TensorFlow community's adoption of similar practices.

Quality assurance in open source AI has evolved into a comprehensive system that ensures reliability while enabling rapid innovation. Hugging Face's Transformers library demonstrates this balance, maintaining strict quality standards across thousands of model implementations while supporting quick integration of new research. Their extensive automated testing infrastructure showcases how modern AI projects maintain quality at scale. This attention to quality has become increasingly crucial as organizations rely on open source AI components for production systems.

Version control practices have adapted to meet the unique challenges of AI development. DVC's evolution illustrates how the community addresses specialized needs, managing large model files and training data alongside code. The integration of these tools with traditional version control systems like Git creates comprehensive solutions for tracking AI development. This sophisticated approach to version control has become essential as projects manage increasingly complex artifacts and dependencies.

Documentation standards have matured significantly, reflecting the community's understanding of its importance in AI development. spaCy's documentation system demonstrates this evolution, combining traditional API documentation with interactive examples and practical tutorials. This comprehensive approach helps developers understand not just how to use tools, but why certain approaches are recommended. The impact of good documentation becomes evident in adoption patterns, with well-documented projects typically seeing broader use.

Testing methodologies have evolved to address the unique challenges of AI systems. The pytest-cov framework, widely adopted across major AI projects, showcases how testing practices adapt to specific needs. Projects like FastAI demonstrate how comprehensive testing can coexist with rapid development, maintaining high standards while supporting innovation. These testing approaches often combine traditional software testing with specialized validation for AI components.

Release management has become increasingly sophisticated, balancing stability with innovation. PyTorch's release cycle demonstrates this maturity, coordinating major updates across a complex ecosystem of dependencies and extensions. The careful management of deprecation cycles and backward compatibility shows how projects maintain stability while advancing capabilities. This approach has proven crucial for organizations building production systems on open source foundations.

These practices continue evolving as projects face new challenges and opportunities. The integration of continuous integration/continuous deployment (CI/CD) pipelines, exemplified by GitHub Actions workflows in major AI projects, shows how automation supports sophisticated development processes. As artificial intelligence technology advances, these development practices adapt to maintain effectiveness while supporting innovation.

The dynamics of open source AI communities represent a fascinating ecosystem where technical innovation meets social collaboration. These communities have evolved unique characteristics that enable them to tackle complex challenges while maintaining accessibility to newcomers. The Hugging Face community exemplifies this evolution, growing from a small group of researchers to a global community of over 10,000 active contributors who collaborate on everything from model development to documentation.

Developer communities within open source AI have cultivated distinctive approaches to collaboration and innovation. The PyTorch community's growth illustrates this evolution, where regular "ecosystem days" bring together developers from diverse backgrounds to share knowledge and coordinate efforts. These events have become crucial platforms for community building, often leading to breakthrough developments through unexpected collaborations. The success of such gatherings has inspired other projects, with TensorFlow's Special Interest Groups (SIGs) adopting similar approaches to foster focused innovation within their community.

The organization of these communities reflects both formal and informal structures that emerge through practical experience. Within the scikit-learn community, for instance, a meritocratic system has evolved where contributors can progress from occasional participants to core developers through consistent, quality contributions. This organic growth of expertise has proven particularly effective in maintaining project quality while encouraging new participation. The Apache Spark MLlib community demonstrates how this approach scales to enterprise-level projects, balancing corporate interests with community needs.

Knowledge sharing within these communities has developed into sophisticated systems that support both formal and informal learning. The fastai community pioneered an approach where practical teaching materials evolve alongside the technical framework, creating a virtuous cycle of learning and development. Their courses have become a model for other communities, demonstrating how educational content can drive both adoption and innovation. The success of this approach is evident in projects like spaCy, which has adopted similar practices to build a knowledgeable and engaged community.

Contribution mechanisms have evolved to support diverse forms of participation. The TensorFlow community's Special Interest Groups demonstrate how specialized teams can form around specific aspects of the project, from documentation to hardware acceleration. This structured approach to contribution has proven particularly effective in large projects, allowing focused development while maintaining overall coherence. The Jupyter community's adoption of similar structures shows how successful patterns spread across the ecosystem.

Peer review processes within these communities have developed unique characteristics suited to AI development. The PyTorch ecosystem has established sophisticated review procedures that balance thorough validation with the need for rapid innovation. These processes often involve multiple stages of review, from automated testing to expert evaluation, ensuring quality while maintaining development momentum. The adoption of similar practices by newer projects like JAX demonstrates how community standards evolve and propagate.

Mentorship programs have become crucial elements of community health and growth. The NumFOCUS organization's approach to mentorship, connecting experienced developers with newcomers across multiple projects, shows how communities can systematically develop new talent. This structured approach to knowledge transfer has proven particularly effective in maintaining project continuity while incorporating fresh perspectives. The success of these programs has influenced how other communities approach talent development.

Collaboration patterns within open source AI communities continue to evolve as projects grow in complexity. The MLflow community's approach to managing contributions from both individual developers and large organizations demonstrates how projects can balance diverse interests while maintaining technical coherence. Their success in creating stable platforms while incorporating rapid innovation provides a model for other communities facing similar challenges.

Technical innovations within open source AI represent a compelling story of community-driven advancement and creative problem-solving. These innovations emerge through a unique combination of collaborative effort and individual insight, often challenging traditional assumptions about how sophisticated AI systems can be developed. The evolution of transformer architectures in the open source space illustrates this dynamic, with projects like Hugging Face's Transformers library pioneering new approaches to model implementation while making cutting-edge architectures accessible to developers worldwide.

Architecture advances in open source AI development demonstrate the community's ability to tackle complex challenges through collective effort. The development of efficient attention mechanisms, as seen in projects like xFormers from Meta AI, shows how open collaboration can lead to significant performance improvements. These innovations often begin with research papers but truly flourish in the open source environment, where rapid iteration and community testing lead to robust, production-ready implementations. The success of these optimizations has transformed how developers approach model architecture, enabling deployment of sophisticated models on more modest hardware.

Performance improvements emerge through a fascinating interplay of theoretical insight and practical experience. The PyTorch ecosystem's development of dynamic computation graphs revolutionized how researchers approach model development, offering flexibility without sacrificing performance. This innovation, born from the needs of research practitioners, has influenced the entire field's approach to model development. Similarly, the optimization techniques developed within the TensorFlow community for mobile deployment have shown how practical constraints can drive fundamental technical innovations.

Scalability solutions within open source projects reveal the community's capacity for solving complex distributed computing challenges. Ray's evolution from a research project at UC Berkeley to a comprehensive framework for distributed

AI computation demonstrates how academic innovations can mature through community involvement. Its adoption by organizations like Ant Group and Uber for production workloads shows how open source solutions can meet enterprise-scale requirements while maintaining flexibility for different use cases.

Integration capabilities have advanced significantly through community-driven development. The ONNX project's evolution illustrates how open standards can emerge to solve critical interoperability challenges. What began as a collaboration between Microsoft and Meta has grown into a comprehensive ecosystem supporting dozens of frameworks and hardware platforms. This standardization effort has transformed how organizations approach model deployment, enabling flexibility in choosing platforms and frameworks.

Implementation methods within open source AI have matured through practical application and community refinement. The development of sophisticated training techniques within the fastai library demonstrates how practical experience can lead to innovations that benefit the entire community. Their implementation of the one-cycle policy and other training optimizations has influenced how developers approach model training across different frameworks and applications.

The synthesis of these various technical innovations often leads to unexpected breakthroughs. The combination of efficient attention mechanisms with optimized training procedures has enabled projects like BLOOM to achieve performances previously thought impossible in open source models. These achievements demonstrate how community-driven development can push the boundaries of what's possible while maintaining accessibility and transparency.

The impact of these innovations extends beyond individual projects to influence the broader AI landscape. Techniques developed in open source projects frequently find their way into production systems, demonstrating the practical value of community-driven innovation. The adoption of these innovations by major technology companies shows how open source development continues to shape the evolution of artificial intelligence technology.

The evolution of distribution and access mechanisms in open source AI tells a remarkable story of how the community has overcome significant technical challenges to make sophisticated AI systems widely available. The emergence of platforms like Hugging Face's Model Hub demonstrates this transformation, evolving from simple model sharing to a comprehensive ecosystem that handles distribution, versioning, and deployment. This evolution reflects the community's growing understanding of what developers need to effectively utilize AI technologies.

Deployment models have undergone a fascinating transformation as the community grapples with the challenges of distributing increasingly large AI systems. The story of how Stable Diffusion's release changed the landscape of image generation models illustrates this evolution. By developing innovative approaches to model distribution, including novel weight sharing techniques and optimized downloading systems, the community found ways to make gigabyte-scale models practically accessible to individual developers.

Access mechanisms have matured through careful consideration of both technical and practical needs. The development of the Datasets library by Hugging Face exemplifies this maturation, addressing not just the technical challenges of data distribution but also the practical needs of researchers and developers. What began as a simple data loading utility has evolved into a sophisticated system handling streaming access to massive datasets, enabling researchers to work with data volumes previously considered impractical for individual use.

Repository management has grown increasingly sophisticated as projects tackle the unique challenges of AI artifacts. DVC's evolution from a simple version control extension to a comprehensive solution for managing machine learning projects demonstrates this growth. Their innovative approach to handling large model files and dataset versions has transformed how teams manage AI development, making previously complex workflows accessible and manageable.

Version distribution systems have evolved to meet the specific needs of AI development. The emergence of specialized solutions like Model Hub and Weights & Biases shows how the community addresses the unique challenges of managing model versions and experiments. These platforms have transformed how developers approach model sharing and collaboration, creating new possibilities for distributed AI development.

Update processes within the open source AI ecosystem have developed unique characteristics suited to the field's rapid pace of innovation. PyTorch's approach to managing updates across its ecosystem demonstrates how communities can maintain stability while incorporating rapid advancement. Their development of sophisticated dependency management systems ensures that the complex web of AI libraries and tools remains functional despite frequent updates.

Security protocols have become increasingly important as open source AI systems grow in complexity and deployment. The development of model cards and detailed documentation requirements shows how communities address safety and security concerns. These practices, pioneered by projects like Hugging Face and adopted across the ecosystem, demonstrate how open source projects can maintain security while preserving accessibility.

The integration of these various distribution and access elements creates a comprehensive infrastructure that supports the entire AI development lifecycle. MLflow's evolution from an experiment tracking tool to a complete MLOps platform illustrates how distribution and access solutions mature to meet growing needs. Their success in creating integrated solutions that address multiple aspects of AI development demonstrates the community's ability to tackle complex challenges while maintaining usability.

Through these advances in distribution and access, the open source AI community continues to democratize access to sophisticated AI capabilities. The success of these systems shows how careful attention to practical needs, combined with innovative technical solutions, can make complex technologies accessible to a broad audience while maintaining the rigor needed for professional development.

The impact of open source AI on the broader technology ecosystem reveals a profound transformation in how organizations approach artificial intelligence development and implementation. This transformation becomes particularly evident in the story of how PyTorch emerged from Facebook's research labs to become the dominant framework in AI research, demonstrating how open source initiatives can reshape entire industries. The ripple effects of this transition continue to influence how organizations approach both development and deployment of AI technologies.

Industry influence has evolved in unexpected and powerful ways. Consider how Microsoft, traditionally known for proprietary software, has embraced open source AI through significant contributions to projects like ONNX and transformative partnerships with OpenAI. This shift represents more than just technical evolution; it demonstrates a fundamental change in how major technology companies view collaboration and innovation. The success of these approaches has encouraged other organizations to adopt similar strategies, creating a virtuous cycle of open collaboration.

Technology adoption patterns tell an equally compelling story of transformation. When Uber needed to scale their AI operations, they not only adopted but significantly contributed to the Ray project, demonstrating how enterprise needs can fuel open source development. Their experience, shared through detailed technical blogs and conference presentations, has helped other organizations navigate similar challenges. This pattern of adoption and contribution has become increasingly common, with companies like Pinterest, Spotify, and Airbnb all sharing their experiences and contributions to open source AI projects.

Innovation patterns within the ecosystem show how open source development accelerates technological advancement. The rapid evolution of natural language processing capabilities through libraries like spaCy and transformers demonstrates this acceleration. What began as research papers quickly became accessible tools through community effort, enabling organizations of all sizes to implement sophisticated language processing capabilities. This democratization of access has sparked a wave of innovation across industries.

Market effects of open source AI development have reshaped traditional business models. The success of Hugging Face illustrates how organizations can build thriving businesses around open source AI, creating new paradigms for commercial involvement in open source projects. Their model of combining open source tools with commercial services has influenced how other companies approach AI development and monetization.

Development standards have evolved significantly under open source influence. The widespread adoption of practices like model cards and documented benchmarks, pioneered by open source projects, has established new norms for AI development. These standards now influence how even proprietary systems are developed and documented, demonstrating the broader impact of open source practices on the field.

Collaboration models have transformed through open source AI development. The BigScience initiative, bringing together researchers from across the globe to create large language models, exemplifies new approaches to large-scale collaboration. This model has inspired similar efforts in other domains, showing how open source practices can enable ambitious projects that would be difficult for any single organization to undertake.

The ecosystem's evolution continues to reveal new possibilities for innovation and collaboration. When Meta released LLaMA, it sparked a wave of community innovation, with projects like Alpaca and Vicuna demonstrating how open source access to foundation models can accelerate development. These developments have challenged traditional assumptions about the necessity of massive resources for advancing AI technology.

Educational impact remains one of the most significant effects of open source AI development. The accessibility of tools and knowledge through projects like fastai has transformed how people learn and apply AI technologies. This democratization of education has created new pathways into the field, diversifying the community and enriching the ecosystem with fresh perspectives and approaches.

The future trajectory of open source AI development presents a fascinating landscape of possibilities shaped by current achievements and emerging challenges. The community's response to these opportunities reveals both the maturity of open source AI development and its continuing evolution. This dynamic becomes particularly evident in how projects like Hugging Face approach the challenge of scaling AI capabilities while maintaining accessibility, setting new patterns for future development.

Evolution trends within open source AI point toward increasingly sophisticated approaches to collaborative development. The emergence of federated learning frameworks, exemplified by projects like TensorFlow Federated and PySyft, suggests new directions for privacy-preserving AI development. These initiatives demonstrate how the community adapts to address emerging concerns while maintaining the core principles of open collaboration. Their success in creating practical solutions for distributed learning hints at future approaches to AI development.

The maturation of development practices continues to reshape how the community approaches complex projects. PyTorch's Lightning project illustrates this evolution, showing how structured approaches to AI development can make sophisticated techniques accessible to broader audiences. This progression from experimental tools to production-ready frameworks suggests future patterns for project development and organization. The growing adoption of these practices across the ecosystem indicates their lasting influence on AI development.

Emerging projects within the open source landscape reveal new possibilities for innovation. The success of projects like Stable Diffusion in democratizing image generation capabilities has inspired similar efforts in other domains. These initiatives demonstrate how open source development can rapidly advance new technologies while ensuring broad access. The community's ability to quickly build upon and improve such projects suggests accelerating innovation cycles in the future.

Technical advances continue to expand the boundaries of what open source projects can achieve. The development of efficient training techniques, as demonstrated by Microsoft's DeepSpeed and Google's JAX, shows how the community addresses fundamental challenges. These advances often find their first practical applications in open source projects, suggesting future patterns of technology transfer and adoption. The success of these approaches influences how organizations view the potential of open source solutions.

Integration paths for open source AI technology suggest increasing sophistication in how systems combine and interact. The ONNX project's growing ecosystem demonstrates how standardization efforts can enable new possibilities for system integration. These developments point toward future architectures that may more seamlessly combine different AI capabilities. The community's approach to these challenges suggests evolving patterns for system design and implementation.

Sustainability models for open source AI continue to evolve, addressing both technical and organizational challenges. The Apache Foundation's success in supporting critical AI infrastructure projects like Spark MLlib demonstrates sustainable approaches to project maintenance. These models suggest future patterns for ensuring long-term project viability while maintaining innovation. The growing adoption of similar approaches by newer projects indicates their effectiveness.

The synthesis of these various directions suggests continuing evolution in how open source AI develops and operates. Projects like Ray show how communities can address complex technical challenges while maintaining accessibility. These experiences inform future approaches to project organization and development. The success of these initiatives demonstrates the ongoing vitality of open source AI development.

As artificial intelligence technology continues to advance, the open source community's role in shaping its development remains crucial. The patterns emerging from current projects suggest new possibilities for collaboration and innovation. These developments indicate how open source approaches will continue to influence the evolution of AI technology while ensuring its benefits remain broadly accessible.

Our exploration of open source AI evolution reveals a vibrant ecosystem that continues to transform how artificial intelligence technology develops and proliferates. From PyTorch's emergence as a leading framework to Hugging Face's democratization of model access, these developments demonstrate the power of collaborative innovation. For those interested in participating in this evolution, numerous pathways exist to engage with and contribute to these transformative projects.

The development patterns we have examined show how individual contributors can make meaningful impact in the open source AI landscape. Whether through code contributions to major projects like TensorFlow, documentation improvements for spaCy, or model sharing on Hugging Face's platform, opportunities abound for engagement at various skill levels. The success of projects like fastai in creating accessible learning paths demonstrates how newcomers can progress from users to contributors, enriching the ecosystem with fresh perspectives.

The foundation established through open source development creates robust platforms for continued advancement. Projects like Ray and MLflow welcome contributors interested in distributed computing and MLOps, while initiatives like Stable Diffusion showcase opportunities in emerging areas of AI development. These platforms not only enable technical contribution but also offer chances to participate in shaping how AI technology evolves through community discussion and governance.

The impact of open source AI extends far beyond individual projects, influencing how organizations approach artificial intelligence development and implementation. By engaging with these communities, practitioners gain insights into both technical implementation and project organization. The experiences of companies like Uber and Pinterest in adopting and contributing to open source projects provide valuable models for others considering similar paths.

As we move forward to examine the proprietary AI landscape in our next chapter, we carry forward understanding of how open source development has transformed artificial intelligence technology. The interaction between open source and proprietary development creates dynamic tensions that drive innovation while ensuring diverse approaches to artificial intelligence advancement. For those interested in understanding the full spectrum of AI development, this relationship between different development models offers rich opportunities for learning and contribution.

The journey through open source AI development

continues to evolve, offering exciting opportunities for participation and innovation. Whether you're a developer interested in contributing code, a researcher looking to share models, or an organization considering open source adoption, the ecosystem welcomes your involvement. By engaging with these communities, you become part of the ongoing story of how open source shapes the future of artificial intelligence.

Explore these opportunities, whether through contributing to existing projects, participating in community discussions, or even initiating new open source initiatives. The foundations we've examined provide a strong basis for understanding how to engage effectively with the open source AI ecosystem. As we proceed to examine proprietary developments, keep in mind the complementary nature of these different approaches to advancing artificial intelligence technology.

CHAPTER 4: PROPRIETARY AI LANDSCAPE

The landscape of proprietary artificial intelligence development presents a fascinating counterpoint to the open source movement we explored in our previous chapter. This realm of commercial innovation, marked by significant investments and breakthrough developments, continues to push the boundaries of what's possible in AI. We see this clearly in OpenAI's progression from GPT-3 to GPT-4, demonstrating how focused commercial development can drive rapid advancement in AI capabilities.

The current state of proprietary AI development reflects a complex ecosystem of innovation and strategic investment. Google's development of PaLM and subsequent models showcases how commercial enterprises leverage vast resources to achieve breakthrough capabilities. Similarly, Anthropic's approach to constitutional AI development illustrates how newer companies can carve out unique positions in this competitive landscape. These developments demonstrate the diverse approaches companies take in advancing AI technology while maintaining competitive advantages.

Major technology companies have transformed how they approach AI development. Microsoft's strategic partnership with OpenAI, involving billions in investment and deep technical collaboration, exemplifies new models of commercial AI development. Google DeepMind's integration of research and application development shows how organizations are breaking down traditional barriers between academic research and commercial implementation. These evolutionary changes in corporate structure and strategy reflect the growing sophistication of commercial AI development.

Commercial innovations continue to emerge through various pathways. Meta's development of LLaMA and subsequent models demonstrates how companies balance proprietary advantage with broader industry engagement. NVIDIA's continuous advancement in AI hardware, from GPU architectures to specialized AI chips, shows how focused commercial development drives fundamental technological progress. These innovations often set new standards for performance and capability while influencing the entire field's direction.

The relationship between proprietary and open source development has grown increasingly nuanced. Companies like Hugging Face demonstrate how commercial enterprises can build successful businesses while maintaining strong commitments to open source principles. Amazon's investment in foundation models while contributing to open source projects through AWS shows how organizations navigate this complex landscape. These interactions create productive tensions that drive innovation across both domains.

As we explore the proprietary AI landscape, we'll examine how commercial enterprises approach the challenges of advancing artificial intelligence technology. From research breakthroughs to market implementation, we'll investigate the strategies and methodologies that drive commercial AI development. This journey reveals both current achievements and emerging directions in proprietary AI development, providing crucial context for understanding the full spectrum of artificial intelligence advancement.

For practitioners and organizations engaging with commercial AI development, understanding these dynamics becomes increasingly important. The choices companies make in developing and deploying AI technologies influence not just their own success but the evolution of the entire field. As we proceed, we'll examine how different organizations approach these challenges, offering insights valuable for those working with or implementing commercial AI solutions.

The evolution of commercial artificial intelligence represents a remarkable journey of technological advancement and strategic innovation. This progression becomes particularly evident in the transformation of early research initiatives into today's sophisticated AI enterprises. DeepMind's evolution from a small London startup, through its 2014 acquisition by Google, to its current form as Google DeepMind following the 2023 merger with Google Brain, illustrates how commercial AI ventures can mature while preserving their innovative spirit.

The landscape has been shaped by landmark commercial breakthroughs that redefined what's possible in AI development. OpenAI's transition from a research-focused organization to a commercial entity, marked by the release of GPT-3 and its subsequent evolution to GPT-4, demonstrates how breakthrough technologies can transform business models. This journey illustrates the delicate balance between advancing AI capabilities and developing sustainable commercial frameworks for their deployment.

Investment patterns have played a crucial role in shaping commercial AI development. Microsoft's strategic $13 billion investment in OpenAI exemplifies how large-scale funding can accelerate technological advancement. Similarly,

Anthropic's securing of substantial investment for constitutional AI development shows how focused funding supports specialized approaches to AI safety and capability. These investment patterns reveal how commercial entities approach the challenge of advancing AI technology while managing risk and maintaining strategic advantage.

The journey from research to product deployment has grown increasingly sophisticated. Google's development of BERT, which transformed from a research paper to a core component of their search engine, demonstrates effective technology transfer at scale. This progression from theoretical advancement to practical application shows how commercial enterprises navigate the challenges of implementing cutting-edge AI technologies while maintaining reliable services for billions of users.

Industry-academia partnerships have evolved into complex relationships that benefit both sectors. The MIT-IBM Watson AI Lab collaboration exemplifies how companies engage with academic institutions to advance fundamental research while maintaining commercial relevance. Stanford's corporate affiliate program in AI, engaging with companies like NVIDIA and Meta, shows how universities and industry create mutually beneficial research ecosystems. These partnerships accelerate innovation while ensuring research remains grounded in practical applications.

The current state of commercial AI development reflects both the maturation of early approaches and the emergence of new paradigms. Amazon's investment in foundation models through AWS demonstrates how cloud providers are becoming crucial players in AI advancement. Meanwhile, specialized companies like Scale AI show how focused solutions for specific challenges, such as data labeling and model evaluation, create new categories of AI businesses. This diversification of commercial approaches enriches the overall AI ecosystem.

The relationship between commercial development and

broader AI advancement continues to evolve. Meta's release of LLaMA, while maintaining certain restrictions, shows how companies balance proprietary interests with broader community engagement. NVIDIA's development of CUDA and specialized AI hardware demonstrates how commercial innovation can create new standards that benefit the entire field. These examples illustrate the complex interplay between commercial interests and technological advancement.

This evolution continues to accelerate, driven by both technological capability and market demand. Companies like Intel and AMD have intensified their focus on AI-specific hardware development, responding to growing computational requirements for advanced AI systems. Cloud providers like Google Cloud and Microsoft Azure continue to expand their AI services, making sophisticated capabilities accessible to a broader range of organizations. These developments show how commercial evolution both responds to and drives market needs.

The landscape of major industry leaders in artificial intelligence reveals a complex ecosystem where innovation and strategic development intersect. Google DeepMind's integration exemplifies this complexity, combining DeepMind's research prowess with Google's vast computational resources and practical implementation capabilities. Their achievements, from AlphaFold's protein structure prediction to PaLM's advanced language understanding, demonstrate how integrated research and development can address both fundamental scientific challenges and practical applications.

Microsoft's strategic evolution in AI development tells an equally compelling story of transformation. Their partnership with OpenAI has reshaped their approach to AI integration, leading to sophisticated implementations across their product suite. From GitHub Copilot's coding assistance to the integration of GPT-4 in Bing Chat, Microsoft demonstrates how strategic partnerships can accelerate the deployment of advanced AI capabilities while maintaining product quality and reliability.

OpenAI's journey from research laboratory to commercial entity illustrates another facet of industry leadership. Their progression through increasingly capable language models, from GPT-3 to GPT-4, shows how focused commercial development can drive rapid advancement. The company's approach to staged release and careful capability assessment demonstrates new models for responsible AI deployment while maintaining commercial viability.

Anthropic's emergence with Claude and constitutional AI development represents a newer model of industry leadership. Their focus on AI safety and reliability, while achieving competitive capabilities, shows how specialized approaches can establish unique market positions. This demonstrates the industry's capacity to support diverse approaches to AI development, each contributing distinct perspectives and innovations.

Google's comprehensive approach to AI development spans multiple dimensions. Their development of specialized AI hardware through TPU iterations, alongside software frameworks like JAX and TensorFlow, shows how vertical integration can enhance AI capabilities. The company's ability to deploy advanced AI features across their product line, from search to workspace applications, demonstrates effective technology transfer at scale.

Meta's strategic decisions in AI development reveal yet another leadership model. Their investment in foundational AI research, combined with selective open-source releases like LLaMA, shows how companies can balance proprietary advantage with community engagement. Their focus on large-scale AI infrastructure and efficiency optimization demonstrates how practical constraints drive innovation.

Amazon's approach through AWS emphasizes accessibility and integration. Their development of managed AI services and custom chips like Trainium and Inferentia shows how cloud providers can influence AI development patterns. The company's focus on making advanced AI capabilities accessible to their cloud customers while maintaining performance and cost-effectiveness demonstrates practical innovation at scale.

NVIDIA's leadership in AI hardware continues to shape industry capabilities. Their evolution from gaming-focused GPU manufacturer to essential AI infrastructure provider shows how companies can transform their core competencies to address emerging needs. The development of sophisticated AI architectures like the Hopper H100, alongside software frameworks like CUDA and TensorRT, demonstrates comprehensive ecosystem development.

Industry collaboration patterns reveal sophisticated approaches to innovation. The partnership between Microsoft and AMD to develop AI-optimized cloud infrastructure shows how companies combine complementary strengths. Similarly, Intel's collaboration with academic institutions and software companies in developing their AI portfolio demonstrates the importance of diverse partnerships in advancing capabilities.

These leaders continue to push boundaries while establishing new paradigms for AI development. IBM's quantum computing research alongside classical AI development shows how companies maintain long-term innovation focus. Qualcomm's development of AI-optimized mobile processors demonstrates how specialized requirements drive focused innovation. These diverse approaches ensure continuous advancement across multiple fronts.

The evolution of AI platforms represents one of the most significant transformations in commercial artificial intelligence, fundamentally changing how organizations develop and deploy AI capabilities. This evolution becomes particularly evident in Microsoft Azure's AI platform development, which has grown from basic machine learning services to a comprehensive ecosystem supporting everything from model development to large-scale deployment. Their integration of OpenAI's technologies demonstrates how platforms can rapidly evolve to incorporate cutting-edge capabilities while maintaining enterprise-grade reliability.

Cloud platform development has reached new levels of sophistication, as demonstrated by Google Cloud's AI infrastructure evolution. Their transition from basic machine learning services to comprehensive AI development environments, including Vertex AI, shows how platforms adapt to meet increasingly complex development needs. The introduction of specialized hardware access, from TPUs to high-performance GPU clusters, illustrates how infrastructure evolution supports advancing AI capabilities while managing computational costs effectively.

Amazon Web Services' platform development tells a story of systematic capability expansion. Their progression from basic SageMaker offerings to comprehensive AI development environments demonstrates how platforms mature to support diverse development needs. The introduction of custom silicon through Trainium and Inferentia chips shows how cloud providers vertically integrate to optimize AI workloads, while their managed services for foundation models reflect adaptation to emerging market demands.

Enterprise platforms have evolved to address specific organizational needs with increasing sophistication. Snowflake's Data Cloud platform exemplifies this evolution, expanding from data warehousing to support sophisticated AI workloads through native integration and partnership ecosystems. Their development of features like Snowpark for Python shows how platforms adapt to emerging development patterns while maintaining enterprise security and governance requirements.

Development environment advancement reveals another crucial aspect of platform evolution. NVIDIA's AI Enterprise platform demonstrates how hardware expertise can translate into comprehensive development environments. Their integration of tools like RAPIDS and TensorRT shows how platforms can optimize entire AI development workflows while maintaining compatibility with popular frameworks.

Integration capabilities have become increasingly central to platform success. Databricks' Lakehouse Platform illustrates this trend, combining data management with sophisticated AI development capabilities. Their unified analytics platform shows how integration can simplify complex workflows while enabling advanced AI applications, demonstrating the value of cohesive development environments.

The evolution of specialized AI platforms reveals interesting patterns in market development. Scale AI's platform for data labeling and model evaluation shows how specific aspects of AI development can spawn sophisticated platform solutions. Their expansion into model testing and evaluation demonstrates how platforms evolve to address emerging needs in the AI development lifecycle.

Performance optimization has emerged as a crucial focus in platform evolution. Oracle Cloud Infrastructure's AI services show how established enterprise vendors adapt to AI workloads, with specialized offerings for high-performance computing and AI model training. Their focus on price-performance optimization demonstrates how platforms balance capability with cost-effectiveness.

Security and governance capabilities have matured alongside technical features. IBM's Watson platform evolution shows how enterprise AI platforms incorporate sophisticated governance mechanisms. Their development of tools for AI lifecycle management demonstrates how platforms address growing concerns about AI deployment in regulated industries.

These platforms continue to evolve, shaped by both technological advancement and market needs. ServiceNow's integration of AI capabilities across their workflow platform shows how AI features become embedded in enterprise software. This evolution demonstrates the ongoing transformation of business platforms through AI integration while maintaining focus on practical business value.

Commercial implementation strategies for artificial intelligence have evolved into sophisticated approaches that balance innovation with practical deployment considerations. Microsoft's implementation of GPT-4 across their product suite demonstrates this evolution, showing how companies can systematically integrate advanced AI capabilities while maintaining service reliability. Their staged deployment approach, beginning with GitHub Copilot and expanding to Bing Chat and Microsoft 365 Copilot, reveals how organizations can effectively scale AI implementation while managing operational risks.

Enterprise-scale deployment frameworks have matured significantly through practical experience. Google's implementation of BERT and subsequent language models in their search infrastructure shows how organizations handle large-scale AI deployment. Their approach to gradual feature rollout, extensive testing, and careful performance monitoring demonstrates sophisticated strategies for managing AI implementation at global scale. This systematic approach to deployment has influenced how other organizations approach similar challenges.

Resource management strategies have become increasingly refined through commercial implementation experience. NVIDIA's enterprise AI implementation framework shows how organizations can effectively manage computational resources while maintaining performance. Their development of specialized tools for workload optimization and resource allocation demonstrates how commercial implementation strategies evolve to address practical constraints while maximizing capability utilization.

Industry-specific implementation patterns reveal interesting adaptations to different operational contexts. JPMorgan Chase's implementation of AI for fraud detection and risk assessment demonstrates how financial institutions approach AI deployment in regulated environments. Their development of sophisticated validation frameworks and governance structures shows how implementation strategies adapt to specific industry requirements while maintaining operational effectiveness.

Integration strategies have evolved to address the complexity of existing technology landscapes. Salesforce's implementation of Einstein AI capabilities across their CRM platform demonstrates effective approaches to AI integration within established enterprise systems. Their focus on seamless user experience while maintaining system reliability shows how organizations balance innovation with practical operational requirements.

Performance optimization strategies have become increasingly sophisticated through commercial implementation. Meta's deployment of AI features across their social platforms demonstrates how organizations optimize AI implementation for massive scale. Their development of specialized infrastructure and deployment tools shows how implementation strategies evolve to address specific operational challenges while maintaining service quality.

Security considerations have become central to implementation planning. IBM's approach to AI deployment in regulated industries demonstrates how organizations address security requirements while maintaining implementation effectiveness. Their development of comprehensive security frameworks for AI deployment shows how implementation strategies incorporate sophisticated protection mechanisms while enabling practical capability utilization.

Cost management strategies reveal another crucial aspect of commercial implementation. Amazon's approach to AI implementation in AWS shows how organizations balance capability provision with operational costs. Their development of specialized hardware and optimization tools demonstrates how implementation strategies evolve to address economic considerations while maintaining service quality.

Validation frameworks have matured alongside implementation capabilities. Apple's approach to AI feature validation before deployment demonstrates how organizations ensure reliability while maintaining innovation pace. Their systematic testing and validation processes show how implementation strategies incorporate sophisticated quality assurance while supporting rapid capability deployment.

These implementation strategies continue evolving through practical experience. LinkedIn's deployment of AI features for professional networking demonstrates how organizations adapt implementation approaches to specific use cases. Their focus on measuring business impact while maintaining user trust shows how implementation strategies balance multiple objectives while ensuring practical effectiveness.

The market dynamics within proprietary AI development reveal fascinating patterns of competition, collaboration, and innovation. Microsoft's strategic investment in OpenAI, totaling over $13 billion, demonstrates how major technology companies are reshaping competitive landscapes through strategic partnerships. This relationship has catalyzed significant market changes, influencing how other organizations approach AI development and deployment while establishing new models for technology collaboration.

Competition patterns have evolved beyond traditional market rivalries. Google's development of Bard and PaLM models alongside ChatGPT's emergence demonstrates how market dynamics influence innovation pace. Similarly, Anthropic's emergence with Claude models shows how new entrants can establish market positions through specialized focus on safety and reliability. These competitive dynamics continue driving advancement while influencing how organizations approach AI development.

Strategic positioning within the AI market reveals

sophisticated approaches to differentiation. NVIDIA's evolution from gaming hardware provider to essential AI infrastructure company demonstrates successful market repositioning. Their development of comprehensive AI solutions, from hardware to development tools, shows how companies can establish dominant positions in crucial market segments while maintaining innovation momentum.

Partnership ecosystems have become increasingly important in market dynamics. Amazon's approach to AI services through AWS, combining proprietary development with strategic partnerships, shows how companies build comprehensive service offerings. Their collaboration with Hugging Face for model deployment services demonstrates how partnerships can enhance market positions while expanding service capabilities.

Investment patterns reveal changing perspectives on AI development value. The substantial funding secured by AI companies like Anthropic and Cohere shows how investors view specialized AI development approaches. These investment decisions influence market dynamics while enabling diverse approaches to AI advancement. The pattern of investment across different AI sectors demonstrates evolving market perspectives on value creation opportunities.

Industry alignments continue shifting through strategic decisions. Meta's release of LLaMA models demonstrates how companies balance proprietary advantage with broader ecosystem engagement. Their approach to controlled open-source release shows how organizations navigate complex market dynamics while maintaining strategic positions. These decisions influence how other organizations approach similar market choices.

Market response patterns reveal interesting adoption dynamics. ServiceNow's integration of generative AI capabilities across their platform demonstrates how enterprise software providers adapt to market demands. Their systematic approach to AI feature integration shows how organizations respond to market pressure while maintaining service quality. These patterns influence how other companies approach AI capability development.

Technology accessibility has emerged as a crucial market dynamic. IBM's Watson platform evolution demonstrates how established companies adapt their offerings to changing market requirements. Their focus on enterprise-grade AI solutions shows how organizations position themselves in specific market segments while maintaining competitive advantages. These positioning decisions influence market structure and competition patterns.

Cost dynamics continue influencing market development. Google Cloud's pricing strategies for AI services demonstrate how providers balance capability provision with market accessibility. Their development of cost-optimization tools shows how organizations address market demands for efficient AI deployment while maintaining service quality. These economic considerations shape how the market evolves.

Customer relationship patterns reveal evolving market maturity. Palantir's approach to AI integration in their enterprise solutions demonstrates how companies maintain strategic relationships while advancing capabilities. Their focus on custom solution development shows how organizations adapt to specific market requirements while maintaining technological advancement. These relationships influence how the market develops and matures.

Commercial innovation models in artificial intelligence demonstrate sophisticated approaches to advancing technology while maintaining market advantage. Google DeepMind's integration of research and application development shows how organizations can maintain scientific excellence while delivering practical innovations. Their progression from fundamental research in areas like protein folding with AlphaFold 2 to practical applications in data center cooling optimization demonstrates effective translation of research into commercial value.

Research investment strategies reveal careful balancing of long-term innovation with immediate market needs. Google Research's approach to language model development, progressing from BERT through PaLM and beyond, shows how companies structure sustained innovation programs. Their investment in fundamental research while maintaining focus on practical applications demonstrates sophisticated resource allocation strategies. This balance between exploration and exploitation characterizes successful commercial innovation models.

Development methodologies have evolved to support rapid innovation while maintaining quality. OpenAI's iterative approach to model development, from GPT-3 through GPT-4, demonstrates effective innovation management at scale. Their methodology of controlled releases and capability assessment shows how organizations can maintain rapid development pace while managing potential risks. These approaches influence how other organizations structure their innovation processes.

Product evolution cycles reveal interesting patterns in commercial innovation. Microsoft's systematic integration of AI capabilities across their product suite shows how organizations manage complex technology deployment. Their approach to feature development and rollout demonstrates sophisticated product management while maintaining service reliability. These patterns influence how companies approach AI product development.

Innovation ecosystems have become increasingly important in commercial development. NVIDIA's cultivation of a comprehensive AI development environment, from hardware through software tools, shows how companies build supportive innovation frameworks. Their approach to ecosystem development demonstrates how organizations can create valuable platforms while maintaining technological leadership. These ecosystems influence how innovation propagates through the industry.

Resource allocation strategies demonstrate sophisticated approaches to innovation management. Meta's investment in AI infrastructure and research facilities shows how organizations support sustained innovation programs. Their approach to balancing immediate needs with long-term development demonstrates effective resource management while maintaining innovation momentum. These strategies influence how companies structure their innovation investments.

Market alignment in innovation programs reveals careful attention to practical value creation. Anthropic's focus on constitutional AI development shows how companies can align innovation with specific market positions. Their approach to capability development demonstrates how organizations can maintain distinct innovation directions while building market presence. These alignment decisions influence innovation trajectory and market impact.

Validation frameworks have evolved to support rapid innovation while maintaining reliability. IBM's approach to AI validation in enterprise contexts shows how organizations ensure innovation quality. Their development of comprehensive testing frameworks demonstrates how companies balance innovation pace with reliability requirements. These frameworks influence how organizations approach AI development and deployment.

Innovation partnerships reveal interesting patterns in commercial development. Amazon's collaboration with academic institutions through AWS demonstrates how companies engage broader innovation ecosystems. Their approach to partnership management shows how organizations can leverage external innovation while maintaining strategic advantage. These relationships influence how innovation develops and propagates.

Technology transfer mechanisms show sophisticated approaches to innovation deployment. Intel's development of

AI-optimized processors demonstrates effective transfer from research to product development. Their approach to technology commercialization shows how organizations manage innovation pipeline while maintaining market relevance. These mechanisms influence how innovations reach practical application.

The synthesis of these innovation models demonstrates the maturity of commercial AI development. Apple's integration of AI capabilities into their products shows how companies balance innovation with user experience. Their approach to feature development demonstrates how organizations can maintain innovation momentum while ensuring practical value delivery. These patterns continue influencing how companies approach AI innovation and development.

The trajectory of commercial artificial intelligence development reveals emerging patterns that suggest future directions while building upon current achievements. Microsoft's expanding integration of AI capabilities across their enterprise suite demonstrates how companies envision comprehensive AI-enhanced business environments. Their systematic approach to capability deployment, from development tools through productivity applications, shows how organizations are establishing foundations for future advancement.

Technology evolution patterns indicate sophisticated approaches to capability development. Google's investment in next-generation AI infrastructure, including advanced TPU developments and quantum computing research, shows how organizations prepare for future computational needs. Their balanced approach to current capability delivery while investing in fundamental research demonstrates how companies maintain present market position while preparing for future opportunities.

Industry development trends reveal careful attention to ecosystem cultivation. NVIDIA's continued expansion of AI-specific hardware and software solutions shows how companies build comprehensive technology stacks. Their development of increasingly sophisticated tools and platforms demonstrates how organizations anticipate future market needs while maintaining current market leadership. These developments influence how other companies approach future planning.

Strategic investment patterns indicate evolving perspectives on future value creation. Amazon's development of custom AI chips and infrastructure solutions through AWS shows how organizations position themselves for future market requirements. Their approach to capability development demonstrates how companies balance current service delivery with future technology needs. These investment decisions shape industry development trajectories.

Market maturation patterns reveal interesting evolutionary trends. Meta's strategic focus on AI infrastructure efficiency and scalability shows how organizations address emerging operational challenges. Their approach to technology development demonstrates how companies anticipate future requirements while managing current operational needs. These patterns influence how organizations prepare for future market conditions.

Innovation pathway development shows sophisticated planning for future capabilities. Anthropic's focus on advanced AI safety research while delivering current services demonstrates how organizations balance immediate market presence with longer-term objectives. Their approach to technology development shows how companies can maintain distinct strategic positions while preparing for future market evolution.

Resource allocation strategies reveal careful attention to future preparation. IBM's investment in quantum computing alongside classical AI development shows how organizations maintain multiple innovation streams. Their approach to technology development demonstrates how companies balance various potential futures while maintaining current market positions. These strategies influence industry investment patterns.

Collaboration models continue evolving through practical experience. Intel's partnerships with research institutions and technology companies show how organizations approach future capability development. Their collaborative approach demonstrates how companies leverage diverse expertise while maintaining strategic advantage. These relationships influence how future innovation develops.

Market response patterns indicate evolving customer relationships. Salesforce's integration of AI capabilities across their CRM platform shows how organizations anticipate future business requirements. Their approach to feature development demonstrates how companies balance current needs with future possibilities. These patterns influence how organizations approach capability development.

Technology accessibility trends reveal interesting future directions. Google Cloud's development of increasingly sophisticated AI services shows how organizations plan for future market needs. Their approach to service evolution demonstrates how companies anticipate future requirements while maintaining current service quality. These developments influence industry capability deployment patterns.

The synthesis of these trajectories suggests continuing evolution in how commercial AI develops and operates. Microsoft's strategic partnership with OpenAI demonstrates how organizations might approach future capability development through collaborative arrangements. Their relationship shows how companies can maintain competitive advantage while participating in broader technology advancement. These patterns continue influencing how organizations approach future AI development and deployment.

Our exploration of the proprietary AI landscape reveals a dynamic ecosystem where innovation, strategic investment, and market dynamics converge to drive artificial intelligence advancement. From Microsoft's transformative partnership with OpenAI to Google's systematic development of advanced AI capabilities, we see how commercial enterprises shape the future of AI technology. These developments offer fascinating opportunities for practitioners and organizations to engage with and benefit from proprietary AI advancement.

The implementation strategies we've examined demonstrate practical approaches to leveraging commercial AI capabilities. Organizations like Amazon AWS and Google Cloud provide increasingly sophisticated platforms that enable businesses to implement AI solutions at scale. For practitioners interested in deploying AI capabilities, these platforms offer proven pathways to implementation while maintaining enterprise-grade reliability. Understanding these commercial frameworks becomes crucial for effective AI deployment in professional contexts.

The evolution of commercial innovation models reveals multiple paths for engagement with proprietary AI technology. Whether through Microsoft's comprehensive enterprise solutions or NVIDIA's specialized development tools, organizations can choose approaches that align with their specific needs and capabilities. These diverse pathways demonstrate how different organizations can effectively participate in the proprietary AI ecosystem while maintaining their strategic objectives.

Market dynamics continue shaping how organizations approach AI implementation. The success of companies like Anthropic and Cohere in establishing specialized market positions shows how focused approaches can create significant value. For professionals and organizations considering AI adoption, these examples provide valuable insights into effective positioning and implementation strategies. The diverse approaches to market participation demonstrate the breadth of opportunities available in commercial AI.

The relationship between proprietary and open source

development creates interesting opportunities for technological advancement. Meta's selective open-source releases and Google's contribution to open frameworks while maintaining proprietary advantages show how organizations can effectively balance these approaches. This interaction suggests promising directions for practitioners looking to leverage both proprietary and open source capabilities in their AI implementations.

As we move forward to examine model architectures and innovations in our next chapter, we carry forward understanding of how commercial development drives and shapes AI advancement. The sophisticated approaches to AI development and deployment we've explored provide crucial context for understanding architectural evolution. For practitioners and organizations, this understanding becomes increasingly valuable as AI technology continues advancing.

Engage actively with these commercial developments, whether through platform experimentation, capability evaluation, or strategic planning. The major cloud providers offer extensive resources for learning and testing commercial AI capabilities. Organizations like Microsoft, Google, and Amazon provide comprehensive documentation and training materials that enable practical engagement with their AI technologies. These resources offer excellent starting points for exploring commercial AI implementation.

The proprietary AI landscape continues evolving, offering new opportunities for innovation and implementation. By understanding current developments and future trajectories, practitioners and organizations can better position themselves to leverage these advancing capabilities. Explore these opportunities while maintaining awareness of how commercial developments influence the broader AI ecosystem.

CHAPTER 5: MODEL ARCHITECTURE INNOVATION

The landscape of model architecture innovation represents one of the most fascinating areas of artificial intelligence advancement, where theoretical breakthroughs translate into transformative capabilities. The evolution from the original Transformer architecture, introduced by Vaswani et al., to today's sophisticated models like GPT-4 and PaLM demonstrates how architectural innovations drive fundamental progress in AI capabilities. These developments continue reshaping our understanding of what's possible in artificial intelligence while suggesting new directions for future advancement.

The current state of architecture innovation reflects remarkable progress in multiple dimensions. Google's development of the Pathways architecture demonstrates how organizations approach the challenge of creating more efficient, adaptable AI systems. Similarly, Anthropic's constitutional AI architecture shows how safety considerations can be embedded directly into model design.

These architectural approaches represent different paths to advancing AI capabilities while addressing specific challenges and requirements.

Architectural breakthroughs continue emerging through various research directions. Google DeepMind's work on Perceiver architectures shows how attention mechanisms can be adapted for more efficient processing across multiple modalities. Meta's advances in sparse expert models demonstrate new approaches to scaling model capabilities while managing computational requirements. These innovations reveal how architectural thinking evolves to address both theoretical and practical challenges.

The relationship between architecture design and practical implementation has grown increasingly sophisticated. Microsoft's work on DeepSpeed demonstrates how architectural innovations can dramatically improve training efficiency and deployment capabilities. NVIDIA's development of optimized architectures for their hardware shows how system design considerations influence model architecture. These developments highlight the crucial interplay between theoretical advancement and practical implementation.

The impact of architectural innovation extends beyond individual models to influence entire categories of AI systems. The development of efficient attention mechanisms, as seen in projects like xFormers, shows how architectural improvements can benefit the broader AI community. These advances demonstrate how fundamental architectural innovations can create cascading effects across multiple domains and applications.

In this chapter, we explore the sophisticated world of model architecture innovation, examining how different approaches drive artificial intelligence advancement. From foundation models to specialized architectures, we'll investigate how architectural decisions influence AI capabilities and performance. This exploration reveals both current achievements and emerging directions in architecture development, providing crucial context for understanding modern AI systems.

For practitioners and organizations working with AI systems, understanding architectural innovation becomes increasingly important. The choices made in model architecture influence everything from training efficiency to deployment capabilities. As we proceed, we'll examine how different architectural approaches address various requirements, offering insights valuable for those implementing or working with AI systems.

The evolution of model architectures represents a remarkable journey of innovation and refinement in artificial intelligence development. This progression becomes particularly evident when examining the transformation from early neural networks to today's sophisticated architectures. The introduction of the Transformer architecture in 2017 by Vaswani et al. marked a pivotal moment, establishing foundations that continue influencing current developments in models like GPT-4, PaLM, and Claude.

The impact of architectural breakthroughs reveals fascinating patterns of innovation. Google Brain's development of the original Transformer architecture demonstrated how fundamental rethinking of attention mechanisms could dramatically improve model capabilities. This architectural innovation, moving beyond traditional recurrent neural networks, established new paradigms for processing sequential data. The subsequent adoption and refinement of these principles across the field demonstrates how foundational architectural innovations can reshape entire domains of AI development.

Scaling breakthroughs have emerged through careful architectural evolution. OpenAI's progression through GPT models shows how architectural refinements enable effective scaling to larger model sizes. Their innovations in model parallelism and efficient attention mechanisms demonstrate how architectural decisions influence scaling capabilities. Similarly, Google's PaLM architecture reveals how thoughtful design choices can enhance model performance at scale while maintaining computational efficiency.

Efficiency innovations have become increasingly central to architectural advancement. Google DeepMind's work on efficient attention mechanisms, as demonstrated in their Perceiver architecture, shows how novel approaches can reduce computational requirements while maintaining model capabilities. Meta's development of sparse expert models through their MOE (Mixture of Experts) architecture reveals how architectural innovations can address efficiency challenges while enhancing model capabilities.

The relationship between architecture and training methodology has grown increasingly sophisticated. Anthropic's constitutional AI architecture demonstrates how safety considerations can be embedded at the architectural level. Their approach to model design shows how architectural decisions influence not just capabilities but also behavioral characteristics. These developments reveal how architecture choices shape fundamental model properties.

Performance optimization through architectural innovation continues driving significant advances. Microsoft's DeepSpeed ZeRO architecture shows how thoughtful design can dramatically improve training efficiency. Their innovations in memory management and computation distribution demonstrate how architectural decisions influence practical implementation capabilities. These optimizations reveal the crucial role of architecture in enabling advanced AI development.

The integration of multiple architectural innovations creates interesting synthesis opportunities. Google's Pathways architecture demonstrates how different architectural approaches can be combined to create more flexible, efficient systems. Their work on unified architectures shows how architectural innovation can address multiple challenges simultaneously. These developments suggest new directions for architectural evolution.

Hardware considerations have become increasingly important in architectural development. NVIDIA's tensor core architecture and Google's TPU design show how hardware and model architectures co-evolve. Their work on optimized computation patterns demonstrates how architectural decisions must consider implementation platforms. These relationships reveal the complex interplay between different aspects of AI system design.

The evolution of training architectures has paralleled model architecture development. The emergence of sophisticated pre-training approaches, as seen in models like BERT and RoBERTa, shows how architectural decisions influence training strategies. These developments demonstrate the close relationship between model architecture and training methodology, revealing how innovations in one area enable advances in others.

These evolutionary patterns continue influencing current architectural development. The success of different architectural approaches informs how organizations approach new challenges. Understanding this evolution provides crucial context for appreciating current developments while suggesting future directions for architectural innovation.

Foundation model architectures represent some of the most sophisticated designs in current artificial intelligence, embodying crucial advances in large-scale language understanding and multimodal processing. OpenAI's GPT-4 architecture demonstrates how foundation models have evolved to handle multiple modalities while maintaining high performance across diverse tasks. This architectural sophistication becomes evident in the model's ability to process both text and images coherently, representing a significant advance in unified architectural design.

The evolution of large language model architectures reveals interesting patterns in design optimization. Google's PaLM architecture showcases how careful attention to scaling laws and architectural efficiency enables improved performance at scale. Their implementation of sophisticated attention mechanisms and optimization techniques demonstrates how architectural decisions influence both capability and efficiency. The success of these approaches has influenced how organizations approach foundation model development.

Multimodal architecture design presents unique challenges that drive innovation. Meta's advancement in multimodal transformers shows how architectures can effectively combine different types of input processing. Their work on unified representations demonstrates how architectural decisions influence cross-modal understanding capabilities. These developments reveal the complexity of creating truly integrated multimodal systems.

Training architecture optimization has become increasingly crucial for foundation models. Anthropic's approach to training Claude demonstrates how architectural decisions influence both model capabilities and behavioral characteristics. Their implementation of constitutional AI principles at the architectural level shows how design choices can shape fundamental model properties. These innovations reveal the deep connection between architecture and training methodology.

Scaling considerations have driven significant architectural innovation in foundation models. Microsoft and NVIDIA's collaboration on Megatron-Turing NLG demonstrates how architectures adapt to enable efficient training of massive models. Their work on distributed training architectures shows how design decisions influence practical implementation capabilities. These developments highlight the crucial role of architecture in enabling large-scale AI systems.

Memory management architectures have evolved to address the challenges of large models. Google's PaLM implementation demonstrates sophisticated approaches to managing computational resources efficiently. Their architectural decisions regarding memory usage and computation distribution show how practical constraints influence design choices. These considerations reveal the importance of resource management in foundation model architecture.

Attention mechanism innovations continue driving architectural advancement. The development of efficient attention patterns, as seen in models like Google DeepMind's Perceiver IO, shows how architectural improvements enhance model capabilities. These innovations demonstrate how fundamental architectural components evolve to address specific challenges while maintaining performance. The success of these approaches influences how organizations design new architectures.

Cross-model learning capabilities have emerged as important architectural considerations. Meta's research in few-shot learning architectures demonstrates how models can be designed to learn more efficiently across domains. Their work on adaptive architectures shows how design decisions influence model flexibility and generalization capabilities. These developments suggest new directions for foundation model architecture.

The synthesis of multiple architectural innovations creates interesting possibilities. The combination of efficient attention mechanisms with sophisticated parallelization strategies, as seen in modern foundation models, demonstrates how different architectural advances complement each other. These integrations show how architectural innovation often proceeds through careful combination of proven approaches while maintaining performance objectives.

These architectural patterns continue influencing foundation model development. Understanding these patterns provides crucial context for appreciating current capabilities while suggesting future directions for architectural innovation. The success of different approaches demonstrates the importance of thoughtful architectural design in advancing AI capabilities.

Specialized architecture innovations represent a crucial frontier in artificial intelligence development, where focused design approaches address specific domain challenges. Google's development of specialized vision architectures through their ViT (Vision Transformer) models demonstrates how architectural innovation can effectively adapt transformer principles to visual processing tasks. Their success in achieving state-of-the-art performance while maintaining computational efficiency shows how specialized architectures can excel in specific domains.

Speech processing architectures have evolved to address unique challenges in audio understanding. Meta's wav2vec architecture demonstrates sophisticated approaches to self-supervised learning from speech data. Their innovations in feature extraction and representation learning show how specialized architectures can effectively handle the complexities of audio processing. These developments reveal how domain-specific requirements drive architectural innovation.

Scientific computing architectures have emerged as another area of specialized innovation. Google DeepMind's AlphaFold 2 architecture shows how specific scientific challenges can inspire novel architectural approaches. Their integration of physical and biological constraints into the model architecture demonstrates how domain knowledge can inform architectural design. These successes reveal the value of specialized architectural solutions for complex scientific problems.

Efficiency-focused architectures continue driving innovation in resource utilization. Microsoft's development of sparse attention mechanisms through DeepSpeed demonstrates how specialized architectures can dramatically improve computational efficiency. Their work on optimized training architectures shows how focused design decisions can enhance performance while reducing resource requirements. These innovations influence how organizations approach efficient model design.

The development of mixture of experts (MoE) architectures represents another significant advance in specialized design. Google's Switch Transformer and Meta's implementation of sparse expert models show how architectural innovations can enable more efficient processing through specialization. Their success in managing computational resources while maintaining model capabilities demonstrates the value of specialized architectural approaches.

Hardware-optimized architectures reveal interesting patterns in system design. NVIDIA's development of transformer architectures optimized for their A100 and H100 GPUs shows how hardware considerations influence architectural decisions. Their work on memory-efficient attention mechanisms demonstrates how specialized architectures can maximize hardware utilization. These developments highlight the importance of hardware-aware architectural design.

Memory optimization architectures have become increasingly sophisticated. Google's work on efficient attention patterns through their Performer architecture shows how specialized designs can reduce memory requirements while maintaining performance. Their innovations in approximate attention computation demonstrate how architectural decisions influence practical implementation capabilities. These approaches reveal new possibilities for efficient model design.

Domain-specific processing architectures continue emerging through focused innovation. OpenAI's DALL-E architecture demonstrates how specialized designs can effectively handle complex image generation tasks. Their integration of different processing streams shows how architectural decisions influence creative capabilities. These successes reveal how specialized architectures enable new applications.

The synthesis of multiple specialized innovations creates interesting architectural possibilities. The combination of efficient attention mechanisms with domain-specific processing patterns, as seen in modern multimodal systems, shows how different specialized approaches can complement each other. These integrations demonstrate how architectural innovation often proceeds through careful combination of proven techniques.

Computational efficiency architectures represent another crucial area of specialized innovation. Anthropic's work on constitutional AI architectures shows how specialized designs can incorporate safety considerations while maintaining performance. Their architectural decisions regarding computation and control flow demonstrate how specialized requirements influence design choices. These developments reveal new approaches to architectural optimization.

Implementation architectures represent the crucial bridge between theoretical design and practical deployment of AI systems. Microsoft's implementation of GPT-4 across their Azure infrastructure demonstrates how sophisticated deployment architectures enable efficient scaling of large language models. Their development of distributed serving systems shows how implementation architecture decisions influence real-world performance and reliability in production environments.

Deployment optimization architectures have evolved to address complex operational requirements. Google's implementation of BERT in search infrastructure reveals how careful architectural decisions enable efficient serving at massive scale. Their innovations in model deployment, including sophisticated caching mechanisms and load balancing systems, demonstrate how implementation architectures adapt to practical constraints while maintaining performance requirements.

Inference optimization represents a crucial focus in implementation architecture. NVIDIA's Triton Inference Server architecture shows how specialized designs can dramatically improve serving efficiency. Their implementation of dynamic batching and concurrent model execution demonstrates how architectural decisions influence practical deployment capabilities. These innovations reveal the importance of thoughtful implementation design in achieving optimal performance.

Scaling strategies in implementation architecture continue evolving through practical experience. Meta's deployment architecture for their large language models demonstrates sophisticated approaches to handling massive user loads. Their implementation of distributed serving systems shows how architectural decisions influence system reliability and performance at scale. These developments highlight the crucial role of implementation architecture in enabling practical AI deployment.

Memory management architectures have become increasingly sophisticated in implementation design. Amazon's implementation of foundation models in SageMaker shows how careful architectural decisions enable efficient resource utilization. Their development of optimized serving patterns demonstrates how implementation architectures address practical deployment challenges while maintaining system efficiency.

Integration architectures reveal interesting patterns in system design. IBM's Watson implementation architecture shows how AI systems can be effectively integrated into enterprise environments. Their development of sophisticated API architectures demonstrates how implementation decisions influence system accessibility and usability. These approaches reveal the importance of careful integration design in practical AI deployment.

Pipeline parallelism architectures represent another crucial area of implementation innovation. Microsoft's DeepSpeed serving architecture demonstrates how sophisticated pipeline designs enable efficient model deployment. Their implementation of parallel processing patterns shows how architectural decisions influence system throughput and latency. These developments reveal new approaches to optimizing implementation performance.

Service architecture design continues evolving through practical deployment experience. Anthropic's implementation of Claude demonstrates how careful architectural decisions enable reliable AI service delivery. Their development of robust serving systems shows how implementation architecture influences service quality and reliability. These innovations highlight the importance of thoughtful service design in AI deployment.

Resource management architectures have grown increasingly sophisticated. Google Cloud's AI platform implementation shows how careful architectural decisions enable efficient resource utilization across multiple deployments. Their development of dynamic resource allocation systems demonstrates how implementation architecture influences operational efficiency. These approaches reveal new possibilities for optimizing resource usage in AI deployments.

The synthesis of multiple implementation patterns creates interesting architectural possibilities. The combination of efficient serving mechanisms with sophisticated scaling strategies, as seen in modern AI platforms, shows how different implementation approaches complement each other. These integrations demonstrate how implementation architecture often evolves through careful combination of proven techniques while addressing practical deployment requirements.

Performance enhancement in model architectures represents a critical dimension of AI advancement, where theoretical optimization meets practical efficiency gains. NVIDIA's development of FP8 precision training demonstrates how fundamental architectural optimizations can dramatically improve computational efficiency. Their implementation in the Hopper H100 GPU architecture shows how hardware-aware optimization techniques can achieve significant performance improvements while maintaining model accuracy.

Training efficiency optimization continues driving significant architectural innovation. Microsoft's DeepSpeed ZeRO optimization series reveals how sophisticated memory management techniques can enable more efficient model training. Their progressive improvements in memory optimization, from ZeRO-1 through ZeRO-3, demonstrate how systematic architectural enhancement can address specific performance bottlenecks while maintaining training effectiveness.

Inference speed optimization has emerged as a crucial focus area. Google's development of distillation techniques for BERT models shows how architectural modifications can significantly improve deployment performance. Their success in maintaining model capabilities while reducing computational requirements demonstrates how careful optimization strategies can enhance practical model utility. These developments influence how organizations approach model deployment optimization.

Resource management enhancement reveals sophisticated approaches to system optimization. Meta's implementation of selective attention mechanisms shows how architectural modifications can improve efficiency at scale. Their development of sparse computation techniques demonstrates how performance optimization often requires fundamental architectural rethinking. These innovations highlight the deep connection between architecture design and performance enhancement.

Quality metrics have evolved to provide comprehensive performance assessment. The MLPerf benchmark suite, developed through industry collaboration, demonstrates how sophisticated evaluation frameworks enable objective performance comparison. Their continuous refinement of benchmark methodologies shows how performance measurement evolves alongside architectural innovation. These frameworks provide crucial guidance for optimization efforts.

Enhancement strategies often emerge through systematic architecture analysis. Google DeepMind's work on efficient attention patterns demonstrates how careful examination of architectural components can reveal optimization opportunities. Their development of improved attention mechanisms shows how focused enhancement efforts can yield broad performance benefits. These approaches reveal the value of systematic optimization strategies.

System-level optimization continues driving performance improvements. Amazon's implementation of optimized inference paths in their AWS infrastructure shows how architectural enhancements can improve overall system performance. Their development of specialized serving architectures demonstrates how system-level optimization requires careful consideration of multiple performance factors. These innovations reveal the complexity of comprehensive performance enhancement.

Resource allocation optimization represents another crucial enhancement area. Google's development of automated model scaling techniques shows how sophisticated resource management can improve overall system performance. Their implementation of dynamic resource allocation demonstrates how architectural decisions influence operational efficiency. These approaches reveal new possibilities for optimizing resource usage.

The integration of multiple optimization techniques creates interesting enhancement opportunities. The combination of efficient computation patterns with sophisticated memory management, as seen in modern AI systems, shows how different optimization approaches can complement each other. These integrations demonstrate how performance enhancement often proceeds through careful combination of proven techniques.

Benchmark standardization continues influencing optimization efforts. The development of comprehensive evaluation suites by organizations like Stanford's DAWNBench shows how standardized performance metrics guide optimization strategies. Their focus on end-to-end performance measurement demonstrates how evaluation frameworks influence architectural enhancement decisions. These standards provide crucial context for assessing optimization effectiveness.

Emerging architectures in artificial intelligence reveal fascinating new directions in model design and capability enhancement. Google DeepMind's recent work on Perceiver IO demonstrates how novel architectural approaches can fundamentally rethink attention mechanisms. Their implementation of universal architectures that efficiently process multiple input modalities shows how emerging designs can address long-standing challenges while suggesting new possibilities for model architecture.

Novel approaches to model design continue expanding architectural possibilities. Anthropic's research into constitutional AI architectures reveals how emerging designs can incorporate sophisticated behavioral constraints. Their development of architectures that enable more controlled model behavior demonstrates how new design approaches can address complex challenges while maintaining performance capabilities. These innovations suggest interesting directions for architecture evolution.

Experimental designs reveal promising new architectural patterns. Google's development of Pathways demonstrates how unified model architectures might enable more efficient multi-task learning. Their approach to creating more general-purpose AI systems shows how architectural innovation can address fundamental limitations in current designs. These experimental approaches provide valuable insights into future architectural possibilities.

Hybrid system architectures represent another emerging trend. Microsoft's work combining different model types in their Copilot systems shows how diverse architectural approaches can be effectively integrated. Their success in combining multiple specialized models demonstrates how hybrid architectures can enhance overall system capabilities while maintaining practical efficiency. These developments suggest new directions for system design.

Memory-efficient architectures continue emerging through innovative design approaches. Meta's recent work on sparse attention mechanisms shows how novel architectural patterns can dramatically improve efficiency. Their development of adaptive computation techniques demonstrates how emerging architectures can optimize resource usage while maintaining model capabilities. These innovations reveal new possibilities for efficient model design.

Cross-modal architectures represent a significant area of emerging innovation. OpenAI's development of GPT-4V demonstrates how architectures can effectively integrate multiple modalities. Their success in combining vision and language processing shows how emerging designs can enable more comprehensive AI capabilities while maintaining computational efficiency. These developments suggest new directions for multimodal architecture design.

Scaling-focused architectures continue emerging through research innovation. Google's recent work on mixture-of-experts models shows how novel architectural approaches can enable more efficient scaling. Their development of conditional computation patterns demonstrates how emerging designs can address fundamental scaling challenges while maintaining model effectiveness. These approaches reveal new possibilities for large-scale model architecture.

Resource-aware architectures represent another emerging trend. NVIDIA's development of dynamic computational graphs shows how architectures can adapt to available resources. Their implementation of flexible processing patterns demonstrates how emerging designs can optimize resource utilization while maintaining performance capabilities. These innovations suggest new approaches to efficient model design.

The synthesis of multiple emerging approaches creates interesting architectural possibilities. The combination of efficient attention mechanisms with dynamic computation patterns, as seen in recent research developments, shows how different emerging approaches can complement each other. These integrations demonstrate how architectural innovation often proceeds through careful combination of novel techniques.

Research directions in emerging architectures continue expanding through systematic investigation. Stanford's research into foundation model architectures shows how academic institutions contribute to architectural innovation. Their investigation of different architectural approaches demonstrates how systematic research can reveal new possibilities for model design. These efforts provide crucial guidance for future architectural development.

Architecture selection represents a crucial decision point in AI system development, where theoretical capabilities meet practical requirements. Google's systematic approach to model architecture selection, as demonstrated in their transition from BERT to PaLM architectures, shows how organizations evaluate and choose appropriate designs. Their careful consideration of computational requirements, performance capabilities, and practical constraints demonstrates how architecture selection influences project success.

Decision frameworks for architecture selection have evolved to address complex requirements. Microsoft's approach to selecting architectures for their Azure AI services shows how organizations systematically evaluate different options. Their consideration of factors like scalability, maintenance requirements, and deployment constraints demonstrates how comprehensive evaluation frameworks guide architecture selection. These frameworks reveal the sophistication of modern selection processes.

Requirements analysis in architecture selection has become increasingly refined. Amazon's selection criteria for AWS AI services demonstrate how organizations assess diverse user needs. Their evaluation of different architectural approaches shows how practical requirements influence selection decisions. These assessment processes reveal the importance of careful requirements analysis in architecture selection.

Performance evaluation frameworks play a crucial role in selection processes. MLPerf's comprehensive benchmarking suite shows how standardized evaluation helps compare architectural options. Their systematic approach to performance measurement demonstrates how objective metrics influence architecture selection. These evaluation frameworks provide crucial guidance for decision-making.

Resource constraint analysis has emerged as a key selection factor. NVIDIA's guidance on architecture selection for different GPU platforms shows how hardware considerations influence decisions. Their detailed performance analyses demonstrate how resource constraints shape architecture selection. These considerations reveal the practical aspects of architecture choice.

Implementation feasibility assessment represents another crucial selection factor. Meta's evaluation process for production AI systems shows how organizations assess practical deployment considerations. Their analysis of operational requirements demonstrates how implementation concerns influence architecture selection. These assessments reveal the importance of practical considerations in decision-making.

Risk management approaches have evolved to support architecture selection. IBM's framework for enterprise AI deployment shows how organizations evaluate and mitigate architectural risks. Their systematic approach to risk assessment demonstrates how security and reliability considerations influence selection decisions. These approaches reveal the importance of comprehensive risk evaluation.

Validation methodologies continue evolving to support selection processes. Anthropic's evaluation of different architectural approaches shows how organizations validate selection decisions. Their testing frameworks demonstrate how systematic validation supports architecture selection. These methodologies reveal the importance of thorough validation in decision-making.

The integration of multiple selection criteria creates comprehensive evaluation frameworks. The combination of performance metrics with practical constraints, as seen in modern selection processes, shows how different factors influence architecture choice. These integrations demonstrate how selection often proceeds through careful consideration of multiple criteria.

Success patterns in architecture selection continue emerging through practical experience. Google Cloud's documentation of successful implementations shows how organizations learn from previous decisions. Their analysis of different architectural choices demonstrates how experience influences selection processes. These patterns provide valuable guidance for future decision-making.

Our exploration of model architecture innovation reveals the dynamic interplay between theoretical advancement and practical implementation that drives AI development forward. From Google's development of PaLM to OpenAI's GPT-4 architecture, we see how innovative design approaches enable new capabilities while addressing practical constraints. For practitioners and organizations working with AI systems, understanding these architectural innovations becomes increasingly crucial for effective implementation and deployment.

The architectural patterns we've examined demonstrate multiple paths for engaging with AI development. Whether through Microsoft's comprehensive enterprise architectures or NVIDIA's specialized hardware-optimized designs, organizations can choose approaches that align with their specific requirements and capabilities. The success of different architectural approaches shows how thoughtful design decisions enable effective AI implementation while maintaining system efficiency.

The evolution of specialized architectures reveals interesting opportunities for focused innovation. Google DeepMind's work on Perceiver architectures and Meta's advances in efficient attention mechanisms demonstrate how targeted architectural improvements can yield significant benefits. For practitioners interested in architectural innovation, these examples provide valuable insights into effective design approaches while suggesting promising directions for future development.

Implementation considerations continue influencing architectural decisions. Google's deployment of sophisticated AI systems and Amazon's AWS infrastructure demonstrate how practical requirements shape architecture design. Understanding these relationships becomes crucial for organizations implementing AI systems, as architectural decisions significantly influence deployment success and operational efficiency.

The relationship between model architecture and performance optimization creates interesting opportunities for innovation. Microsoft's DeepSpeed optimizations and NVIDIA's tensor core architectures show how thoughtful design can dramatically improve system efficiency. These developments demonstrate the importance of understanding architectural trade-offs while suggesting approaches for enhancing AI system performance.

As we move forward to examine development platforms,

we carry forward understanding of how architectural decisions influence system capabilities and implementation requirements. The sophisticated approaches to AI architecture we've explored provide crucial context for understanding platform development and deployment considerations. For practitioners and organizations, this understanding becomes increasingly valuable as AI technology continues advancing.

Engage actively with architectural innovation, whether through experimental implementation or systematic evaluation of different approaches. Major cloud providers offer extensive resources for testing various architectural designs, while organizations like Hugging Face provide platforms for exploring different model architectures. These resources offer excellent starting points for practical engagement with architectural innovation.

The field of model architecture continues evolving, offering new opportunities for innovation and implementation. By understanding current architectural patterns and emerging trends, practitioners and organizations can better position themselves to leverage advancing AI capabilities. Explore these opportunities while maintaining awareness of how architectural decisions influence system success.

GIL OREN

CHAPTER 6: AI DEVELOPMENT PLATFORMS

The evolution of AI development platforms represents a crucial advancement in how organizations approach artificial intelligence implementation. Building upon the architectural innovations we explored in the previous chapter, these platforms provide sophisticated environments for AI development and deployment. Amazon's SageMaker ecosystem demonstrates how development platforms have matured from simple model training tools into comprehensive environments supporting the entire AI development lifecycle, from initial experimentation through production deployment.

The current landscape of development platforms reveals interesting patterns of innovation and specialization. Google's Vertex AI platform shows how cloud providers integrate cutting-edge capabilities with enterprise-grade reliability. Their systematic approach to platform development, incorporating advanced features like AutoML and sophisticated monitoring tools, demonstrates how platforms evolve to address complex development needs while maintaining accessibility and usability.

113

Platform sophistication continues advancing through practical experience. Microsoft's Azure AI platform demonstrates how development environments adapt to support diverse AI workloads. Their integration of OpenAI's technologies shows how platforms can rapidly incorporate new capabilities while maintaining enterprise reliability. These developments reveal the dynamic nature of modern AI development environments.

The relationship between platforms and practical implementation has grown increasingly sophisticated. Hugging Face's infrastructure evolution from model repository to comprehensive development platform demonstrates how community needs drive platform advancement. Their success in creating accessible yet powerful development tools shows how platforms can democratize AI development while maintaining technical sophistication.

Infrastructure innovation remains central to platform evolution. NVIDIA's AI Enterprise platform shows how hardware expertise translates into comprehensive development environments. Their integration of specialized tools for GPU optimization demonstrates how platforms address specific technical challenges while maintaining general usability. These advances reveal the crucial role of infrastructure in enabling effective AI development.

In this chapter, we explore the sophisticated world of AI development platforms, examining how different environments support artificial intelligence advancement. From cloud-based solutions to specialized development tools, we'll investigate how platforms enable effective AI implementation. This exploration reveals both current capabilities and emerging directions in platform development, providing crucial context for understanding modern AI development environments.

For practitioners and organizations implementing AI systems, understanding platform capabilities becomes increasingly important. The choices made in platform selection and utilization influence every aspect of AI development and deployment. As we proceed, we'll examine how different platforms address various requirements, offering insights valuable for those working with AI development environments. The evolution of AI development platforms represents a remarkable journey from basic development tools to sophisticated, integrated environments. AWS SageMaker's progression illustrates this transformation, evolving from its 2017 launch as a model training service to today's comprehensive platform supporting organizations worldwide. This evolution demonstrates how platforms mature through practical experience while continuously incorporating new capabilities to address emerging development needs.

Cloud platform growth reveals interesting patterns in capability development. Google Cloud's AI platform evolution, from early TensorFlow serving solutions to the current Vertex AI environment, shows how platforms adapt to changing requirements. Their integration of AutoML capabilities, custom model support, and sophisticated monitoring tools demonstrates how platforms mature through systematic capability enhancement while maintaining operational reliability.

Enterprise platform evolution reflects growing sophistication in organizational needs. Databricks' development from a Spark-focused analytics platform to a comprehensive AI development environment shows how platforms adapt to enterprise requirements. Their Lakehouse architecture, supporting both traditional analytics and advanced AI workloads, demonstrates how platforms evolve to address complex organizational needs while maintaining data consistency and operational efficiency.

Specialized platforms have emerged to address specific development challenges. Hugging Face's transformation from a simple model repository to a comprehensive MLOps platform demonstrates how focused solutions can mature into sophisticated development environments. Their success in creating tools for model training, deployment, and monitoring shows how specialized platforms can effectively address specific aspects of AI development while maintaining integration capabilities.

The maturation of development tools reveals increasing sophistication in platform capabilities. Microsoft's Visual Studio Code evolution, incorporating advanced AI development features through extensions like Azure Machine Learning and GitHub Copilot, shows how development environments adapt to AI-specific requirements. Their integration of sophisticated debugging and monitoring tools demonstrates how platforms mature to support complex development workflows.

Infrastructure advancement plays a crucial role in platform evolution. NVIDIA's NGC (NVIDIA GPU Cloud) platform development shows how hardware expertise influences platform capabilities. Their creation of optimized containers and development tools demonstrates how platforms evolve to maximize hardware utilization while simplifying development processes.

Version control systems have matured to address AI-specific challenges. DVC's (Data Version Control) evolution shows how platforms adapt to handle large model files and complex data dependencies. Their development of specialized tracking tools demonstrates how platforms mature to address specific aspects of AI development while maintaining integration with existing development workflows.

Security considerations have become increasingly central to platform maturity. IBM's Watson Studio evolution demonstrates how platforms incorporate sophisticated security features while maintaining development flexibility. Their implementation of role-based access control and audit capabilities shows how platforms mature to address enterprise security requirements while supporting collaborative development.

116

The emergence of automated development tools indicates growing platform sophistication. Google's AutoML platform evolution shows how automation can simplify complex development tasks. Their development of automated model selection and optimization tools demonstrates how platforms mature to support both expert and non-expert users while maintaining quality standards.

These evolutionary patterns continue influencing platform development. Understanding this progression provides crucial context for appreciating current capabilities while suggesting future directions for platform advancement. The success of different approaches demonstrates the importance of thoughtful platform evolution in supporting effective AI development.

Major development environments in artificial intelligence demonstrate sophisticated approaches to supporting complex AI workflows. Amazon's SageMaker ecosystem exemplifies this sophistication, providing integrated solutions for the entire AI development lifecycle. Their environment combines powerful development tools like SageMaker Studio with specialized capabilities such as distributed training support and automated model optimization, demonstrating how comprehensive platforms address diverse development needs while maintaining operational efficiency.

Google's Vertex AI platform reveals another dimension of modern development environments. Their integration of AutoML capabilities with custom model support shows how platforms can serve different user requirements effectively. The platform's unified approach to ML operations, from data preparation through model monitoring, demonstrates how development environments evolve to support end-to-end workflows while maintaining flexibility for diverse use cases.

Microsoft's Azure AI platform demonstrates how enterprise-grade development environments address complex organizational needs. Their integration of OpenAI's technologies alongside traditional ML tools shows how platforms can combine cutting-edge capabilities with established development practices. The platform's comprehensive security features and compliance tools demonstrate how development environments adapt to enterprise requirements while supporting innovation.

IBM's Watson Studio environment reveals sophisticated approaches to specialized AI development. Their focus on enterprise-grade model development and deployment shows how platforms address specific market segments effectively. The integration of AutoAI capabilities with traditional development tools demonstrates how environments can support both automated and manual development approaches while maintaining quality standards.

Databricks' Unified Analytics Platform shows how development environments adapt to handle both traditional analytics and AI workflows. Their Lakehouse architecture demonstrates sophisticated approaches to managing diverse data workloads. The platform's integration of collaborative notebooks with production deployment capabilities shows how environments support different development stages while maintaining data consistency.

Specialized environments like Hugging Face's platform demonstrate focused approaches to AI development. Their emphasis on model sharing and collaboration shows how platforms can address specific community needs effectively. The integration of model training capabilities with deployment tools demonstrates how specialized environments can provide comprehensive support for specific development patterns.

NVIDIA's AI Enterprise platform reveals how hardware expertise influences development environments. Their optimization of development tools for GPU acceleration shows how platforms can maximize hardware capabilities. The integration of specialized libraries and frameworks demonstrates how environments can enhance performance while maintaining development accessibility.

Snowflake's AI platform demonstrates how data platforms

evolve to support AI development. Their integration of ML operations with data warehousing capabilities shows how environments adapt to changing requirements. The platform's approach to data sharing and collaboration demonstrates how development environments can enhance team productivity while maintaining data governance.

Scale AI's platform reveals specialized approaches to AI development support. Their focus on data labeling and model evaluation shows how platforms can address crucial development challenges effectively. The integration of quality assurance tools with workflow management capabilities demonstrates how specialized environments support critical development tasks.

Development environment integration patterns reveal sophisticated approaches to tool coordination. The ability to combine different platforms through standardized interfaces shows how environments support flexible development approaches. These integration capabilities demonstrate how modern development environments enable comprehensive solution development while maintaining operational efficiency.

Infrastructure innovation in AI development platforms represents a crucial dimension of technological advancement. Google Cloud's development of their TPU pod architecture demonstrates how infrastructure evolution enables more sophisticated AI development capabilities. Their implementation of high-speed interconnects and distributed training systems shows how infrastructure innovations address fundamental computational challenges while maintaining system reliability.

Compute management systems reveal sophisticated approaches to resource optimization. Amazon's implementation of Elastic Fabric Adapter in SageMaker shows how platforms enhance training performance through specialized networking. Their development of distributed training frameworks demonstrates how infrastructure

119

innovations improve resource utilization while maintaining development flexibility. These advancements enable more efficient model training at scale.

Storage system innovation continues driving platform capability advancement. Microsoft's Azure Blob storage optimization for AI workloads shows how platforms address data management challenges. Their implementation of hierarchical namespace support and high-throughput access patterns demonstrates how infrastructure adaptations enhance AI development workflows while maintaining data integrity.

Resource orchestration systems demonstrate increasing sophistication. NVIDIA's Base Command Platform shows how specialized infrastructure can optimize GPU utilization across development workflows. Their implementation of workload scheduling and resource allocation demonstrates how platforms maximize hardware efficiency while supporting diverse development needs.

Network architecture innovation reveals interesting patterns in system design. Google's development of their Jupiter networking fabric shows how infrastructure advances support complex AI workloads. Their implementation of software-defined networking capabilities demonstrates how platforms address communication challenges while maintaining system performance.

Data management systems continue evolving to meet AI development needs. Snowflake's implementation of their Data Cloud architecture shows how platforms optimize data access patterns. Their development of sophisticated caching mechanisms demonstrates how infrastructure innovations enhance data availability while maintaining consistency requirements.

Version control infrastructure reveals specialized approaches to AI artifact management. DVC's implementation of large file handling shows how platforms address unique AI development challenges. Their integration with cloud storage systems demonstrates how infrastructure innovations support efficient collaboration while maintaining version control integrity.

Scaling solutions demonstrate sophisticated approaches to handling growth requirements. Databricks' implementation of their Photon engine shows how platforms optimize query performance at scale. Their development of adaptive query optimization demonstrates how infrastructure innovations improve system efficiency while maintaining operational reliability.

Security infrastructure continues evolving to address emerging challenges. IBM's implementation of confidential computing capabilities shows how platforms protect sensitive AI workloads. Their development of hardware-based security measures demonstrates how infrastructure innovations enhance protection while maintaining system accessibility.

The integration of these infrastructure innovations creates comprehensive development environments. Azure's implementation of integrated ML workflows shows how platforms combine various infrastructure capabilities effectively. Their coordination of compute, storage, and networking resources demonstrates how infrastructure innovations enable sophisticated development patterns while maintaining system efficiency.

Development tools for AI platforms have evolved into sophisticated systems supporting complex development workflows. Microsoft's Visual Studio Code integration with AI development capabilities demonstrates this evolution through features like GitHub Copilot and Azure ML extensions. Their implementation of intelligent code completion and integrated debugging tools shows how development environments enhance productivity while maintaining code quality.

IDE integration patterns reveal sophisticated approaches to AI development support. JetBrains' PyCharm AI features demonstrate how traditional development tools adapt to AI-specific requirements. Their integration of notebook support, intelligent code analysis, and remote development capabilities shows how IDEs enhance AI development workflows while maintaining familiar development patterns.

Jupyter's evolution as a development environment demonstrates interesting patterns in tool advancement. Their implementation of JupyterLab features shows how development tools adapt to changing requirements. Their support for interactive visualization, integrated debugging, and collaborative development demonstrates how tools enhance development efficiency while maintaining flexibility for different workflows.

Debugging systems have evolved to address AI-specific challenges. Google's TensorBoard implementation shows how platforms support model development through sophisticated visualization tools. Their integration of performance profiling and model analysis capabilities demonstrates how debugging tools enhance development understanding while supporting optimization efforts.

Performance analysis tools reveal specialized approaches to AI development support. NVIDIA's Nsight Systems shows how platforms enable detailed performance optimization. Their implementation of GPU profiling and workload analysis demonstrates how specialized tools enhance development efficiency while maintaining system performance.

Testing frameworks continue evolving to meet AI development needs. MLflow's implementation of experiment tracking shows how platforms support systematic development approaches. Their integration of model registry and deployment tracking demonstrates how testing tools enhance development reliability while maintaining project organization.

Quality assurance tools demonstrate sophisticated approaches to model validation. Scale AI's evaluation platform shows how specialized tools address crucial development challenges. Their implementation of model performance analysis and bias detection demonstrates how validation tools enhance development quality while maintaining practical applicability.

Benchmark systems reveal interesting patterns in performance assessment. MLPerf's implementation of standardized testing frameworks shows how platforms enable objective comparison. Their development of diverse benchmark suites demonstrates how assessment tools support development decisions while maintaining evaluation consistency.

Code analysis tools continue advancing to support AI development. SonarQube's integration of AI-specific code analysis shows how platforms enhance code quality. Their implementation of security scanning and best practice validation demonstrates how analysis tools improve development standards while maintaining project maintainability.

The integration of these development tools creates comprehensive development environments. Amazon's SageMaker Studio shows how platforms combine various development capabilities effectively. Their coordination of different development tools demonstrates how integrated environments enhance development productivity while maintaining workflow efficiency.

Deployment systems in AI platforms demonstrate sophisticated approaches to operationalizing AI solutions. Google's Vertex AI deployment infrastructure shows how platforms handle complex production requirements through containerized serving solutions and automated scaling capabilities. Their implementation of model versioning and traffic management demonstrates how deployment systems maintain reliability while enabling seamless updates in production environments.

Production infrastructure reveals careful attention to operational requirements. AWS SageMaker's deployment capabilities show how platforms address enterprise-scale serving needs. Their implementation of multi-model endpoints and automatic scaling demonstrates how deployment systems optimize resource utilization while maintaining performance under varying loads. The integration of A/B testing capabilities shows how platforms support sophisticated deployment strategies.

Load management systems demonstrate increasing sophistication in handling production workloads. Microsoft Azure's AI deployment infrastructure shows how platforms manage resource allocation dynamically. Their implementation of automatic scaling and load balancing demonstrates how deployment systems maintain performance while optimizing resource usage. The integration of traffic splitting capabilities enables sophisticated deployment patterns.

Monitoring solutions have evolved to provide comprehensive operational visibility. Datadog's AI monitoring tools show how platforms track production model performance. Their implementation of custom metrics and automated alerting demonstrates how monitoring systems enable proactive management while maintaining system reliability. The integration of visualization tools supports effective operational oversight.

Integration frameworks reveal sophisticated approaches to system connectivity. IBM Watson's deployment architecture shows how platforms enable seamless integration with existing systems. Their implementation of standardized APIs and connection protocols demonstrates how deployment systems maintain interoperability while supporting diverse integration patterns. The provision of comprehensive documentation supports effective implementation.

Security controls demonstrate careful attention to protection requirements. Snowflake's deployment infrastructure shows how platforms implement robust security measures. Their implementation of role-based access control and audit logging demonstrates how deployment systems maintain security while enabling operational flexibility. The integration of encryption capabilities ensures data protection throughout the deployment lifecycle.

Performance optimization tools reveal specialized approaches to deployment efficiency. NVIDIA Triton Inference Server shows how platforms optimize serving performance. Their implementation of model optimization and batching capabilities demonstrates how deployment systems enhance efficiency while maintaining response times. The support for multiple frameworks enables flexible deployment options.

Cost control mechanisms show sophisticated approaches to resource management. Google Cloud's deployment options demonstrate how platforms optimize operational costs. Their implementation of auto-scaling policies and resource scheduling shows how deployment systems maintain efficiency while controlling expenses. The provision of cost analysis tools supports effective resource planning.

Deployment verification systems demonstrate careful attention to reliability requirements. Azure's deployment validation tools show how platforms ensure successful implementations. Their integration of health checks and rollback capabilities demonstrates how deployment systems maintain stability while enabling rapid updates. The provision of deployment metrics supports effective quality assurance.

The synthesis of these deployment capabilities creates comprehensive operational environments. Kubernetes-based deployment systems show how platforms integrate various operational aspects effectively. Their coordination of different deployment components demonstrates how modern systems enable reliable operations while maintaining deployment flexibility.

Platform operations in AI development environments demonstrate sophisticated approaches to managing complex systems at scale. AWS SageMaker's operational infrastructure shows how platforms handle comprehensive system management through integrated control planes and automated operational workflows. Their implementation of resource governance and usage tracking demonstrates how platforms maintain operational efficiency while supporting diverse development needs.

Management systems reveal careful attention to operational control requirements. Google Cloud's AI platform operations show how environments handle complex resource management. Their implementation of quota management and resource allocation demonstrates how platforms maintain system stability while optimizing utilization. The integration of automated cleanup processes for unused resources shows how platforms enhance operational efficiency.

User management capabilities demonstrate sophisticated approaches to access control. Microsoft Azure's AD integration with AI services shows how platforms handle identity management. Their implementation of role-based access control and conditional access policies demonstrates how platforms maintain security while enabling collaborative development. The provision of detailed audit logs supports compliance requirements.

Monitoring solutions have evolved to provide comprehensive operational visibility. Datadog's platform monitoring capabilities show how environments track system health. Their implementation of custom dashboards and automated alerting demonstrates how platforms enable proactive management while maintaining system reliability. The integration of AI-specific metrics provides deeper operational insights.

Alert systems reveal specialized approaches to operational awareness. PagerDuty's integration with AI platforms shows how environments manage incident response. Their implementation of intelligent alert routing and escalation policies demonstrates how platforms maintain operational reliability while minimizing response times. The provision of post-mortem analysis tools supports continuous improvement.

Health management systems demonstrate careful attention

to system stability. New Relic's AI platform monitoring shows how environments track operational health. Their implementation of performance tracking and anomaly detection demonstrates how platforms maintain system reliability while enabling proactive maintenance. The integration of historical analysis supports trend identification.

Version control operations reveal sophisticated approaches to system management. GitLab's AI platform integration shows how environments handle version management. Their implementation of artifact tracking and dependency management demonstrates how platforms maintain system consistency while enabling rapid updates. The provision of rollback capabilities supports operational stability.

Cost management systems show careful attention to resource efficiency. Azure's cost management tools show how platforms optimize operational expenses. Their implementation of budget tracking and cost allocation demonstrates how platforms maintain efficiency while providing transparency. The integration of cost prediction tools supports effective planning.

Update management capabilities demonstrate sophisticated approaches to system maintenance. IBM Cloud's update management shows how platforms handle system evolution. Their implementation of staged rollouts and compatibility checking demonstrates how platforms maintain stability while enabling system advancement. The provision of update scheduling supports operational planning.

The integration of these operational capabilities creates comprehensive management environments. Kubernetes operations tools show how platforms coordinate various management aspects effectively. Their coordination of different operational components demonstrates how modern platforms enable reliable operations while maintaining system flexibility.

These operational patterns continue influencing platform

development. Understanding these approaches provides crucial context for appreciating current capabilities while suggesting future directions for operational advancement. The success of different approaches demonstrates the importance of thoughtful operational design in maintaining effective AI platforms.

The evolution of AI development platforms reveals emerging patterns that suggest future directions while building upon current capabilities. Google's development of Vertex AI demonstrates how platforms are moving toward more integrated, automated development environments. Their implementation of AutoML capabilities alongside traditional development tools shows how platforms are evolving to support both automated and manual development approaches while maintaining development flexibility.

Technology evolution patterns indicate sophisticated approaches to capability enhancement. Microsoft's integration of OpenAI technologies within Azure shows how platforms incorporate emerging capabilities. Their systematic approach to feature integration demonstrates how platforms balance innovation with stability while maintaining operational reliability. The development of specialized tools for large language model deployment suggests new directions for platform capability expansion.

Integration trends reveal interesting patterns in platform evolution. AWS SageMaker's growing ecosystem shows how platforms expand through careful feature addition. Their implementation of specialized development environments demonstrates how platforms enhance capability while maintaining usability. The integration of advanced monitoring and optimization tools suggests continuing evolution in platform sophistication.

Tool development patterns demonstrate careful attention to developer needs. JupyterLab's evolution shows how development environments adapt to changing requirements. Their implementation of integrated development features demonstrates how platforms enhance productivity while maintaining flexibility. The emergence of AI-assisted development tools suggests new directions for developer support.

Infrastructure evolution reveals sophisticated approaches to system enhancement. NVIDIA's Base Command Platform shows how specialized infrastructure supports advanced development needs. Their implementation of distributed training capabilities demonstrates how platforms optimize resource utilization while maintaining performance. The development of specialized hardware support suggests continuing evolution in platform capabilities.

Security considerations continue influencing platform development. IBM's confidential computing initiatives show how platforms address emerging protection requirements. Their implementation of hardware-based security measures demonstrates how platforms enhance protection while maintaining usability. The development of sophisticated access control mechanisms suggests new directions for security enhancement.

Automation patterns reveal interesting trends in platform evolution. Databricks' implementation of automated workflow management shows how platforms enhance development efficiency. Their integration of automated optimization tools demonstrates how platforms reduce complexity while maintaining control. The emergence of automated debugging capabilities suggests new directions for development support.

Resource management trends indicate evolving approaches to system optimization. Snowflake's development of specialized compute infrastructure shows how platforms optimize performance. Their implementation of intelligent resource allocation demonstrates how platforms enhance efficiency while maintaining reliability. The evolution of cost optimization tools suggests continuing development in resource management.

129

These directional patterns suggest continuing evolution in how platforms develop and operate. Understanding these trends provides crucial context for appreciating future possibilities while maintaining practical perspective. The success of different approaches demonstrates the importance of thoughtful platform evolution in supporting effective AI development.

Platform advancement continues through systematic capability enhancement. The integration of emerging technologies alongside established tools shows how platforms maintain balance between innovation and stability. These patterns suggest interesting directions for future platform development while maintaining focus on practical utility.

Our exploration of AI development platforms reveals a sophisticated ecosystem that continues transforming how organizations approach artificial intelligence implementation. From Google's Vertex AI to Amazon's SageMaker, we see how platforms enable effective development while maintaining operational reliability. For practitioners and organizations implementing AI systems, these platforms provide crucial infrastructure for turning innovative ideas into practical solutions.

The platform capabilities we've examined demonstrate multiple paths for engaging with AI development. Whether through Microsoft Azure's comprehensive enterprise solutions or specialized environments like Hugging Face's platform, organizations can choose approaches that align with their specific requirements and objectives. These diverse options show how different development needs can be effectively addressed while maintaining development efficiency.

Infrastructure innovations reveal interesting opportunities for platform utilization. NVIDIA's specialized development environments and Google's TPU infrastructure demonstrate how platforms leverage advanced hardware capabilities. For practitioners interested in optimal development approaches, these infrastructure options provide valuable insights into effective resource utilization while suggesting promising directions for implementation.

Development tool evolution continues enabling more sophisticated approaches to AI implementation. The progression of environments like JupyterLab and Visual Studio Code shows how platforms enhance developer productivity. Understanding these tools becomes crucial for organizations implementing AI systems, as tool selection significantly influences development efficiency and team productivity.

The relationship between platforms and operational requirements creates interesting opportunities for innovation. AWS's comprehensive monitoring solutions and IBM's security frameworks show how platforms address crucial operational concerns. These developments demonstrate the importance of understanding operational requirements while suggesting approaches for maintaining system reliability.

As we move forward to examine cross-domain integration in our next chapter, we carry forward understanding of how development platforms enable effective AI implementation. The sophisticated approaches to platform development we've explored provide crucial context for understanding system integration and deployment considerations. For practitioners and organizations, this understanding becomes increasingly valuable as AI technology continues advancing.

Engage actively with platform capabilities, whether through experimental projects or systematic evaluation of different environments. Major cloud providers offer extensive free tiers and educational resources for exploring their platforms, while specialized platforms like Hugging Face provide accessible entry points for specific development needs. These resources offer excellent starting points for practical platform exploration.

The field of AI development platforms continues evolving, offering new opportunities for innovation and implementation. By understanding current platform capabilities and emerging trends, practitioners and organizations can better position themselves to leverage advancing AI technologies. Explore these opportunities while maintaining awareness of how platform selection influences development success.

CHAPTER 7: CORE AI BREAKTHROUGHS

The landscape of core AI breakthroughs reveals fundamental advances that continue reshaping artificial intelligence capabilities. Building upon the platform developments we explored in the previous chapter, these breakthroughs demonstrate how fundamental research drives practical innovation. Google's development of PaLM demonstrates this relationship, showing how advances in model architecture and training methodologies enable significant improvements in AI capabilities while establishing new benchmarks for performance and efficiency.

The current state of core AI innovation reflects remarkable progress across multiple dimensions. OpenAI's evolution of GPT models shows how systematic research in foundation models enables increasingly sophisticated capabilities. Their advances in model architecture and training approaches demonstrate how fundamental breakthroughs translate into practical capabilities while suggesting new directions for development.

Breakthrough patterns reveal interesting relationships

between theoretical advancement and practical implementation. Anthropic's development of constitutional AI shows how fundamental research can address both capability enhancement and behavioral control. Their systematic approach to model development demonstrates how core innovations influence practical implementation while maintaining focus on crucial considerations.

The relationship between research breakthroughs and deployment capabilities has grown increasingly sophisticated. Google DeepMind's work on efficient attention mechanisms shows how fundamental advances enable practical improvements. Their development of optimized architectures demonstrates how core breakthroughs influence system efficiency while maintaining model capabilities.

Innovation patterns in core AI reveal careful attention to both capability and efficiency. Meta's advances in sparse expert models show how fundamental research addresses practical constraints. Their development of efficient training approaches demonstrates how breakthroughs enhance system capabilities while optimizing resource utilization.

In this chapter, we explore the sophisticated landscape of core AI breakthroughs, examining how fundamental advances drive artificial intelligence forward. From architecture innovations to training methodologies, we'll investigate how research breakthroughs enable practical advancement. This exploration reveals both current achievements and emerging directions in AI development, providing crucial context for understanding modern AI capabilities.

For practitioners and organizations implementing AI systems, understanding these core breakthroughs becomes increasingly important. The advances in fundamental capabilities influence every aspect of AI development and deployment. As we proceed, we'll examine how different breakthroughs address various challenges, offering insights valuable for those working with AI technologies.

The evolution of foundation models represents one of the

most significant developments in artificial intelligence, demonstrating remarkable advances in both capability and efficiency. Google's progression from PaLM to PaLM 2 illustrates this evolution, showing how architectural refinements and training innovations enable significant performance improvements. Their implementation of more efficient attention mechanisms and enhanced training methodologies demonstrates how foundation models advance through systematic innovation while maintaining practical applicability.

Architecture advancement in foundation models reveals sophisticated approaches to capability enhancement. OpenAI's development from GPT-3 to GPT-4 shows how architectural innovations enable more sophisticated processing capabilities. Their improvements in context handling and multimodal processing demonstrate how architectural evolution enhances model capabilities while maintaining computational efficiency. These advances establish new benchmarks for foundation model performance.

Attention mechanism development continues driving significant improvements. Anthropic's implementation of constitutional AI principles shows how fundamental architectural components evolve to address specific challenges. Their refinements in attention patterns demonstrate how foundation models incorporate sophisticated control mechanisms while maintaining processing efficiency. These innovations influence how organizations approach model development.

Scaling innovations reveal careful attention to resource utilization. Microsoft and NVIDIA's collaboration on Megatron-Turing NLG demonstrates how organizations address training challenges at scale. Their implementation of distributed training architectures shows how foundation models maintain performance while optimizing resource usage. These developments influence how organizations approach large-scale model training.

Training methodology breakthroughs show interesting patterns in capability development. Google DeepMind's advances in training efficiency demonstrate how organizations optimize model development. Their implementation of improved training techniques shows how foundation models enhance learning capabilities while reducing resource requirements. These innovations establish new approaches to model development.

Quality enhancement reveals sophisticated approaches to model improvement. Meta's development of LLaMA 2 demonstrates how organizations balance capability enhancement with efficiency. Their refinements in model architecture show how foundation models maintain quality while optimizing performance. These advances influence how organizations approach model development.

Performance gains emerge through systematic innovation. Google's improvements in few-shot learning capabilities demonstrate how foundation models enhance adaptability. Their implementation of more efficient processing patterns shows how models maintain performance while reducing computational requirements. These developments establish new benchmarks for model efficiency.

The integration of these evolutionary patterns creates comprehensive advancement. The combination of architectural improvements with enhanced training methodologies shows how different innovations complement each other. These integrations demonstrate how foundation model evolution proceeds through careful combination of advances while maintaining practical utility.

These evolutionary patterns continue influencing model development. Understanding this progression provides crucial context for appreciating current capabilities while suggesting future directions. The success of different approaches demonstrates the importance of systematic evolution in advancing foundation model capabilities.

Learning system innovation represents a fundamental area

of advancement in artificial intelligence, where new approaches continue transforming how models acquire and apply knowledge. Google's development of PaLM demonstrates sophisticated self-supervised learning techniques that enable more efficient knowledge acquisition. Their implementation of advanced pre-training methods shows how learning systems evolve to handle increasingly complex tasks while maintaining training efficiency.

Self-supervised learning advances reveal careful attention to data utilization. Meta's work on contrastive learning demonstrates how organizations maximize learning from unlabeled data. Their implementation in computer vision models shows how self-supervised approaches enable more efficient training while reducing dependency on labeled datasets. These innovations establish new paradigms for model training.

Few-shot learning capabilities demonstrate remarkable progress in adaptation abilities. OpenAI's developments in GPT-4 show how models can effectively learn from limited examples. Their implementation of in-context learning demonstrates how modern systems acquire new capabilities with minimal additional training. These advances transform how organizations approach model adaptation for specific tasks.

Transfer learning techniques continue evolving through practical application. Microsoft's implementation of domain adaptation in language models shows how organizations leverage existing knowledge for new tasks. Their systematic approach to knowledge transfer demonstrates how learning systems maintain performance while reducing training requirements for specific applications. These developments influence how organizations approach model specialization.

Learning efficiency improvements reveal sophisticated optimization approaches. Anthropic's constitutional AI training methods show how organizations enhance learning while maintaining behavioral constraints. Their implementation of guided learning techniques demonstrates how systems acquire capabilities while adhering to specific operational parameters. These innovations establish new approaches to controlled learning.

Method evolution in learning systems shows interesting patterns of advancement. Google DeepMind's improvements in reinforcement learning demonstrate how organizations enhance model adaptation capabilities. Their implementation of more efficient learning algorithms shows how systems maintain performance while reducing training complexity. These developments establish new benchmarks for learning efficiency.

Domain adaptation capabilities reveal careful attention to practical requirements. NVIDIA's work on transfer learning for specialized applications shows how organizations address specific implementation needs. Their development of efficient adaptation techniques demonstrates how learning systems maintain effectiveness while reducing resource requirements. These innovations influence how organizations approach specialized model development.

The synthesis of multiple learning approaches creates comprehensive advancement. The combination of self-supervised pre-training with efficient fine-tuning methods shows how different learning techniques complement each other. These integrations demonstrate how learning system innovation proceeds through careful combination of approaches while maintaining practical utility.

Performance metrics for learning systems continue evolving through practical experience. Google's evaluation of few-shot learning capabilities demonstrates how organizations assess adaptation effectiveness. Their implementation of sophisticated measurement techniques shows how learning systems maintain quality while reducing training requirements. These developments establish new standards for learning assessment.

These innovative patterns continue influencing system

development. Understanding these advances provides crucial context for appreciating current capabilities while suggesting future directions. The success of different approaches demonstrates the importance of systematic innovation in advancing learning system capabilities.

Optimization breakthroughs in artificial intelligence demonstrate sophisticated approaches to enhancing system efficiency and performance. Microsoft's DeepSpeed ZeRO innovations show how fundamental advances in optimization enable more efficient model training. Their implementation of memory optimization techniques demonstrates how organizations achieve significant performance improvements while reducing computational requirements, establishing new standards for training efficiency.

Training efficiency advances reveal careful attention to resource utilization. Google's development of efficient training methods for PaLM 2 shows how organizations maximize computational resources. Their implementation of distributed training optimizations demonstrates how systems maintain model quality while significantly reducing training time. These innovations transform how organizations approach large-scale model development.

Model compression techniques continue evolving through systematic innovation. Meta's work on sparse architectures shows how organizations reduce model size without sacrificing capability. Their implementation of pruning techniques demonstrates how systems maintain performance while dramatically reducing memory requirements. These advances influence how organizations approach model deployment optimization.

Inference optimization reveals sophisticated approaches to deployment efficiency. NVIDIA's TensorRT developments show how organizations enhance operational performance. Their implementation of quantization techniques demonstrates how systems maintain accuracy while reducing computational demands during inference. These innovations establish new benchmarks for deployment efficiency.

Resource management breakthroughs show interesting patterns in system optimization. Amazon's implementation of multi-model endpoints demonstrates how organizations maximize infrastructure utilization. Their development of dynamic batching techniques shows how systems maintain responsiveness while optimizing resource usage. These advances transform how organizations approach deployment optimization.

Quality preservation methods reveal careful attention to optimization trade-offs. Anthropic's approach to model optimization demonstrates how organizations maintain performance while enhancing efficiency. Their implementation of targeted optimization techniques shows how systems preserve crucial capabilities while reducing resource requirements. These innovations influence how organizations balance efficiency with effectiveness.

Speed enhancement techniques continue evolving through practical application. Intel's work on neural network optimization shows how hardware-specific optimizations improve performance. Their development of specialized computation patterns demonstrates how systems maximize throughput while maintaining accuracy. These advances establish new approaches to performance optimization.

The integration of multiple optimization approaches creates comprehensive improvements. The combination of model compression with inference optimization shows how different techniques complement each other. These integrations demonstrate how optimization advances proceed through careful combination of methods while maintaining system reliability.

These optimization patterns continue influencing system development. Understanding these advances provides crucial context for appreciating current capabilities while suggesting future directions. The success of different approaches demonstrates the importance of systematic optimization in advancing AI system capabilities.

Performance measurement for optimization continues evolving through practical experience. MLPerf's benchmark developments show how organizations assess optimization effectiveness. Their implementation of standardized testing demonstrates how systems evaluate improvements while maintaining comparison validity. These developments establish new standards for optimization assessment.

Architecture innovations in artificial intelligence reveal sophisticated approaches to system design and capability enhancement. Google DeepMind's development of Perceiver architectures demonstrates how fundamental rethinking of attention mechanisms enables more efficient processing across multiple modalities. Their implementation of flexible input processing shows how architectural innovations address scalability challenges while maintaining processing efficiency.

Network design advances show careful attention to structural optimization. Google's development of PaLM architecture demonstrates how organizations enhance model capabilities through innovative design patterns. Their implementation of sophisticated parameter sharing techniques shows how architectural decisions influence both performance and efficiency. These innovations establish new approaches to model architecture that influence industry development.

Processing pattern evolution reveals interesting approaches to computation management. Meta's implementation of sparse expert models shows how architectural innovations enable more efficient resource utilization. Their development of conditional computation paths demonstrates how systems maintain capability while reducing computational requirements. These advances transform how organizations approach model design.

Memory management innovations demonstrate sophisticated approaches to resource optimization. Microsoft's work on efficient attention patterns shows how architectural decisions influence system performance. Their implementation of optimized memory access patterns demonstrates how systems maintain processing capability while reducing resource requirements. These developments establish new standards for architectural efficiency.

Scaling approaches reveal careful attention to growth management. NVIDIA's implementation of distributed training architectures shows how organizations address large-scale computation challenges. Their development of efficient communication patterns demonstrates how systems maintain coordination while optimizing resource usage. These innovations influence how organizations approach system scaling.

Component integration methods show interesting patterns in architecture design. Anthropic's constitutional AI architecture demonstrates how organizations incorporate behavioral constraints into fundamental design. Their implementation of controlled processing patterns shows how systems maintain desired characteristics while preserving performance. These advances establish new approaches to architectural control.

Resource utilization patterns continue evolving through practical application. AWS's implementation of efficient inference architectures shows how organizations optimize deployment performance. Their development of specialized serving patterns demonstrates how systems maximize throughput while maintaining reliability. These innovations transform how organizations approach operational architecture.

The synthesis of multiple architectural innovations creates comprehensive improvements. The combination of efficient attention mechanisms with optimized memory management shows how different architectural advances complement each other. These integrations demonstrate how architecture innovation proceeds through careful combination of approaches while maintaining system effectiveness.

Architectural validation methods reveal sophisticated approaches to design assessment. Google's evaluation of different attention mechanisms shows how organizations assess architectural decisions. Their implementation of comparative analysis demonstrates how systems validate improvements while maintaining objective assessment. These developments establish new standards for architecture evaluation.

These architectural patterns continue influencing system development. Understanding these advances provides crucial context for appreciating current capabilities while suggesting future directions. The success of different approaches demonstrates the importance of systematic architecture innovation in advancing AI capabilities.

Quality advancement in artificial intelligence demonstrates sophisticated approaches to enhancing system reliability and performance. Anthropic's development of constitutional AI shows how organizations systematically improve model behavior while maintaining capabilities. Their implementation of advanced training protocols demonstrates how quality considerations can be embedded at fundamental levels while preserving system performance.

Reliability enhancement reveals careful attention to consistent operation. Google's work on model robustness shows how organizations improve system dependability through systematic innovation. Their implementation of enhanced validation techniques demonstrates how systems maintain performance stability across diverse conditions. These developments establish new standards for operational reliability in AI systems.

Error reduction methods continue evolving through practical experience. Microsoft's implementation of advanced testing frameworks shows how organizations systematically identify and address potential issues. Their development of comprehensive validation protocols demonstrates how systems maintain quality while reducing error rates. These

143

innovations transform how organizations approach quality assurance.

Consistency improvement reveals sophisticated approaches to output stability. OpenAI's work on GPT-4 demonstrates how organizations enhance output reliability across different contexts. Their implementation of improved processing patterns shows how systems maintain response consistency while handling diverse inputs. These advances influence how organizations approach quality management.

Performance optimization shows interesting patterns in capability enhancement. Google DeepMind's improvements in model accuracy demonstrate how organizations systematically enhance system capabilities. Their implementation of refined training methods shows how systems achieve higher performance levels while maintaining operational stability. These innovations establish new benchmarks for AI system performance.

Robustness improvement reveals careful attention to system resilience. Meta's work on adversarial training demonstrates how organizations enhance system stability under challenging conditions. Their implementation of sophisticated defense mechanisms shows how systems maintain performance while handling unexpected inputs. These developments transform how organizations approach system hardening.

Validation methods continue evolving through systematic innovation. IBM's implementation of comprehensive testing protocols shows how organizations ensure system quality. Their development of automated validation techniques demonstrates how systems maintain reliability while scaling operations. These advances establish new approaches to quality assurance.

The integration of multiple quality advancement approaches creates comprehensive improvements. The combination of enhanced validation methods with improved robustness techniques shows how different quality measures complement each other. These integrations demonstrate how quality advancement proceeds through careful combination of approaches while maintaining system effectiveness.

Recovery capabilities show sophisticated approaches to handling exceptions. Amazon's implementation of fallback mechanisms demonstrates how organizations maintain service quality during challenges. Their development of graceful degradation patterns shows how systems maintain functionality while addressing unexpected conditions. These innovations influence how organizations approach operational reliability.

These quality advancement patterns continue influencing system development. Understanding these advances provides crucial context for appreciating current capabilities while suggesting future directions. The success of different approaches demonstrates the importance of systematic quality enhancement in advancing AI capabilities.

Implementation advances in artificial intelligence reveal sophisticated approaches to deploying and operating complex systems. Google's deployment of PaLM demonstrates how organizations successfully implement large-scale AI systems while maintaining operational efficiency. Their systematic approach to service deployment shows how implementation innovations enable reliable operation of advanced AI capabilities while ensuring consistent performance.

System integration reveals careful attention to operational requirements. Microsoft's implementation of GPT-4 across their service portfolio shows how organizations effectively incorporate AI capabilities into existing systems. Their development of sophisticated integration patterns demonstrates how implementation advances enable seamless operation while maintaining system reliability. These innovations establish new standards for AI system deployment.

Performance monitoring continues evolving through practical experience. Amazon's SageMaker implementation shows how organizations track and maintain system effectiveness. Their development of comprehensive monitoring frameworks demonstrates how systems maintain operational awareness while enabling proactive management. These advances transform how organizations approach implementation oversight.

Resource management innovations show interesting patterns in operational optimization. NVIDIA's implementation of AI Enterprise platform demonstrates how organizations effectively manage computational resources. Their development of sophisticated scheduling mechanisms shows how systems maintain performance while optimizing resource utilization. These developments influence how organizations approach implementation efficiency.

Maintenance methodologies reveal sophisticated approaches to system upkeep. IBM's Watson platform implementation shows how organizations ensure continued system effectiveness. Their development of automated maintenance procedures demonstrates how systems maintain operational quality while reducing manual intervention. These innovations establish new approaches to implementation maintenance.

Update processes show careful attention to system evolution. Meta's deployment of LLaMA 2 demonstrates how organizations manage system advancement effectively. Their implementation of staged rollout procedures shows how systems maintain stability while incorporating improvements. These advances influence how organizations approach implementation updates.

Quality control mechanisms continue evolving through systematic innovation. Anthropic's implementation of Claude demonstrates how organizations maintain output quality across deployments. Their development of comprehensive validation procedures shows how systems ensure consistent performance while scaling operations. These developments establish new standards for implementation quality.

The synthesis of multiple implementation advances creates comprehensive improvements. The combination of sophisticated monitoring with effective resource management shows how different implementation aspects complement each other. These integrations demonstrate how implementation innovation proceeds through careful combination of approaches while maintaining operational effectiveness.

Interface design reveals careful attention to system accessibility. Hugging Face's implementation of model serving infrastructure shows how organizations enable effective system utilization. Their development of standardized interfaces demonstrates how systems maintain usability while supporting diverse applications. These innovations transform how organizations approach implementation accessibility.

These implementation patterns continue influencing system development. Understanding these advances provides crucial context for appreciating current capabilities while suggesting future directions. The success of different approaches demonstrates the importance of systematic implementation innovation in advancing AI capabilities.

The trajectory of core AI breakthroughs reveals emerging patterns that suggest promising directions for continued advancement. Google's research into Pathways demonstrates how organizations approach the development of more flexible, efficient AI systems. Their investigation of unified architectures shows how research directions focus on enhancing system capabilities while improving operational efficiency.

Research trends reveal careful attention to fundamental challenges. Google DeepMind's work on more efficient attention mechanisms shows how organizations address core computational constraints. Their investigation of novel architectural approaches demonstrates how research continues advancing basic capabilities while maintaining practical applicability. These investigations suggest interesting directions for future development.

Method development patterns show sophisticated approaches to capability enhancement. Microsoft's research into advanced training methodologies demonstrates how organizations systematically improve AI systems. Their investigation of efficient learning approaches shows how development focuses on enhancing capabilities while reducing resource requirements. These advances indicate promising directions for training innovation.

Integration approaches reveal interesting patterns in system advancement. Meta's research into cross-modal processing shows how organizations enhance system versatility. Their investigation of unified processing architectures demonstrates how development aims to improve system capabilities while maintaining operational efficiency. These developments suggest new directions for system integration.

Capability enhancement reveals careful attention to practical requirements. Anthropic's research into constitutional AI principles shows how organizations address both performance and control considerations. Their investigation of enhanced training methods demonstrates how development focuses on improving capabilities while maintaining system reliability. These advances indicate promising directions for controlled advancement.

Technology evolution patterns demonstrate systematic approaches to advancement. NVIDIA's research into specialized AI architectures shows how organizations enhance processing efficiency. Their investigation of optimized computation patterns demonstrates how development aims to improve performance while reducing resource requirements. These developments suggest new directions for hardware-software integration.

Implementation methods continue evolving through systematic investigation. Amazon's research into efficient serving architectures shows how organizations enhance deployment capabilities. Their investigation of optimized delivery patterns demonstrates how development focuses on improving operational efficiency while maintaining system reliability. These advances indicate promising directions for practical implementation.

The synthesis of multiple research directions creates comprehensive advancement opportunities. The combination of architectural innovation with enhanced training methods shows how different research streams complement each other. These integrations demonstrate how future development may proceed through careful combination of advances while maintaining practical utility.

Domain expansion reveals interesting patterns in capability growth. IBM's research into specialized AI applications shows how organizations address specific operational requirements. Their investigation of domain-adapted systems demonstrates how development aims to enhance specific capabilities while maintaining general applicability. These developments suggest new directions for specialized advancement.

These directional patterns continue influencing research and development. Understanding these trends provides crucial context for appreciating future possibilities while maintaining practical perspective. The success of different approaches demonstrates the importance of systematic innovation in advancing AI capabilities.

Our exploration of core AI breakthroughs reveals the fundamental advances driving artificial intelligence forward. From Google's development of PaLM architectures to OpenAI's progression through GPT models, we see how systematic innovation enables significant capability enhancement while maintaining practical applicability. For practitioners and organizations working with AI systems, these breakthroughs provide crucial insights into both current capabilities and future possibilities.

The innovation patterns we've examined demonstrate multiple paths for engaging with AI advancement. Whether through Microsoft's comprehensive AI implementations or Anthropic's focused development of constitutional AI, organizations can choose approaches that align with their specific requirements and objectives. The success of different approaches shows how various development paths can effectively address distinct challenges while maintaining operational effectiveness.

Learning system innovations reveal interesting opportunities for capability enhancement. Google DeepMind's advances in efficient training methodologies and Meta's development of self-supervised learning techniques demonstrate how organizations can improve system capabilities. For practitioners interested in AI development, these innovations provide valuable insights into effective learning approaches while suggesting promising directions for implementation.

Implementation considerations continue influencing how organizations approach AI advancement. Amazon's deployment of sophisticated AI services and NVIDIA's development of optimized computation systems show how practical requirements shape innovation. Understanding these relationships becomes crucial for organizations implementing AI systems, as implementation decisions significantly influence operational success.

The relationship between architecture and performance creates interesting opportunities for innovation. Google's development of efficient attention mechanisms and Microsoft's advances in distributed training show how thoughtful design enables significant improvements. These developments demonstrate the importance of understanding architectural trade-offs while suggesting approaches for enhancing AI system capabilities.

As we move forward to examine language AI frontiers in our next chapter, we carry forward understanding of how core breakthroughs enable specific capability advancements. The sophisticated approaches to AI development we've explored provide crucial context for understanding specialized applications and implementations. For practitioners and organizations, this understanding becomes increasingly valuable as AI technology continues advancing.

Engage actively with these core breakthroughs, whether through experimental implementation or systematic evaluation of different approaches. Major AI platforms provide extensive resources for exploring these innovations, while research publications offer detailed insights into breakthrough developments. These resources offer excellent starting points for practical engagement with AI advancement.

The field of core AI development continues evolving, offering new opportunities for innovation and implementation. By understanding current breakthroughs and emerging trends, practitioners and organizations can better position themselves to leverage advancing AI capabilities. Explore these opportunities while maintaining awareness of how fundamental advances influence practical implementation success.

CHAPTER 8: LANGUAGE AI FRONTIERS

The frontier of language AI represents one of the most dynamic areas of artificial intelligence advancement, building upon the core breakthroughs we explored in our previous chapter. OpenAI's progression from GPT-3 to GPT-4 demonstrates how fundamental innovations enable increasingly sophisticated language processing capabilities. Their systematic advancement in model architecture and training approaches shows how language AI continues evolving while establishing new benchmarks for performance and capability.

The current landscape of language AI reveals remarkable progress across multiple dimensions. Google's development of PaLM 2 demonstrates how organizations enhance language understanding and generation capabilities through architectural innovation. Their advances in multilingual processing and context understanding show how language models achieve increasingly sophisticated capabilities while maintaining computational efficiency.

Implementation patterns reveal interesting approaches to

practical deployment. Anthropic's development of Claude shows how organizations balance advanced capabilities with controlled behavior. Their systematic approach to model development demonstrates how language AI addresses both performance requirements and operational constraints while maintaining reliable operation.

The relationship between model scale and capability has grown increasingly sophisticated. Meta's LLaMA 2 shows how organizations optimize model architecture for efficient operation. Their development of advanced training approaches demonstrates how language models enhance capabilities while managing computational requirements. These advances influence how organizations approach language AI implementation.

Specialized applications continue emerging through focused development. GitHub's Copilot demonstrates how language models enable sophisticated code generation and programming support. Their implementation of context-aware assistance shows how language AI addresses specific operational needs while maintaining general language capabilities.

In this chapter, we explore the sophisticated world of language AI, examining how different approaches enable advanced natural language processing. From foundation models to specialized applications, we'll investigate how language AI continues advancing. This exploration reveals both current achievements and emerging directions in language processing, providing crucial context for understanding modern capabilities.

For practitioners and organizations implementing language AI systems, understanding these developments becomes increasingly important. The advances in language processing capabilities influence every aspect of implementation and deployment. As we proceed, we'll examine how different approaches address various challenges, offering insights valuable for those working with language AI technologies.

Foundation model advancement in language AI demonstrates sophisticated approaches to enhancing natural language processing capabilities. Google's development of PaLM 2 illustrates how architectural innovations enable significant improvements in language understanding and generation. Their implementation of enhanced attention mechanisms shows how foundation models advance through systematic innovation while maintaining computational efficiency.

Architecture evolution reveals careful attention to processing capability enhancement. OpenAI's progression through GPT models demonstrates how organizations systematically improve language model architectures. Their advances in context processing and response generation show how foundation models achieve increasingly sophisticated capabilities while managing computational requirements. These developments establish new standards for language model performance.

Scale progression patterns show interesting approaches to capability enhancement. Anthropic's Claude series demonstrates how organizations balance model size with processing efficiency. Their implementation of optimized architectures shows how foundation models maintain performance while managing resource utilization. These innovations influence how organizations approach model development.

Attention mechanism advancement continues driving significant improvements. Microsoft's implementation of advanced transformer architectures shows how organizations enhance processing capabilities. Their refinements in attention patterns demonstrate how foundation models improve understanding while maintaining processing efficiency. These developments establish new approaches to language processing.

Context processing capabilities reveal sophisticated approaches to understanding enhancement. Meta's development of LLaMA 2 shows how organizations improve contextual comprehension. Their implementation of advanced context modeling demonstrates how foundation models maintain understanding across complex discussions while preserving computational efficiency. These advances transform how models handle extended interactions.

Generation quality improvements show careful attention to output refinement. Google DeepMind's language model developments demonstrate how organizations enhance response quality. Their implementation of sophisticated generation techniques shows how foundation models maintain output coherence while improving relevance. These innovations establish new standards for language generation.

Task adaptation capabilities demonstrate interesting patterns in model versatility. Google's implementation of instruction tuning shows how organizations enhance model flexibility. Their development of improved adaptation techniques demonstrates how foundation models maintain performance across diverse tasks while preserving core capabilities. These advances influence how organizations approach model deployment.

Processing efficiency reveals sophisticated approaches to resource optimization. NVIDIA's work on inference optimization shows how organizations enhance operational efficiency. Their implementation of advanced computation patterns demonstrates how foundation models maintain performance while reducing resource requirements. These developments establish new benchmarks for operational efficiency.

The integration of these advancement patterns creates comprehensive improvements. The combination of enhanced architecture with improved processing efficiency shows how different innovations complement each other. These integrations demonstrate how foundation model advancement proceeds through careful combination of approaches while maintaining practical utility.

Multilingual processing capabilities in language AI demonstrate sophisticated approaches to cross-linguistic understanding and generation. Google's development of Universal Language Model (ULM) shows how organizations achieve advanced multilingual capabilities through unified architectures. Their implementation of shared representations across languages demonstrates how models maintain performance while handling diverse linguistic structures, establishing new standards for multilingual processing.

Cross-lingual understanding reveals careful attention to semantic preservation. Meta's advances in multilingual models demonstrate how organizations enhance cross-language comprehension. Their implementation of M2M-100, capable of direct translation between 100 languages without English as an intermediate, shows how models achieve sophisticated understanding while maintaining translation quality. These innovations transform how systems handle cross-linguistic communication.

Translation system advancement continues driving significant improvements. Google DeepMind's translation architecture developments show how organizations enhance translation accuracy. Their implementation of context-aware translation demonstrates how systems maintain meaning across language boundaries while preserving cultural nuances. These developments establish new benchmarks for translation quality.

Cultural context processing demonstrates sophisticated approaches to nuance preservation. Anthropic's implementation of cultural awareness in Claude shows how models handle cultural-specific expressions. Their development of context-sensitive processing demonstrates how systems maintain appropriateness across cultural boundaries while preserving communication intent. These advances influence how organizations approach global deployment.

Generation capabilities across languages reveal interesting

patterns in output quality. Microsoft's multilingual GPT implementations show how organizations achieve consistent generation across languages. Their development of language-specific optimization demonstrates how systems maintain generation quality while addressing linguistic particularities. These innovations establish new standards for multilingual generation.

Style adaptation capabilities show careful attention to linguistic variation. OpenAI's GPT-4 demonstrates sophisticated handling of language-specific writing styles. Their implementation of style-aware generation shows how systems maintain appropriate tone across languages while preserving content integrity. These developments transform how models handle stylistic elements.

Integration approaches reveal sophisticated methods for language handling. Google's Vertex AI translation services show how organizations implement seamless language switching. Their development of integrated processing demonstrates how systems maintain context while transitioning between languages. These advances establish new approaches to multilingual service delivery.

Quality maintenance across languages demonstrates interesting patterns in consistency management. AWS's implementation of multilingual validation shows how organizations ensure consistent performance. Their development of language-specific quality metrics demonstrates how systems maintain standards while addressing linguistic diversity. These innovations influence how organizations approach quality assurance.

The synthesis of these capabilities creates comprehensive multilingual solutions. The combination of enhanced understanding with sophisticated generation shows how different capabilities complement each other. These integrations demonstrate how multilingual processing advances through careful combination of approaches while maintaining practical effectiveness.

Specialized applications of language AI demonstrate sophisticated approaches to domain-specific challenges. GitHub's Copilot represents a significant advancement in code generation and programming support, processing over 40% of newly written code in supported languages. Their implementation of context-aware programming assistance shows how language models address specific development needs while maintaining code quality and consistency.

Code generation capabilities reveal careful attention to development requirements. Amazon's CodeWhisperer demonstrates how organizations enhance programming productivity through AI assistance. Their implementation of security-aware code suggestions shows how specialized systems maintain development efficiency while addressing crucial security considerations. These innovations transform how organizations approach automated programming support.

Documentation creation systems show interesting patterns in technical writing assistance. Google's technical documentation tools demonstrate how language AI enhances documentation quality. Their implementation of context-aware documentation generation shows how systems maintain technical accuracy while improving clarity. These developments establish new standards for automated documentation support.

Content creation capabilities reveal sophisticated approaches to text generation. Microsoft's implementation of enterprise content assistance shows how organizations enhance writing productivity. Their development of style-aware generation demonstrates how systems maintain brand consistency while adapting to different content types. These advances influence how organizations approach content development.

Editorial support systems demonstrate careful attention to quality enhancement. Grammarly's advanced writing assistance shows how specialized applications improve text quality. Their implementation of contextual suggestions demonstrates how systems maintain writing effectiveness while enhancing clarity. These innovations establish new approaches to automated editing.

Analysis systems reveal interesting patterns in text understanding. Bloomberg's implementation of financial text analysis shows how organizations extract valuable insights from complex documents. Their development of domain-specific processing demonstrates how systems maintain accuracy while handling specialized terminology. These advances transform how organizations approach document analysis.

Pattern recognition capabilities show sophisticated approaches to content understanding. Databricks' implementation of contract analysis demonstrates how organizations enhance document processing. Their development of specialized recognition patterns shows how systems maintain accuracy while handling complex legal language. These innovations influence how organizations approach document processing.

Insight generation reveals careful attention to practical utility. IBM's Watson Discovery shows how organizations derive actionable insights from unstructured text. Their implementation of domain-adapted processing demonstrates how systems maintain relevance while handling diverse content types. These developments establish new standards for automated insight extraction.

The integration of these specialized capabilities creates comprehensive solutions. The combination of enhanced understanding with sophisticated generation shows how different specializations complement each other. These integrations demonstrate how specialized applications advance through careful combination of approaches while maintaining practical effectiveness.

These specialized application patterns continue influencing development directions. Understanding these advances provides crucial context for appreciating current capabilities while suggesting future possibilities. The success of different approaches demonstrates the importance of domain-specific optimization in advancing language AI applications.

Enhancement technologies in language AI demonstrate sophisticated approaches to improving system capabilities and performance. Anthropic's implementation of constitutional AI shows how organizations enhance model behavior through advanced control mechanisms. Their development of structured enhancement techniques, resulting in Claude's demonstrated improvement in truthfulness and reliability, shows how systems maintain capability while improving output quality.

Context processing advances reveal careful attention to understanding depth. Google's PaLM 2 demonstrates significant improvements in contextual comprehension, handling complex references across extended discussions. Their implementation of enhanced memory systems shows how organizations improve context retention while maintaining processing efficiency. These innovations transform how models manage extended interactions.

Reference management capabilities show interesting patterns in information handling. OpenAI's GPT-4 demonstrates sophisticated management of internal references and citations. Their implementation of enhanced fact-checking mechanisms shows how systems maintain accuracy while processing complex information, demonstrating measurable reductions in hallucination rates. These developments establish new standards for information reliability.

Memory systems reveal sophisticated approaches to information retention. Meta's development of long-term memory architectures shows how organizations enhance contextual understanding across extended interactions. Their implementation of structured memory management demonstrates how systems maintain conversation coherence while preserving important details. These advances influence how models handle extended dialogues.

Quality control mechanisms demonstrate careful attention to output reliability. Microsoft's implementation of enhanced validation systems shows how organizations ensure consistent output quality. Their development of real-time verification processes demonstrates how systems maintain accuracy while operating at scale. These innovations establish new approaches to quality assurance.

Performance optimization reveals interesting patterns in efficiency enhancement. NVIDIA's Triton Inference Server shows how organizations improve response speed while maintaining quality. Their implementation of optimized processing patterns demonstrates how systems reduce latency while preserving capability. These advances transform how organizations approach operational efficiency.

Resource efficiency shows sophisticated approaches to optimization. AWS's implementation of dynamic batching and caching strategies shows how organizations enhance processing efficiency. Their development of resource management techniques demonstrates how systems maintain performance while reducing computational requirements. These innovations influence how organizations approach system scaling.

The integration of these enhancement technologies creates comprehensive improvements. Google DeepMind's combination of advanced memory systems with sophisticated validation demonstrates how different enhancements complement each other. These integrations show how enhancement technologies advance through careful combination of approaches while maintaining practical utility.

Scaling approaches reveal careful attention to growth management. Google Cloud's implementation of distributed enhancement systems shows how organizations maintain quality at scale. Their development of coordinated optimization techniques demonstrates how systems preserve performance while expanding capabilities. These developments establish new standards for scalable enhancement.

These enhancement patterns continue influencing system development. Understanding these advances provides crucial context for appreciating current capabilities while suggesting future directions. The success of different approaches demonstrates the importance of systematic enhancement in advancing language AI capabilities.

Implementation advances in language AI demonstrate sophisticated approaches to deploying and managing complex language systems. Microsoft's integration of GPT-4 across their product suite shows how organizations successfully implement advanced language capabilities at scale. Their deployment across GitHub Copilot, Bing Chat, and Microsoft 365 demonstrates how systematic implementation approaches enable reliable operation while maintaining consistent performance across diverse applications.

Deployment systems reveal careful attention to operational requirements. Google's implementation of PaLM 2 services shows how organizations handle complex serving requirements. Their development of sophisticated load balancing and request routing demonstrates how systems maintain sub-second response times while managing massive query volumes.

Load management capabilities show interesting patterns in resource optimization. OpenAI's API infrastructure demonstrates how organizations handle variable demand effectively. Their implementation of dynamic scaling systems shows how deployment architectures maintain performance under varying loads, automatically adjusting resources to handle substantial peak demands.

Resource management reveals sophisticated approaches to computation optimization. AWS's implementation of multi-model endpoints shows how organizations maximize infrastructure utilization. Their development of efficient serving patterns demonstrates how systems maintain performance while optimizing resource usage, significantly reducing costs through intelligent resource allocation.

Integration methods demonstrate careful attention to system connectivity. Anthropic's API design shows how organizations enable effective system utilization. Their implementation of structured interaction patterns demonstrates how systems maintain capability while supporting diverse integration needs. These innovations establish new standards for API design in language AI.

Service coordination reveals interesting patterns in system management. Meta's implementation of language services shows how organizations handle complex service dependencies. Their development of sophisticated service mesh architectures demonstrates how systems maintain reliability while managing intricate service relationships. These advances transform how organizations approach service management.

Monitoring tools show sophisticated approaches to system oversight. Datadog's language AI monitoring capabilities demonstrate how organizations track complex system behavior. Their implementation of specialized metrics and alerts shows how systems maintain operational awareness while enabling proactive management. These innovations influence how organizations approach operational monitoring.

The synthesis of these implementation advances creates comprehensive operational improvements. IBM's Watson platform shows how organizations combine various implementation capabilities effectively. Their coordination of different operational aspects demonstrates how implementation advances proceed through careful combination of approaches while maintaining system reliability.

Compatibility management reveals careful attention to system integration. Snowflake's implementation of language

AI capabilities shows how organizations maintain effective system interaction. Their development of standardized interfaces demonstrates how systems preserve functionality while enabling broad integration. These developments establish new approaches to system compatibility.

These implementation patterns continue influencing operational approaches. Understanding these advances provides crucial context for appreciating current capabilities while suggesting future directions. The success of different approaches demonstrates the importance of systematic implementation in advancing language AI operations.

Operational excellence in language AI reveals sophisticated approaches to maintaining high-performance systems at scale. Google Cloud's language AI operations demonstrate how organizations achieve consistent reliability while serving millions of users. Their achievement of 99.99% availability while processing over a billion daily requests shows how careful operational practices enable sustained performance while maintaining service quality.

Quality maintenance reveals careful attention to output consistency. OpenAI's operational framework demonstrates how organizations ensure reliable performance across diverse applications. Their implementation of continuous quality monitoring shows how systems maintain response quality while handling varied user interactions, with automated systems continuously checking outputs for accuracy and appropriateness.

Performance tracking capabilities show interesting patterns in system optimization. Microsoft's Azure AI operations demonstrate sophisticated approaches to monitoring and enhancement. Their implementation of real-time performance analytics shows how organizations maintain service quality while identifying optimization opportunities, resulting in consistent rapid response times for most applications.

Resource optimization reveals sophisticated approaches to efficiency management. AWS's implementation of dynamic resource allocation shows how organizations maximize operational efficiency. Their development of automated scaling systems demonstrates how operations maintain performance while optimizing costs, achieving substantial reductions in resource utilization through intelligent management.

Usage management capabilities demonstrate careful attention to resource allocation. Anthropic's operational systems show how organizations balance capacity with demand. Their implementation of sophisticated usage tracking demonstrates how operations maintain service quality while optimizing resource distribution, ensuring consistent performance across varying load patterns.

Cost control mechanisms reveal interesting patterns in efficiency optimization. Databricks' operational practices show how organizations manage resources effectively. Their implementation of automated cost optimization demonstrates how operations maintain performance while reducing expenses, achieving significant savings through intelligent workload management.

Service management shows sophisticated approaches to system maintenance. Meta's operational framework demonstrates how organizations ensure consistent service delivery. Their implementation of automated health checks shows how operations maintain system reliability while enabling proactive maintenance, preventing potential issues before they impact users.

Update processes reveal careful attention to system evolution. IBM's Watson platform operations show how organizations manage system advancement effectively. Their implementation of zero-downtime updates demonstrates how operations maintain service continuity while incorporating improvements, enabling continuous enhancement without disrupting users.

Support systems demonstrate sophisticated approaches to issue resolution. Google's operational support framework shows how organizations maintain service quality through effective problem management. Their implementation of automated diagnostic systems demonstrates how operations maintain reliability while expediting issue resolution, significantly reducing mean time to recovery.

These operational patterns continue influencing system management approaches. Understanding these advances provides crucial context for appreciating current capabilities while suggesting future directions. The success of different approaches demonstrates the importance of operational excellence in maintaining effective language AI systems.

The trajectory of language AI reveals emerging patterns that suggest promising directions for continued advancement. Google's development of PaLM architecture demonstrates how organizations approach the evolution of more sophisticated language understanding capabilities. Their systematic progression in model architecture shows how research directions focus on enhancing comprehension while improving efficiency, with each iteration achieving measurable improvements in both capability and resource utilization.

Technical evolution reveals careful attention to fundamental enhancement. Microsoft's research into advanced language model architectures shows how organizations address core processing challenges. Their investigation of more efficient attention mechanisms demonstrates how development continues advancing basic capabilities while maintaining practical applicability. Current implementations achieving 40% efficiency improvements suggest promising directions for future optimization.

Capability enhancement patterns show sophisticated approaches to improving model performance. Anthropic's development of constitutional AI principles demonstrates how organizations systematically enhance model behavior. Their research into controlled response generation shows how development focuses on improving reliability while maintaining performance, with current systems showing significant reductions in unwanted outputs.

Integration approaches reveal interesting patterns in system advancement. Meta's research into cross-modal language processing shows how organizations enhance system versatility. Their development of unified processing architectures demonstrates how future systems might handle multiple input types more effectively, with current prototypes showing promising results in combined text and visual understanding.

Application growth reveals careful attention to practical implementation. OpenAI's expansion of language model applications shows how organizations explore new use cases. Their systematic investigation of different application domains demonstrates how development aims to broaden utility while maintaining reliability, with current implementations successfully extending into specialized professional domains.

Service evolution patterns demonstrate systematic approaches to enhancement. AWS's research into advanced serving architectures shows how organizations improve deployment efficiency. Their investigation of optimized delivery patterns demonstrates how development aims to improve operational efficiency while maintaining system reliability, with current implementations showing substantial improvements in resource utilization.

Implementation methods continue evolving through systematic investigation. Google DeepMind's research into efficient deployment architectures shows how organizations enhance practical application. Their investigation of optimized serving patterns demonstrates how development focuses on improving operational efficiency while maintaining system reliability, with current systems achieving significant performance gains.

The synthesis of multiple advancement directions creates comprehensive improvement opportunities. The combination of architectural innovation with enhanced training methods shows how different research streams complement each other.

These integrations demonstrate how future development may proceed through careful combination of advances while maintaining practical utility.

These directional patterns continue influencing research and development approaches. Understanding these trends provides crucial context for appreciating future possibilities while maintaining practical perspective. The success of different approaches demonstrates the importance of systematic innovation in advancing language AI capabilities.

Our exploration of language AI frontiers reveals the sophisticated evolution of natural language processing capabilities. From Google's PaLM 2 to OpenAI's GPT-4, we see how systematic innovation enables increasingly advanced language understanding and generation while maintaining practical applicability. For practitioners and organizations working with language AI, these developments provide crucial insights into both current capabilities and implementation approaches.

The advancement patterns we've examined demonstrate multiple paths for engaging with language AI technology. Whether through Microsoft's enterprise-scale implementations or Anthropic's focused development of controlled language models, organizations can choose approaches that align with their specific requirements and objectives. The success of different approaches shows how various development paths can effectively address distinct challenges while maintaining operational effectiveness.

Implementation considerations continue influencing how organizations approach language AI deployment. Amazon's sophisticated serving architectures and Google's advanced deployment systems demonstrate how practical requirements shape operational decisions. Understanding these relationships becomes crucial for organizations implementing language AI systems, as deployment choices significantly influence operational success.

The relationship between capability and efficiency creates

interesting opportunities for innovation. Meta's advances in multilingual processing and Google DeepMind's improvements in context understanding show how thoughtful design enables significant improvements. These developments demonstrate the importance of understanding technical trade-offs while suggesting approaches for enhancing language AI capabilities.

As we move forward to examine data AI innovations in our next chapter, we carry forward understanding of how language processing capabilities enable sophisticated data analysis. The advanced approaches to language understanding we've explored provide crucial context for understanding how AI systems process and derive insights from structured and unstructured data. For practitioners and organizations, this understanding becomes increasingly valuable as AI technology continues advancing.

Engage actively with these language AI developments, whether through experimental implementation or systematic evaluation of different approaches. Major cloud providers offer extensive resources for exploring language AI capabilities, while specialized platforms provide focused environments for specific applications. These resources offer excellent starting points for practical engagement with language AI advancement.

The field of language AI continues evolving, offering new opportunities for innovation and implementation. By understanding current capabilities and emerging trends, practitioners and organizations can better position themselves to leverage advancing language AI technologies. Explore these opportunities while maintaining awareness of how language processing capabilities influence practical implementation success.

CHAPTER 9: DATA AI INNOVATIONS

The frontier of data AI innovations represents a crucial advancement in how organizations process and derive value from complex information, building upon the language processing capabilities we explored in our previous chapter. Databricks' development of their Lakehouse architecture demonstrates how organizations are revolutionizing data processing through AI innovation. Their systematic advancement in unified analytics, processing over 20 exabytes of data daily across thousands of organizations, shows how data AI continues evolving while establishing new benchmarks for performance and capability.

The current landscape of data AI reveals remarkable progress across multiple dimensions. Snowflake's Data Cloud platform demonstrates how organizations enhance data processing capabilities through architectural innovation. Their advances in hybrid processing and automated optimization show how data systems achieve increasingly sophisticated capabilities while maintaining computational efficiency, handling millions of queries per hour with sub-second response times.

Implementation patterns reveal interesting approaches to practical deployment. Google BigQuery's ML capabilities show how organizations balance advanced analytics with operational efficiency. Their systematic approach to integrated machine learning demonstrates how data AI addresses both performance requirements and scalability constraints while maintaining reliable operation across petabyte-scale datasets.

The relationship between processing scale and capability has grown increasingly sophisticated. AWS's Redshift ML shows how organizations optimize analytics architecture for efficient operation. Their development of advanced query optimization approaches demonstrates how data systems enhance capabilities while managing computational requirements, processing billions of rows per second while maintaining consistency.

Specialized applications continue emerging through focused development. MongoDB's Atlas platform demonstrates how data AI enables sophisticated real-time analytics and automation. Their implementation of predictive optimization shows how data systems address specific operational needs while maintaining general processing capabilities across diverse workloads.

In this chapter, we explore the sophisticated world of data AI, examining how different approaches enable advanced analytics and processing. From fundamental innovations to specialized applications, we'll investigate how data AI continues advancing. This exploration reveals both current achievements and emerging directions in data processing, providing crucial context for understanding modern capabilities.

For practitioners and organizations implementing data AI systems, understanding these developments becomes increasingly important. The advances in data processing capabilities influence every aspect of implementation and deployment. As we proceed, we'll examine how different approaches address various challenges, offering insights valuable for those working with data AI technologies.

Analytics evolution in data AI demonstrates sophisticated approaches to processing and deriving insights from complex information systems. Snowflake's implementation of dynamic optimization shows how organizations enhance analytical capabilities through AI-driven processing. Their advances in hybrid processing and automated optimization show how data systems achieve increasingly sophisticated capabilities while maintaining computational efficiency, processing massive volumes of data daily.

Pattern recognition capabilities reveal careful attention to insight discovery. Databricks' implementation of automated pattern detection shows how organizations enhance understanding of complex datasets. Their development of sophisticated recognition algorithms demonstrates how analytics systems identify subtle patterns across massive datasets, processing millions of data points per second while maintaining accuracy above 99%. These innovations transform how organizations approach data understanding.

Predictive analytics reveals sophisticated approaches to future insight generation. Amazon's SageMaker implementation demonstrates how organizations enhance forecasting capabilities. Their development of automated model selection and optimization shows how analytics systems maintain prediction accuracy while processing diverse data types. These advances establish new standards for predictive capability, with demonstrable accuracy improvements of 30-40% over traditional methods.

Real-time analysis capabilities show interesting patterns in immediate insight generation. MongoDB's Atlas platform demonstrates how organizations achieve sophisticated real-time processing. Their implementation of streaming analytics shows how systems maintain accuracy while processing millions of events per second. These innovations influence how organizations approach immediate decision-making requirements.

Automated discovery mechanisms reveal careful attention to insight extraction. Google's BigQuery ML shows how organizations enhance automated analysis capabilities. Their implementation of sophisticated discovery algorithms demonstrates how systems identify valuable insights while maintaining processing efficiency. These developments establish new approaches to automated analytics.

Correlation detection capabilities demonstrate sophisticated approaches to relationship identification. Microsoft's Azure Synapse Analytics shows how organizations discover complex data relationships. Their implementation of advanced correlation analysis demonstrates how systems maintain accuracy while processing interconnected data streams. These advances transform how organizations understand data relationships.

Trend identification reveals interesting patterns in temporal analysis. Splunk's implementation of trend detection shows how organizations enhance understanding of data evolution. Their development of adaptive trend analysis demonstrates how systems maintain accuracy while processing historical and real-time data. These innovations establish new standards for temporal analysis.

The integration of these analytical capabilities creates comprehensive insights. The combination of enhanced pattern recognition with sophisticated prediction shows how different analytical approaches complement each other. These integrations demonstrate how analytics evolution proceeds through careful combination of techniques while maintaining practical utility.

Performance enhancement reveals careful attention to processing efficiency. Oracle's implementation of autonomous databases shows how organizations optimize analytical processing. Their development of AI-driven optimization demonstrates how systems maintain performance while reducing resource requirements. These advances influence how organizations approach analytical processing.

Data processing innovations demonstrate sophisticated approaches to handling complex information streams at scale. Apache Kafka's evolution shows how stream processing capabilities continue advancing through systematic innovation, handling massive volumes of events daily across major organizations. Their implementation of intelligent partitioning and AI-driven optimization demonstrates how modern systems maintain performance while handling massive data volumes.

Stream processing capabilities reveal careful attention to real-time handling requirements. Confluent Cloud's implementation of intelligent stream processing shows how organizations manage continuous data flows effectively. Their system processes massive volumes of events while maintaining sub-millisecond latency, demonstrating how modern architectures balance throughput with responsiveness. These innovations transform how organizations approach real-time data handling.

Event processing systems show sophisticated approaches to immediate data analysis. Apache Flink's advancement in complex event processing demonstrates how organizations handle sophisticated event patterns. Their implementation of AI-enhanced pattern detection shows how systems maintain accuracy while processing millions of events per second, achieving pattern recognition rates above 99% in real-time scenarios.

Batch processing reveals interesting patterns in large-scale data handling. Databricks' implementation of photon engine shows how organizations optimize massive data processing. Their system processes petabytes of data while reducing processing time by up to 12x compared to traditional methods, demonstrating how modern architectures balance throughput with resource efficiency.

Distributed computing capabilities demonstrate careful

attention to resource utilization. Apache Spark's implementation of adaptive query execution shows how organizations optimize processing across clusters. Their system automatically adjusts resource allocation while maintaining processing efficiency, showing significant improvement in resource utilization across large-scale deployments.

Lambda architecture implementations reveal sophisticated approaches to hybrid processing. LinkedIn's data processing infrastructure shows how organizations balance real-time and batch processing needs. Their system handles over 20 petabytes of data daily while maintaining both speed and accuracy, demonstrating how modern architectures address diverse processing requirements.

Kappa architecture adoption shows interesting patterns in unified stream processing. Netflix's implementation of stream-first processing demonstrates how organizations simplify data architectures. Their system processes billions of events daily through a single processing paradigm, showing how modern approaches reduce complexity while maintaining capability.

Integration methods reveal careful attention to system coordination. Google Cloud Dataflow's implementation shows how organizations manage complex processing pipelines. Their system automatically optimizes processing paths while maintaining data consistency, demonstrating how modern architectures handle complex processing requirements.

Resource management capabilities show sophisticated approaches to optimization. Amazon Kinesis's implementation of adaptive sharding demonstrates how organizations manage processing resources effectively. Their system automatically adjusts processing capacity while maintaining performance, showing how modern architectures handle variable workloads efficiently.

These processing innovations continue influencing system development. Understanding these advances provides crucial context for appreciating current capabilities while suggesting future directions. The success of different approaches demonstrates the importance of systematic innovation in advancing data processing capabilities.

Advanced analytics applications demonstrate sophisticated approaches to deriving actionable insights from complex data landscapes. Tableau's integration with Salesforce's Einstein Analytics shows how organizations enhance business intelligence through AI-driven analysis. Their system processes vast numbers of customer interactions, automatically identifying patterns and trends while maintaining high accuracy rates in prediction models.

Business intelligence applications reveal careful attention to decision support requirements. Microsoft's Power BI implementation demonstrates how organizations leverage AI for automated insight discovery. Their system analyzes trillions of data points monthly, automatically surfacing relevant patterns and anomalies while significantly reducing analysis time compared to traditional methods. These innovations transform how organizations approach data-driven decision making.

Automated analysis capabilities show sophisticated approaches to pattern recognition. Looker's integration with Google Cloud reveals how organizations enhance analytical automation. Their implementation processes vast numbers of queries annually, automatically identifying significant trends and correlations while maintaining context relevance. These advances establish new standards for automated business analysis.

Scientific computing applications demonstrate careful attention to research requirements. CERN's implementation of data analysis systems shows how organizations handle complex scientific data. Their system processes over 1 petabyte of particle physics data daily, automatically identifying significant events while maintaining accuracy in pattern detection. These innovations influence how research organizations approach data analysis.

Research analysis capabilities reveal interesting patterns in scientific discovery. The Allen Institute for AI's implementation shows how organizations enhance research productivity. Their system automatically analyzes millions of scientific papers, identifying connections and patterns that significantly accelerate research discovery. These developments establish new approaches to scientific data analysis.

Operational analytics show sophisticated approaches to process optimization. GE's Predix platform demonstrates how organizations enhance industrial operations through AI-driven analytics. Their system monitors millions of sensor data points in real-time, automatically identifying optimization opportunities while improving operational efficiency. These advances transform how organizations approach operational improvement.

Performance monitoring capabilities reveal careful attention to system optimization. Splunk's implementation of predictive analytics shows how organizations enhance operational oversight. Their system processes massive volumes of operational data daily, automatically predicting potential issues while significantly reducing mean time to resolution.

Efficiency enhancement reveals sophisticated approaches to resource optimization. Palantir's Foundry platform demonstrates how organizations optimize complex operations. Their system analyzes billions of operational data points, automatically identifying efficiency opportunities while maintaining operational stability. These innovations establish new standards for operational analytics.

The integration of these analytical applications creates comprehensive improvement opportunities. The combination of enhanced business intelligence with sophisticated operational analytics shows how different applications complement each other. These integrations demonstrate how advanced analytics proceed through careful combination of approaches while maintaining practical utility.

Data quality management demonstrates sophisticated approaches to ensuring information accuracy and reliability in modern AI systems. Informatica's intelligent data quality platform shows how organizations systematically enhance data reliability through AI-driven validation. Their system processes massive volumes of cloud transactions monthly, automatically identifying and correcting quality issues while maintaining high accuracy in anomaly detection.

Validation systems reveal careful attention to accuracy requirements. Talend's Data Fabric implementation demonstrates how organizations ensure data integrity at scale. Their platform automatically validates enormous volumes of data points daily, identifying quality issues in real-time while significantly reducing error rates compared to traditional methods. These innovations transform how organizations approach data validation.

Consistency verification capabilities show sophisticated approaches to data reliability. Collibra's data intelligence platform demonstrates how organizations maintain data consistency across complex environments. Their system automatically monitors data patterns across enterprises, effectively detecting inconsistencies while processing petabytes of information daily. These advances establish new standards for data consistency management.

Enhancement methods reveal interesting patterns in quality improvement. Precisely's data integrity suite shows how organizations systematically improve data quality. Their implementation automatically enriches billions of records monthly, showing substantial improvement in data completeness while maintaining accuracy standards. These developments influence how organizations approach data enhancement.

Data cleaning capabilities demonstrate careful attention to quality maintenance. Alation's data catalog platform shows how organizations automate quality improvement. Their system processes millions of data assets, automatically identifying and addressing quality issues while substantially reducing manual intervention. These innovations establish new approaches to automated data cleaning.

Monitoring systems reveal sophisticated approaches to quality tracking. Datadog's implementation shows how organizations maintain ongoing quality oversight. Their platform automatically monitors data quality metrics across thousands of sources, detecting anomalies within seconds while maintaining high accuracy. These advances transform how organizations approach quality monitoring.

Issue detection capabilities show careful attention to problem identification. Snowflake's data quality features demonstrate how organizations identify quality concerns proactively. Their system automatically analyzes data patterns across workloads, identifying potential issues before they impact operations while maintaining high detection accuracy. These developments establish new standards for automated quality control.

Resolution management reveals interesting patterns in quality maintenance. MongoDB Atlas's data quality tools show how organizations address quality issues efficiently. Their implementation automatically suggests and implements corrective actions, significantly reducing resolution time while maintaining data integrity. These innovations influence how organizations approach quality management.

The integration of these quality management capabilities creates comprehensive improvement systems. The combination of enhanced validation with sophisticated monitoring shows how different quality approaches complement each other. These integrations demonstrate how quality management advances through careful combination of techniques while maintaining practical effectiveness.

These quality management patterns continue influencing system development. Understanding these advances provides crucial context for appreciating current capabilities while suggesting future directions. The success of different approaches demonstrates the importance of systematic quality management in advancing data AI capabilities.

Integration capabilities in modern data AI systems demonstrate sophisticated approaches to connecting diverse data ecosystems. Databricks' Unity Catalog shows how organizations achieve seamless data integration across complex environments. Their platform enables unified access while maintaining strict governance standards and processing efficiency.

Source integration reveals careful attention to data collection requirements. Fivetran's automated data integration platform demonstrates how organizations streamline data acquisition. Their system, supporting over 300 pre-built connectors, automatically processes millions of daily updates while significantly reducing integration time. These innovations transform how organizations approach data consolidation.

Format handling capabilities show sophisticated approaches to data diversity. Informatica's Intelligent Data Management Cloud demonstrates how organizations manage varied data types. Their platform automatically processes structured and unstructured data from thousands of sources while maintaining data fidelity. These advances establish new standards for heterogeneous data integration.

Pipeline management reveals interesting patterns in data flow optimization. Apache NiFi's implementation shows how organizations handle complex data routing. Their system processes petabytes of data daily across diverse workflows, automatically optimizing data paths while maintaining sub-second latency. These developments influence how organizations approach data movement.

Resource coordination demonstrates careful attention to processing efficiency. Azure Synapse Analytics shows how organizations balance integration workloads. Their platform automatically distributes processing across available resources, improving resource utilization while maintaining performance standards. These innovations establish new approaches to integrated processing.

Output integration reveals sophisticated approaches to result distribution. Snowflake's Data Cloud demonstrates how organizations manage complex data sharing requirements. Their implementation enables secure data sharing across thousands of organizations, processing billions of queries monthly while maintaining strict access controls. These advances transform how organizations approach data distribution.

System connection capabilities show careful attention to interoperability. Google Cloud's BigQuery federation features demonstrate how organizations enable cross-system analysis. Their implementation automatically connects diverse data sources, enabling unified analysis while maintaining query performance. These developments establish new standards for system interoperability.

Format translation reveals interesting patterns in data transformation. AWS Glue demonstrates how organizations handle complex data conversions. Their system automatically processes millions of ETL jobs daily, reducing transformation overhead by 50% while maintaining data accuracy. These innovations influence how organizations approach data standardization.

The synthesis of these integration capabilities creates comprehensive data ecosystems. The combination of enhanced source integration with sophisticated distribution shows how different integration approaches complement each other. These integrations demonstrate how connectivity advances through careful combination of techniques while maintaining practical utility.

These integration patterns continue influencing system development. Understanding these advances provides crucial context for appreciating current capabilities while suggesting future directions. The success of different approaches demonstrates the importance of systematic integration in advancing data AI capabilities.

Operational frameworks in modern data AI systems demonstrate sophisticated approaches to managing complex analytical environments. Snowflake's platform shows how organizations achieve operational excellence at scale. Their implementation of automated resource management and workload optimization demonstrates how modern frameworks balance performance with efficiency.

Resource management reveals careful attention to computational optimization. Google BigQuery's implementation shows how organizations handle massive processing requirements efficiently. Their system automatically allocates resources across millions of concurrent queries, efficiently improving resource utilization while maintaining consistent performance. These innovations transform how organizations approach operational efficiency.

Storage optimization capabilities show sophisticated approaches to data management. Azure Data Lake demonstrates how organizations handle exabyte-scale storage requirements. Their system automatically optimizes data placement and access patterns while maintaining millisecond access times. These advances establish new standards for large-scale data operations.

Network utilization reveals interesting patterns in data movement optimization. AWS's Aurora demonstrates how organizations manage complex data transfer requirements. Their implementation automatically optimizes data routing and replication while maintaining global consistency. These developments influence how organizations approach data distribution.

Performance optimization demonstrates careful attention to processing efficiency. MongoDB Atlas shows how organizations enhance operational performance. Their platform automatically optimizes query execution across distributed systems while maintaining data consistency. These innovations establish new approaches to operational optimization.

System maintenance reveals sophisticated approaches to operational reliability. Databricks' implementation shows how organizations maintain complex data environments. Their system automatically manages updates and patches across thousands of clusters while reducing maintenance overhead. These advances transform how organizations approach system upkeep.

Health monitoring capabilities show careful attention to system reliability. DataDog's platform demonstrates how organizations maintain operational awareness. Their implementation automatically monitors millions of metrics in real-time, quickly detecting potential issues. These developments establish new standards for operational monitoring.

Issue resolution reveals interesting patterns in problem management. New Relic's platform shows how organizations handle operational challenges. Their system automatically identifies and diagnoses issues across complex environments while maintaining service quality. These innovations influence how organizations approach operational stability.

The integration of these operational frameworks creates comprehensive management systems. The combination of enhanced resource management with sophisticated monitoring shows how different operational approaches complement each other. These integrations demonstrate how operational excellence advances through careful combination of techniques while maintaining practical effectiveness.

These operational patterns continue influencing system development. Understanding these advances provides crucial context for appreciating current capabilities while suggesting future directions. The success of different approaches demonstrates the importance of systematic operations in advancing data AI capabilities.

184

AI FRONTIER: NAVIGATING THE CUTTING EDGE

The trajectory of data AI innovations reveals emerging patterns that suggest promising directions for continued advancement. Google Cloud's BigQuery demonstrates how organizations approach the evolution of more sophisticated analytical capabilities. Their implementation of ML-powered query optimization and automated workload management shows how research directions focus on enhancing processing efficiency while improving analytical depth.

Technical evolution reveals careful attention to fundamental enhancement. Snowflake's development of their elastic compute engine shows how organizations address core processing challenges. Recent implementations show significant improvements in query performance, suggesting promising directions for optimization.

Processing enhancement patterns show sophisticated approaches to improving system efficiency. Databricks' photon engine demonstrates how organizations systematically enhance processing capabilities. Their current achievement of significantly faster processing speeds than traditional methods shows how development focuses on improving performance while maintaining reliability. These advances indicate promising directions for processing optimization.

Application growth reveals interesting patterns in use case expansion. MongoDB's implementation of sophisticated analytics capabilities shows how organizations explore new application domains. Their system currently supports real-time analytics across numerous documents, demonstrating how development aims to broaden utility while maintaining performance. These innovations suggest new directions for practical application.

Integration patterns demonstrate careful attention to system connectivity. Amazon's Redshift implementation shows how organizations enhance data integration capabilities. Their current support for federated queries across multiple data sources demonstrates how development focuses on improving connectivity while maintaining security. These advances indicate promising directions for system integration.

Service evolution patterns reveal sophisticated approaches to capability enhancement. Microsoft's Synapse Analytics shows how organizations improve service delivery. Their implementation of unified analytics, processing numerous queries daily, demonstrates how development aims to enhance service capabilities while maintaining operational efficiency. These developments suggest new directions for service advancement.

Implementation methods continue evolving through systematic innovation. Oracle's autonomous database features show how organizations enhance operational automation. Their current achievement of self-tuning capabilities across thousands of workloads demonstrates how development focuses on improving automation while maintaining control. These advances indicate promising directions for implementation enhancement.

The synthesis of multiple advancement directions creates comprehensive improvement opportunities. The combination of enhanced processing capabilities with sophisticated automation shows how different innovation streams complement each other. These integrations demonstrate how future development may proceed through careful combination of advances while maintaining practical utility.

Research directions reveal careful attention to emerging capabilities. IBM's quantum-ready data systems show how organizations prepare for future technological advances. Their current development of quantum-resistant encryption and data structures demonstrates how research aims to address future challenges while maintaining current functionality. These innovations suggest new directions for data security and processing.

These directional patterns continue influencing development approaches. Understanding these trends provides crucial context for appreciating future possibilities while maintaining practical perspective. The success of different approaches demonstrates the importance of systematic innovation in advancing data AI capabilities.

Our exploration of data AI innovations reveals the sophisticated evolution of analytical and processing capabilities in modern systems. From Google BigQuery's processing of massive data volumes daily to Snowflake's handling of numerous daily queries, we see how systematic innovation enables increasingly advanced data processing while maintaining practical applicability. For practitioners and organizations working with data AI, these developments provide crucial insights into both current capabilities and implementation approaches.

The advancement patterns we've examined demonstrate multiple paths for engaging with data AI technology. Whether through Databricks' unified analytics processing massive volumes of data or MongoDB's real-time analytics across numerous documents, organizations can choose approaches that align with their specific requirements and objectives. The success of different approaches shows how various development paths can effectively address distinct challenges while maintaining operational effectiveness.

Implementation considerations continue influencing how organizations approach data AI deployment. Amazon's sophisticated query optimization and Microsoft's advanced workload management demonstrate how practical requirements shape operational decisions. Understanding these relationships becomes crucial for organizations implementing data AI systems, as deployment choices significantly influence operational success.

The relationship between processing scale and efficiency creates interesting opportunities for innovation. Informatica's processing of numerous cloud transactions monthly and Talend's validation of extensive daily data points show how thoughtful design enables significant improvements. These developments demonstrate the importance of understanding technical trade-offs while suggesting approaches for enhancing data AI capabilities.

As we move forward to examine audio/vision AI evolution in our next chapter, often referred to as audio-visual AI, which encompasses technologies and developments that integrate auditory and visual data processing, we carry forward understanding of how data processing capabilities enable sophisticated media analysis. The advanced approaches to data handling we've explored provide crucial context for understanding how AI systems process and analyze complex audio and visual information. For practitioners and organizations, this understanding becomes increasingly valuable as AI technology continues advancing.

Engage actively with these data AI developments, whether through experimental implementation or systematic evaluation of different approaches. Major cloud providers offer extensive resources for exploring data AI capabilities, while specialized platforms provide focused environments for specific applications. These resources offer excellent starting points for practical engagement with data AI advancement.

The field of data AI continues evolving, offering new opportunities for innovation and implementation. By understanding current capabilities and emerging trends, practitioners and organizations can better position themselves to leverage advancing data AI technologies. Explore these opportunities with awareness of how data processing affects implementation success.

CHAPTER 10: AUDIO/VISION AI EVOLUTION

The evolution of audio/vision AI represents a transformative advancement in how machines perceive and interact with the world, building upon the data processing capabilities we explored in our previous chapter. NVIDIA's development of their Maxine platform demonstrates how organizations are revolutionizing audiovisual processing through AI innovation. Their implementation of real-time video enhancement and AI-powered features optimizes video streaming while significantly reducing bandwidth requirements

The current landscape of audio/vision AI reveals remarkable progress across multiple dimensions. Google's advancement in computer vision through their Cloud Vision AI shows how organizations enhance visual understanding capabilities. Their system processes vast numbers of images while maintaining high accuracy in object detection and scene understanding, demonstrating how visual AI continues evolving while establishing new benchmarks for performance.

Implementation patterns reveal sophisticated approaches

189

to practical deployment. OpenAI's DALL-E 2 shows how organizations balance advanced generation capabilities with practical applications. Their system generates numerous unique images while maintaining high quality and consistency, demonstrating how visual AI addresses both creative requirements and practical constraints.

The relationship between audio and visual processing has grown increasingly sophisticated. Meta's advancement in multimodal understanding shows how organizations optimize joint processing for enhanced comprehension. Their development of advanced integration approaches demonstrates how audio/vision systems maintain performance while managing complex multi-stream processing requirements.

Specialized applications continue emerging through focused development. Microsoft's Azure Cognitive Services demonstrates how audio/vision AI enables sophisticated real-world applications. Their implementation of combined audio-visual analysis shows how systems address specific operational needs while maintaining general processing capabilities across diverse scenarios.

In this chapter, we explore the sophisticated world of audio/vision AI, examining how different approaches enable advanced media processing and understanding. From fundamental innovations to specialized applications, we'll investigate how audio/visual AI continues advancing. This exploration reveals both current achievements and emerging directions in media processing, providing crucial context for understanding modern capabilities.

For practitioners and organizations implementing audio/vision AI systems, understanding these developments becomes increasingly important. The advances in media processing capabilities influence every aspect of implementation and deployment. As we proceed, we'll examine how different approaches address various challenges, offering insights valuable for those working with audio/visual

190

AI technologies.

Vision processing advances demonstrate sophisticated approaches to understanding visual information through AI innovation. Google's Vision AI platform shows how organizations achieve advanced visual comprehension at scale. Their system processes images at scale while achieving high accuracy in object detection with rapid response times, demonstrating how modern vision systems balance accuracy with performance.

Object detection capabilities reveal careful attention to real-world recognition requirements. Meta's latest computer vision models demonstrate how organizations enhance object understanding. Their implementation identifies numerous distinct object types with high accuracy across diverse conditions. These innovations transform how machines interpret visual scenes while maintaining reliability in challenging conditions.

Scene understanding shows sophisticated approaches to contextual comprehension. NVIDIA's implementation of advanced scene analysis demonstrates how organizations process complex visual environments. Their system analyzes multiple scene elements simultaneously, understands spatial relationships and object interactions while maintaining real-time processing capabilities.

Feature extraction reveals interesting patterns in visual analysis. Microsoft's Azure Computer Vision services show how organizations identify crucial visual elements. Their system automatically extracts thousands of visual features from images, enabling sophisticated analysis while maintaining processing efficiency. These developments influence how organizations approach visual data understanding.

Visual analysis capabilities demonstrate careful attention to detail recognition. AWS Rekognition shows how organizations enhance image processing precision. Their implementation analyzes facial features with high precision while maintaining privacy standards. These advances establish new approaches to detailed visual analysis.

Pattern recognition reveals sophisticated approaches to visual understanding. IBM's Watson Visual Recognition demonstrates how organizations identify complex patterns across diverse imagery. Their system recognizes intricate visual patterns while maintaining high-speed processing, showing how modern systems balance detail with processing speed.

Movement tracking capabilities show careful attention to dynamic scene analysis. Intel's OpenVINO toolkit demonstrates how organizations process motion effectively. Their implementation maintains real-time tracking of multiple moving objects simultaneously, establishing new benchmarks for real-time motion analysis.

The integration of these visual processing capabilities creates comprehensive understanding systems. The combination of enhanced object detection with sophisticated scene analysis shows how different visual processing approaches complement each other. These integrations demonstrate how vision processing advances through careful combination of techniques while maintaining practical utility.

Performance optimization reveals interesting patterns in processing efficiency. Qualcomm's AI Engine shows how organizations enhance visual processing speed. Their implementation achieves high computational performance while maintaining energy efficiency, demonstrating how modern systems balance performance with resource utilization.

These vision processing patterns continue influencing system development. Understanding these advances provides crucial context for appreciating current capabilities while suggesting future directions. The success of different approaches demonstrates the importance of systematic innovation in advancing visual AI capabilities.

Audio processing innovation demonstrates sophisticated approaches to understanding and analyzing sound through AI advancement. Google's Speech-to-Text API shows how organizations achieve advanced audio comprehension at scale. Their system processes speech at scale with high accuracy across numerous languages, demonstrating how modern audio systems balance comprehensive coverage with precision.

Speech recognition capabilities reveal careful attention to human voice understanding. Microsoft's Azure Speech Services demonstrates how organizations enhance voice processing accuracy. Their implementation achieves high accuracy in real-time transcription while handling multiple speakers and ambient noise. These innovations transform how machines interpret human speech while maintaining reliability in challenging environments.

Language understanding shows sophisticated approaches to speech comprehension. Amazon's Transcribe Medical demonstrates how organizations process specialized audio content. Their system accurately transcribes medical terminology while maintaining HIPAA compliance, showing how audio processing adapts to specific domain requirements without compromising performance.

Accent handling capabilities demonstrate careful attention to speech variation. Nuance's Dragon Speech Recognition shows how organizations process diverse speech patterns. Their system maintains high accuracy across diverse regional accents and dialects while adapting to individual speaking styles. These advances establish new standards for inclusive speech recognition.

Sound classification reveals interesting patterns in audio analysis. NVIDIA's Audio Effects SDK shows how organizations identify and process diverse audio types. Their implementation classifies thousands of distinct sound patterns while maintaining real-time processing capabilities, enabling sophisticated audio scene understanding. These developments influence how organizations approach environmental sound analysis.

Noise reduction capabilities show sophisticated approaches to audio enhancement. Adobe's audio processing technology demonstrates how organizations improve sound quality. Their system effectively reduces unwanted noise while preserving speech clarity, processing audio in real-time while maintaining natural sound characteristics. These innovations establish new approaches to audio quality enhancement.

Environmental adaptation reveals careful attention to context awareness. Apple's audio processing algorithms show how organizations handle varying acoustic environments. Their implementation automatically adjusts processing parameters based on ambient conditions, maintaining clarity while optimizing power usage. These advances transform how systems adapt to real-world conditions.

The integration of these audio processing capabilities creates comprehensive understanding systems. The combination of enhanced speech recognition with sophisticated noise reduction shows how different audio processing approaches complement each other. These integrations demonstrate how audio processing advances through careful combination of techniques while maintaining practical utility.

Signal processing optimization reveals interesting patterns in processing efficiency. Qualcomm's Hexagon DSP shows how organizations enhance audio processing speed. Their implementation achieves sophisticated audio processing while consuming 50% less power than previous generations, demonstrating how modern systems balance performance with energy efficiency.

These audio processing patterns continue influencing system development. Understanding these advances provides crucial context for appreciating current capabilities while suggesting future directions. The success of different approaches demonstrates the importance of systematic innovation in advancing audio AI capabilities.

Multimodal integration demonstrates sophisticated approaches to combining audio and visual processing in modern AI systems. OpenAI's GPT-4V (formerly GPT-4

Vision) shows how organizations achieve advanced multimodal understanding at scale. Their system processes combined visual and textual information with unprecedented accuracy, demonstrating how modern systems effectively integrate multiple input types while maintaining coherent understanding.

Combined processing capabilities reveal careful attention to synchronization requirements. Google's LaMDA 2 demonstrates how organizations enhance multimodal comprehension. Their implementation processes visual and audio inputs simultaneously, processes visual and audio inputs simultaneously while maintaining high accuracy in combined understanding while maintaining real-time performance. These innovations transform how machines interpret complex multimodal scenes while preserving context across modalities.

Audio-visual fusion shows sophisticated approaches to integrated processing. Meta's latest multimodal models demonstrate how organizations combine different input streams effectively. Their system processes synchronized audio-visual data while maintaining temporal alignment and high accuracy. These advances establish new standards for multimodal processing.

Context integration reveals interesting patterns in comprehensive understanding. Microsoft's multimodal AI shows how organizations maintain contextual coherence across inputs. Their implementation analyzes visual scenes while processing associated audio, enabling rich environmental understanding while maintaining processing efficiency. These developments influence how organizations approach complex scene analysis.

Signal alignment capabilities demonstrate careful attention to temporal coordination. NVIDIA's Maxine platform shows how organizations synchronize multiple input streams. Their system maintains precise alignment between audio and visual signals in real-time. These innovations establish new approaches to synchronized processing.

195

Pattern correlation reveals sophisticated approaches to cross-modal understanding. Intel's neural processing units demonstrate how organizations identify relationships across modalities. Their implementation recognizes complex patterns across audio and visual inputs while maintaining energy efficiency, processing multiple streams simultaneously. These advances transform how systems understand related signals.

Real-time processing capabilities show careful attention to performance requirements. Qualcomm's AI Engine demonstrates how organizations handle multiple streams efficiently. Their system processes synchronized audio-visual inputs while consuming minimal power, achieving sophisticated analysis without compromising response times. These developments establish new benchmarks for efficient multimodal processing.

The integration of these multimodal capabilities creates comprehensive understanding systems. The combination of enhanced audio processing with sophisticated visual analysis shows how different modal approaches complement each other. These integrations demonstrate how multimodal processing advances through careful combination of techniques while maintaining practical utility.

Situational analysis reveals interesting patterns in environmental understanding. IBM's Watson multimodal systems show how organizations process complex scenarios. Their implementation analyzes multiple input streams to achieve comprehensive scene understanding, maintaining context while processing diverse environmental inputs. These innovations influence how organizations approach complex scenario analysis.

These multimodal integration patterns continue influencing system development. Understanding these advances provides crucial context for appreciating current capabilities while suggesting future directions. The success of different approaches demonstrates the importance of systematic innovation in advancing multimodal AI capabilities.

Generation capabilities in audio-visual AI demonstrate sophisticated approaches to creating media content. Midjourney V6's image generation capabilities show how organizations achieve unprecedented quality in visual synthesis. Their system creates photorealistic images from text descriptions with remarkable detail and consistency, processing millions of generation requests daily while maintaining high artistic quality and anatomical accuracy.

Image generation reveals careful attention to visual quality requirements. Stability AI's latest models demonstrate how organizations enhance creative capabilities. Their SDXR (Stable Diffusion XL) implementation generates high-resolution images with precise detail control, achieving professional-quality output while processing thousands of requests per second. These innovations transform how machines create visual content while maintaining artistic coherence.

Style transfer capabilities show sophisticated approaches to visual modification. Adobe's Firefly demonstrates how organizations implement controlled creative systems. Their implementation maintains brand consistency and design standards while enabling creative flexibility, processing millions of style transformations daily. These advances establish new standards for commercial-grade AI image generation.

Audio synthesis reveals interesting patterns in sound generation. Eleven Labs' voice synthesis technology shows how organizations create natural-sounding speech. Their system generates human-like voices across multiple languages and emotions while maintaining natural prosody, demonstrating how modern systems balance authenticity with flexibility. These developments influence how organizations approach audio content creation.

Speech synthesis capabilities demonstrate careful attention to voice quality. Microsoft's Azure Neural TTS shows how organizations achieve natural speech generation. Their implementation creates human-like voice output across 400 voices in over 100 languages while maintaining natural intonation and rhythm. These innovations establish new approaches to voice generation.

Music generation reveals sophisticated approaches to audio creation. Google's AudioLM demonstrates how organizations synthesize complex musical content. Their system generates coherent musical sequences while maintaining style consistency, showing how AI systems can create sophisticated audio content while preserving musical structure. These advances transform how systems approach creative audio generation.

Combined creation capabilities show careful attention to synchronization requirements. Meta's AudioCraft shows how organizations generate synchronized audio-visual content. Their implementation creates matching audio for visual scenes while maintaining temporal alignment, processing complex generation tasks with consistent quality. These developments establish new benchmarks for multimodal generation.

The integration of these generation capabilities creates comprehensive creative systems. OpenAI's DALL-E 3 demonstrates how organizations combine various generation techniques effectively. Their system maintains coherence across multiple generation tasks while providing precise control over output characteristics. These integrations show how generation capabilities advance through careful combination of approaches.

Quality control reveals interesting patterns in output validation. Runway's Gen-2 shows how organizations ensure generation reliability. Their implementation maintains quality standards across diverse generation tasks while providing consistent results, demonstrating how modern systems balance creativity with reliability. These innovations influence how organizations approach content generation.

These generation patterns continue influencing system development. Understanding these advances provides crucial context for appreciating current capabilities while suggesting future directions. The success of different approaches demonstrates the importance of systematic innovation in advancing AI generation capabilities.

Implementation frameworks for audio-visual AI demonstrate sophisticated approaches to deploying complex media processing systems. NVIDIA's Metropolis platform shows how organizations achieve scalable deployment of vision AI applications. Their framework currently processes massive volumes of video frames across numerous companies, demonstrating how modern systems balance processing capability with deployment efficiency.

Service integration reveals careful attention to operational requirements. Google Cloud's Video AI platform demonstrates how organizations implement comprehensive media processing. Their system processes extensive amounts of video while maintaining rapid response times and high availability across global deployments. These innovations transform how organizations deploy audio-visual AI while ensuring reliable operation.

Load management capabilities show sophisticated approaches to resource optimization. AWS Media Services demonstrates how organizations handle variable processing demands. Their implementation automatically scales across numerous concurrent streams while maintaining consistent performance. These advances establish new standards for deployment flexibility.

Performance monitoring reveals interesting patterns in system oversight. Microsoft's Azure Media Services shows how organizations maintain operational awareness. Their framework monitors complex media processing pipelines in real-time, automatically detecting and addressing performance issues while maintaining service quality. These developments influence how organizations approach system management.

Resource management demonstrates careful attention to processing efficiency. Intel's OpenVINO deployment toolkit shows how organizations optimize computational resources. Their implementation significantly optimizes CPU utilization while maintaining processing quality. These innovations establish new approaches to resource optimization.

Memory efficiency reveals sophisticated approaches to resource utilization. Qualcomm's AI Engine demonstrates how organizations manage processing constraints. Their framework effectively reduces memory requirements while maintaining real-time processing capabilities, showing how modern systems balance capability with resource limitations. These advances transform how organizations approach deployment optimization.

Scaling solutions show careful attention to growth requirements. AMD's ROCm platform demonstrates how organizations handle expanding processing needs. Their implementation enables efficient scaling across diverse hardware configurations while maintaining consistent performance. These developments establish new benchmarks for deployment flexibility.

The integration of these implementation frameworks creates comprehensive deployment systems. The combination of enhanced service integration with sophisticated resource management shows how different deployment approaches complement each other. These integrations demonstrate how implementation frameworks advance through careful combination of techniques while maintaining practical utility.

Quality assurance reveals interesting patterns in deployment validation. Oracle's Media Flow platform shows how organizations ensure reliable operation. Their implementation maintains consistent quality across diverse deployment scenarios while providing automated verification. These innovations influence how organizations approach system reliability.

These implementation patterns continue influencing deployment approaches. Understanding these advances provides crucial context for appreciating current capabilities while suggesting future directions. The success of different approaches demonstrates the importance of systematic implementation in advancing audio-visual AI deployments.

Practical applications of audio-visual AI demonstrate sophisticated real-world implementations across diverse industries. Tesla's autonomous driving system shows how organizations implement advanced vision AI in safety-critical applications. Their implementation processes multiple camera feeds simultaneously while maintaining real-time decision making, demonstrating how modern systems handle complex environmental understanding in dynamic conditions.

Commercial applications reveal careful attention to business requirements. Amazon's Just Walk Out technology demonstrates how organizations implement sophisticated visual tracking. Their system simultaneously monitors numerous shoppers and products in real-time with high accuracy in transaction processing. These innovations transform how businesses approach automated retail operations.

Industrial systems show sophisticated approaches to quality control. Siemens' visual inspection systems demonstrate how organizations enhance manufacturing processes. Their implementation detects defects with high accuracy in high-speed production environments, showing how AI vision systems maintain quality standards in high-speed production environments. These advances establish new standards for automated inspection.

Healthcare implementation reveals interesting patterns in medical applications. Phillips' medical imaging AI shows how organizations enhance diagnostic capabilities. Their system rocesses medical images with high accuracy in anomaly detection while maintaining HIPAA compliance. These developments influence how healthcare providers approach diagnostic support.

Security systems demonstrate careful attention to surveillance requirements. Axis Communications' audio-visual security platforms show how organizations implement comprehensive monitoring. Their system processes feeds from numerous cameras globally while maintaining precise threat detection capabilities. These innovations establish new approaches to security monitoring.

Entertainment applications reveal sophisticated approaches to content creation. Unity's AI-enhanced game development tools demonstrate how organizations implement creative assistance. Their system processes real-time visual and audio effects while maintaining consistent frame rates, showing how modern systems enhance gaming experiences. These advances transform how developers approach content creation.

System connection capabilities show careful attention to integration requirements. Honeywell's building management systems demonstrate how organizations implement connected audio-visual monitoring. Their implementation coordinates thousands of sensors and cameras while maintaining real-time response capabilities. These developments establish new benchmarks for integrated system management.

The integration of these practical applications creates comprehensive solution frameworks. The combination of enhanced visual processing with sophisticated audio analysis shows how different applications complement each other. These integrations demonstrate how practical applications advance through careful combination of approaches while maintaining operational effectiveness.

Service coordination reveals interesting patterns in system management. Bosch's IoT Suite shows how organizations coordinate complex audio-visual implementations. Their system manages millions of connected devices while maintaining consistent service quality, demonstrating how modern platforms handle diverse application requirements. These innovations influence how organizations approach integrated solutions.

These application patterns continue influencing

implementation approaches. Understanding these advances provides crucial context for appreciating current capabilities while suggesting future directions. The success of different approaches demonstrates the importance of systematic innovation in advancing practical audio-visual AI applications.

The trajectory of audio-visual AI reveals emerging patterns that suggest promising directions for continued advancement. Google's work on next-generation visual transformers demonstrates how organizations approach enhanced perceptual capabilities. Their current research exhibits significant improvement in visual understanding efficiency while reducing computational requirements.

Technical evolution reveals careful attention to fundamental improvements. NVIDIA's development of advanced neural rendering demonstrates how organizations address core processing challenges. Their current implementation achieves photorealistic rendering at high frame rates while optimizing power consumption, showing how development continues advancing basic capabilities while maintaining practical applicability.

Processing enhancement patterns show sophisticated approaches to efficiency improvement. AMD's work on unified audio-visual processing architectures demonstrates how organizations systematically enhance processing capabilities. Their current achievements in significantly reducing latency while maintaining quality shows how development focuses on improving performance without compromising accuracy.

Application growth reveals interesting patterns in use case expansion. Microsoft's research into enhanced holographic communication shows how organizations explore new application domains. Their current prototype achieves realistic 3D presence while maintaining real-time interaction capabilities, demonstrating how development aims to broaden utility while maintaining performance standards.

Integration patterns demonstrate careful attention to

system connectivity. Apple's advancement in spatial computing shows how organizations enhance environmental understanding. Their current development in combining visual, audio, and spatial data demonstrates how future systems might achieve more comprehensive environmental awareness while maintaining user privacy.

Service evolution patterns reveal sophisticated approaches to capability enhancement. Meta's research into advanced virtual presence shows how organizations improve interaction capabilities. Their current implementation achieves natural conversation flow with high accuracy in emotion recognition, demonstrating how development aims to enhance human-computer interaction while maintaining natural feel.

Implementation methods continue evolving through systematic innovation. Intel's work on neuromorphic computing shows how organizations enhance processing efficiency. Their current research significantly reduces power consumption while maintaining processing capability, demonstrating how development focuses on improving efficiency while maintaining performance standards.

Research directions reveal careful attention to emerging capabilities. Samsung's development of advanced display processing shows how organizations prepare for future visual computing needs. Their current work on 8K real-time processing with AI enhancement demonstrates how research aims to address future challenges while maintaining current functionality.

The synthesis of multiple advancement directions creates comprehensive improvement opportunities. The combination of enhanced sensory processing with sophisticated understanding shows how different innovation streams complement each other. These integrations demonstrate how future development may proceed through careful combination of advances while maintaining practical utility.

These directional patterns continue influencing development approaches. Understanding these trends provides crucial context for appreciating future possibilities while maintaining practical perspective. The success of different approaches demonstrates the importance of systematic innovation in advancing audio-visual AI capabilities.

Our exploration of audio-visual AI evolution reveals the sophisticated advancement of machine perception capabilities. From NVIDIA's large-scale video processing to Google's multilingual real-time translation capabilities, we see how systematic innovation enables increasingly advanced media understanding while maintaining practical applicability. For practitioners and organizations working with audio-visual AI, these developments provide crucial insights into both current capabilities and implementation approaches.

The advancement patterns we've examined demonstrate multiple paths for engaging with audio-visual technology. Whether through Microsoft's enterprise-scale video analytics processing millions of streams or OpenAI's DALL-E 3 generating photorealistic images, organizations can choose approaches that align with their specific requirements and objectives. The success of different approaches shows how various development paths can effectively address distinct challenges while maintaining operational effectiveness.

Implementation considerations continue influencing how organizations approach audio-visual AI deployment. Amazon's sophisticated retail tracking systems and Tesla's autonomous driving implementations demonstrate how practical requirements shape operational decisions. Understanding these relationships becomes crucial for organizations implementing audio-visual AI systems, as deployment choices significantly influence operational success.

The relationship between processing capability and efficiency creates interesting opportunities for innovation. Intel's advancement in neuromorphic computing and AMD's unified processing architectures show how thoughtful design enables significant improvements. These developments demonstrate the importance of understanding technical trade-offs while suggesting approaches for enhancing audio-visual AI capabilities.

As we move forward to examine healthcare AI breakthroughs in our next chapter, we carry forward understanding of how audio-visual processing enables sophisticated medical analysis. The advanced approaches to media understanding we've explored provide crucial context for understanding how AI systems process and analyze complex medical imagery and diagnostic information. For practitioners and organizations, this understanding becomes increasingly valuable as AI technology continues advancing.

Engage actively with these audio-visual AI developments, whether through experimental implementation or systematic evaluation of different approaches. Major technology providers offer extensive resources for exploring audio-visual AI capabilities, while specialized platforms provide focused environments for specific applications. These resources offer excellent starting points for practical engagement with audio-visual AI advancement.

The field of audio-visual AI continues evolving, offering new opportunities for innovation and implementation. By understanding current capabilities and emerging trends, practitioners and organizations can better position themselves to leverage advancing audio-visual AI technologies. Explore these opportunities while maintaining awareness of how media processing capabilities influence practical implementation success.

CHAPTER 11: HEALTHCARE AI
BREAKTHROUGHS

Healthcare AI represents one of the most transformative applications of artificial intelligence, building upon the audio-visual processing capabilities we explored in our previous chapter. Google DeepMind's advancement in protein structure prediction through AlphaFold demonstrates how AI revolutionizes fundamental medical research. Their system has predicted structures for over 200 million proteins with atomic accuracy, transforming our understanding of biological systems while accelerating drug discovery and disease research.

The current landscape of healthcare AI reveals remarkable progress across multiple dimensions. Siemens Healthineers' AI-Rad Companion shows how organizations enhance diagnostic capabilities through sophisticated image analysis. Their system processes vast numbers of medical images annually while maintaining high accuracy in anomaly detection, demonstrating how AI continues evolving while establishing new benchmarks for clinical support.

Implementation patterns reveal sophisticated approaches to practical deployment. Philips' patient monitoring systems show how organizations balance advanced capabilities with clinical requirements. Their implementation processes real-time data from millions of devices while maintaining sub-second response times, demonstrating how healthcare AI addresses both performance requirements and patient safety constraints.

The relationship between diagnosis and treatment planning has grown increasingly sophisticated. IBM Watson for Oncology demonstrates how organizations optimize therapeutic decision-making. Their development of evidence-based treatment recommendations shows how AI systems maintain accuracy while processing complex medical information, supporting clinicians across thousands of cases daily.

Specialized applications continue emerging through focused development. Butterfly Network's ultrasound AI demonstrates how portable devices enable sophisticated diagnostics. Their implementation of real-time image analysis shows how AI addresses specific clinical needs while maintaining diagnostic accuracy, processing millions of scans annually while enabling point-of-care assessment.

In this chapter, we explore the sophisticated world of healthcare AI, examining how different approaches enable advanced medical applications. From diagnostic innovation to treatment optimization, we'll investigate how healthcare AI continues advancing. This exploration reveals both current achievements and emerging directions in medical AI, providing crucial context for understanding modern capabilities.

For practitioners and organizations implementing healthcare AI systems, understanding these developments becomes increasingly important. The advances in medical AI capabilities influence every aspect of implementation and deployment. As we proceed, we'll examine how different approaches address various challenges, offering insights valuable for those working with healthcare AI technologies.

Diagnostic innovation in healthcare AI demonstrates sophisticated approaches to medical analysis and disease detection. Google Health's breast cancer screening AI shows how organizations enhance early detection capabilities. Their reduces false negatives and false positives compared to human radiologists alone, processing mammograms for millions of patients while maintaining consistent accuracy across diverse populations.

Medical imaging analysis reveals careful attention to diagnostic precision. NVIDIA's Clara Imaging demonstrates how organizations enhance radiological processing. Their platform accelerates image analysis significantly while maintaining high accuracy in lesion detection, processing over 100,000 images daily across multiple healthcare institutions. These innovations transform how healthcare providers approach diagnostic imaging while ensuring reliability.

Pathology assessment capabilities show sophisticated approaches to tissue analysis. Philips' Digital Pathology platform demonstrates how organizations enhance microscopic examination. Their system processes whole slide images rapidly while achieving high concordance with traditional microscopy, enabling remote consultation and automated screening across thousands of samples daily.

Pattern recognition reveals interesting applications in diagnostic support. Arterys's FDA-cleared AI platform shows how organizations implement sophisticated diagnostic tools. Their system processes cardiac MRI studies in minutes rather than hours, maintaining high accuracy while enabling real-time collaboration between clinicians. These developments influence how organizations approach complex diagnostics.

Clinical decision support demonstrates careful attention to diagnostic assistance. IBM's Watson for Genomics shows how organizations enhance genetic analysis. Their implementation processes complex genomic data from thousands of patients monthly, identifying relevant mutations and matching them to potential treatments while maintaining up-to-date knowledge of current research.

Risk assessment capabilities reveal sophisticated approaches to predictive diagnostics. Mayo Clinic's collaboration with nference demonstrates how organizations enhance early warning systems. Their platform analyzes millions of patient records while maintaining privacy, identifying potential health risks significantly earlier than traditional diagnosis methods.

Treatment planning shows careful attention to therapeutic optimization. Siemens Healthineers' AI-Pathway Companion demonstrates how organizations enhance care planning. Their system significantly reduces planning time while providing evidence-based recommendations. These innovations establish new approaches to personalized care.

The integration of these diagnostic capabilities creates comprehensive medical support systems. The combination of enhanced imaging analysis with sophisticated clinical decision support shows how different diagnostic approaches complement each other. These integrations demonstrate how diagnostic innovation advances through careful combination of techniques while maintaining clinical utility.

Performance enhancement reveals interesting patterns in diagnostic efficiency. Intel's OpenVINO toolkit shows how organizations optimize medical AI processing. Their implementation achieves significantly faster inference times while maintaining diagnostic accuracy, demonstrating how modern systems balance performance with reliability.

These diagnostic patterns continue influencing healthcare development. Understanding these advances provides crucial context for appreciating current capabilities while suggesting future directions. The success of different approaches demonstrates the importance of systematic innovation in advancing healthcare AI capabilities.

Treatment planning systems demonstrate sophisticated approaches to therapeutic optimization in modern healthcare. Varian Medical Systems' Ethos therapy platform shows how organizations enhance radiation treatment planning through AI innovation. Their system processes real-time adaptive therapy plans rapidly compared to traditional approaches requiring days.

Therapy optimization reveals careful attention to treatment efficacy. RaySearch Laboratories' RayStation demonstrates how organizations enhance treatment precision. Their platform significantly reduces planning time while improving dose optimization. These innovations transform how healthcare providers approach complex treatment planning while ensuring patient safety.

Outcome prediction capabilities show sophisticated approaches to treatment assessment. Tempus's precision medicine platform demonstrates how organizations enhance therapeutic decision-making. Their system analyzes molecular and clinical data from over 1 million patients, predicting treatment outcomes with high accuracy while maintaining HIPAA compliance. These developments influence how organizations approach personalized medicine.

Protocol adaptation reveals interesting patterns in treatment customization. Adaptive Biotechnologies' immunoSequence platform shows how organizations implement precision therapy. Their system processes immune system data from thousands of patients monthly, enabling personalized treatment adaptation while maintaining high accuracy in response prediction. These advances establish new standards for personalized care.

Personalized medicine demonstrates careful attention to patient-specific factors. Foundation Medicine's FoundationOne CDx shows how organizations enhance treatment selection. Their platform analyzes 324 genes across all solid tumor types, providing FDA-approved companion diagnostic claims for 15 targeted therapies while processing thousands of tests monthly. These innovations establish new approaches to targeted treatment.

Response prediction reveals sophisticated approaches to therapeutic assessment. Roche's NAVIFY decision support platform demonstrates how organizations enhance treatment planning. Their implementation processes patient data across multiple therapeutic areas, response rates with high accuracy while reducing planning complexity. These developments influence how organizations approach treatment optimization.

Clinical integration shows careful attention to workflow enhancement. Epic Systems' AI integration demonstrates how organizations implement treatment planning tools. Their system processes millions of patient records daily, enabling automated protocol suggestions while maintaining seamless workflow integration. These advances transform how healthcare providers approach treatment planning.

The integration of these planning capabilities creates comprehensive therapeutic systems. The combination of enhanced protocol optimization with sophisticated outcome prediction shows how different planning approaches complement each other. These integrations demonstrate how treatment planning advances through careful combination of techniques while maintaining clinical effectiveness.

Quality assurance reveals interesting patterns in treatment validation. Siemens Healthineers' syngo.via platform shows how organizations ensure treatment accuracy. Their implementation validates thousands of treatment plans daily, significantly reducing verification time while maintaining rigorous safety standards. These innovations influence how organizations approach treatment quality control.

These treatment planning patterns continue influencing healthcare development. Understanding these advances provides crucial context for appreciating current capabilities while suggesting future directions. The success of different approaches demonstrates the importance of systematic innovation in advancing healthcare AI capabilities.

Patient monitoring systems demonstrate sophisticated approaches to continuous health assessment through AI innovation. Philips' eICU program shows how organizations enhance critical care monitoring at scale. Their platform simultaneously monitors ICU patients across hundreds of hospitals, reducing mortality rates while processing massive amounts of data through AI-driven analysis.

Real-time analysis reveals careful attention to immediate health assessment. GE Healthcare's Portrait Mobile system demonstrates how organizations enhance patient surveillance. Their implementation processes vital signs from hundreds of thousands of patients simultaneously, detecting deterioration significantly earlier than traditional methods while maintaining high accuracy. These innovations transform how healthcare providers approach patient monitoring.

Vital sign processing shows sophisticated approaches to physiological assessment. Masimo's SafetyNet platform demonstrates how organizations enhance remote monitoring capabilities. Their system processes continuous data from numerous connected devices worldwide, maintaining clinical-grade accuracy while enabling hospital-grade monitoring in home settings. These developments influence how organizations approach continuous patient assessment.

Trend detection capabilities reveal interesting patterns in health monitoring. Current Health's AI platform shows how organizations implement predictive monitoring. Their system processes patient data across multiple parameters, identifying concerning trends accurately while significantly reducing false alarms. These advances establish new standards for proactive patient care.

Remote monitoring demonstrates careful attention to telehealth requirements. Dexcom's G7 continuous glucose monitoring system shows how organizations enhance chronic disease management. Their platform processes real-time data, enabling automated insulin adjustment while maintaining high accuracy in glucose prediction. These innovations establish new approaches to remote patient care.

Alert generation reveals sophisticated approaches to clinical notification. AliveCor's KardiaMobile system demonstrates how organizations enhance cardiac monitoring. Their implementation processes ECG readings, detecting atrial fibrillation with high accuracy while enabling immediate physician notification. These developments influence how organizations approach urgent care response.

Data integration shows careful attention to comprehensive monitoring. Apple's HealthKit platform demonstrates how organizations implement health data consolidation. Their system processes health information from users worldwide, enabling seamless integration of patient-generated data while maintaining privacy standards. These advances transform how healthcare providers approach patient data management.

The synthesis of these monitoring capabilities creates comprehensive surveillance systems. The combination of enhanced vital sign processing with sophisticated trend detection shows how different monitoring approaches complement each other. These integrations demonstrate how patient monitoring advances through careful combination of techniques while maintaining clinical reliability.

Early warning systems reveal interesting patterns in preventive care. Edwards Lifesciences' HemoSphere platform shows how organizations enhance hemodynamic monitoring. Their implementation processes continuous cardiovascular data, predicting adverse events accurately while enabling proactive intervention. These innovations influence how organizations approach preventive care.

These monitoring patterns continue influencing healthcare development. Understanding these advances provides crucial context for appreciating current capabilities while suggesting future directions. The success of different approaches demonstrates the importance of systematic innovation in advancing healthcare AI capabilities.

Research applications in healthcare AI demonstrate

sophisticated approaches to advancing medical knowledge and drug discovery. Google DeepMind's AlphaFold system shows how organizations revolutionize biological research through AI innovation. Their platform has predicted structures for over 200 million proteins with atomic accuracy, accelerating drug discovery while significantly reducing experimental costs compared to traditional methods.

Drug discovery reveals careful attention to molecular screening efficiency. Atomwise's AI platform demonstrates how organizations enhance compound identification. Their system screens vast numbers of molecules daily against biological targets, identifying promising candidates with significantly greater accuracy than conventional methods while reducing discovery timelines from years to months. These innovations transform how pharmaceutical companies approach drug development.

Trial design shows sophisticated approaches to clinical research optimization. Unlearn.AI's digital twin technology demonstrates how organizations enhance clinical trials. Their platform generates synthetic control arms for trials, reducing the required patient enrollment while maintaining statistical validity. These developments influence how organizations approach clinical research design.

Efficacy prediction reveals interesting patterns in therapeutic assessment. BenevolentAI's platform shows how organizations implement sophisticated drug evaluation. Their system processes biomedical data across vast numbers of data points, predicting drug efficacy with high accuracy while identifying novel drug targets. These advances establish new standards for pharmaceutical research.

Clinical research demonstrates careful attention to data analysis requirements. Flatiron Health's oncology platform shows how organizations enhance cancer research. Their implementation analyzes real-world data from millions of patient records, identifying treatment patterns while maintaining patient privacy. These innovations establish new approaches to evidence generation.

Pattern discovery reveals sophisticated approaches to research insight. nference's nferX platform demonstrates how organizations enhance medical knowledge discovery. Their system processes over 100 million biomedical documents annually, identifying novel connections while significantly reducing research time. These developments influence how organizations approach medical research.

Literature analysis shows careful attention to knowledge synthesis. Semantic Scholar's AI platform demonstrates how organizations implement research aggregation. Their system processes millions of academic papers, enabling sophisticated meta-analysis with high accuracy. These advances transform how researchers approach literature review.

The integration of these research applications creates comprehensive discovery systems. The combination of enhanced molecular screening with sophisticated trial design shows how different research approaches complement each other. These integrations demonstrate how medical research advances through careful combination of techniques while maintaining scientific rigor.

Knowledge integration reveals interesting patterns in research synthesis. IBM Watson for Drug Discovery shows how organizations enhance research understanding. Their implementation processes scientific literature and clinical data, identifying potential therapeutic targets while significantly reducing research time. These innovations influence how organizations approach medical discovery.

These research patterns continue influencing healthcare development. Understanding these advances provides crucial context for appreciating current capabilities while suggesting future directions. The success of different approaches demonstrates the importance of systematic innovation in advancing medical research capabilities.

Implementation advances in healthcare AI demonstrate sophisticated approaches to clinical integration and deployment. Epic Systems' machine learning integration shows how organizations achieve large-scale AI deployment in healthcare settings. Their platform supports millions of patient records while maintaining high system availability across thousands of hospitals, demonstrating how modern systems balance sophisticated capability with reliable operation.

Clinical integration reveals careful attention to workflow requirements. Cerner's Millennium platform demonstrates how organizations enhance healthcare operations through AI. Their implementation processes billions of clinical transactions daily while significantly reducing documentation time, showing how AI systems integrate seamlessly into clinical workflows. These innovations transform how healthcare providers approach technology adoption.

System deployment shows sophisticated approaches to implementation management. Microsoft's Cloud for Healthcare demonstrates how organizations handle complex healthcare deployments. Their platform manages AI implementations across thousands of healthcare facilities maintaining high availability while ensuring HIPAA compliance. These developments influence how organizations approach healthcare technology deployment.

User adoption reveals interesting patterns in clinical acceptance. Nuance's Dragon Medical One shows how organizations implement AI-enhanced documentation. Their system processes millions of patient stories annually, achieving high accuracy while significantly reducing documentation time. These advances establish new standards for clinical technology integration.

Data management demonstrates careful attention to privacy requirements. Meditech's Expanse platform shows how organizations handle sensitive healthcare information. Their implementation manages millions of patient records while maintaining compliance across multiple regulatory frameworks, processing millions of transactions daily while maintaining compliance. These innovations establish new approaches to secure health data management.

Privacy protection reveals sophisticated approaches to data security. Google Cloud Healthcare API demonstrates how organizations implement secure health data processing. Their platform handles billions of API requests monthly while maintaining zero trust security architecture, enabling sophisticated AI applications while protecting patient privacy. These developments influence how organizations approach healthcare data security.

Access control shows careful attention to compliance requirements. Azure Health Data Services demonstrates how organizations implement regulated data handling. Their system processes petabytes of healthcare data while maintaining granular access control, enabling AI applications while ensuring regulatory compliance. These advances transform how organizations approach healthcare data governance.

The integration of these implementation capabilities creates comprehensive deployment frameworks. The combination of enhanced clinical integration with sophisticated privacy protection shows how different implementation approaches complement each other. These integrations demonstrate how healthcare AI implementation advances through careful combination of techniques while maintaining operational effectiveness.

Quality assurance reveals interesting patterns in implementation validation. Oracle's Healthcare Foundation platform shows how organizations ensure implementation reliability. Their system validates millions of clinical transactions daily while maintaining data integrity, demonstrating how modern platforms balance innovation with reliability. These innovations influence how organizations approach healthcare AI deployment.

These implementation patterns continue influencing healthcare development. Understanding these advances provides crucial context for appreciating current capabilities while suggesting future directions. The success of different approaches demonstrates the importance of systematic implementation in advancing healthcare AI capabilities.

Operational excellence in healthcare AI demonstrates sophisticated approaches to maintaining high-performance medical systems. Mayo Clinic's Clinical Data Analytics Platform shows how organizations achieve operational efficiency at scale. Their system processes millions of patient interactions annually while maintaining high uptime and significantly reducing diagnostic waiting times, demonstrating how modern healthcare organizations balance advanced capabilities with reliable operation.

Resource optimization reveals careful attention to efficiency requirements. Cleveland Clinic's AI command center demonstrates how organizations enhance resource allocation. Their implementation processes real-time data managing hospital beds across multiple facilities, reducing patient wait times while improving resource utilization. These innovations transform how healthcare providers approach operational management.

Workflow efficiency shows sophisticated approaches to process optimization. Kaiser Permanente's AI operations platform demonstrates how organizations enhance clinical workflows. Their system manages care delivery for millions of members, significantly reducing administrative overhead while maintaining quality metrics. These developments influence how organizations approach healthcare operations.

Cost management reveals interesting patterns in resource utilization. Providence Health's AI implementation shows how organizations optimize operational expenses. Their platform manages resources across over fifty hospitals, achieving substantial annual savings while maintaining quality standards. These advances establish new standards for healthcare resource management.

Performance monitoring demonstrates careful attention to

system reliability. Intermountain Healthcare's AI operations center shows how organizations maintain operational awareness. Their implementation monitors thousands of clinical systems simultaneously, detecting potential issues with high accuracy while enabling proactive maintenance. These innovations establish new approaches to healthcare system management.

Update processes reveal sophisticated approaches to system maintenance. UPMC's health technology management platform demonstrates how organizations handle system evolution. Their implementation manages updates across 40 hospitals while maintaining continuous operation, enabling seamless capability enhancement. These developments influence how organizations approach healthcare technology maintenance.

Maintenance protocols show careful attention to system reliability. Johns Hopkins' AI infrastructure demonstrates how organizations implement sustainable operations. Their system maintains 99.99% availability while processing millions of clinical transactions daily, showing how modern healthcare organizations balance innovation with stability. These advances transform how providers approach system maintenance.

The integration of these operational capabilities creates comprehensive management systems. The combination of enhanced resource optimization with sophisticated maintenance protocols shows how different operational approaches complement each other. These integrations demonstrate how healthcare operations advance through careful combination of techniques while maintaining clinical effectiveness.

Quality control reveals interesting patterns in operational validation. Mount Sinai's AI quality management system shows how organizations ensure operational excellence. Their implementation monitors clinical outcomes across 8 hospitals, identifying quality variations accurately while enabling rapid improvement. These innovations influence how organizations approach healthcare quality management.

These operational patterns continue influencing healthcare development. Understanding these advances provides crucial context for appreciating current capabilities while suggesting future directions. The success of different approaches demonstrates the importance of systematic operations in advancing healthcare AI capabilities.

The trajectory of healthcare AI reveals emerging patterns that suggest promising directions for continued advancement. Google Health's research into next-generation diagnostic AI demonstrates how organizations approach enhanced medical capabilities. Their current development of multimodal disease detection, achieving significantly higher accuracy than traditional methods while reducing false positives, shows how development focuses on balancing diagnostic power with clinical reliability.

Technical evolution reveals careful attention to fundamental improvements. Nvidia's development of Clara Holoscan demonstrates how organizations address core processing challenges. Their current implementation achieves real-time processing of multiple medical imaging streams while significantly reducing latency, showing how development continues advancing basic capabilities while maintaining clinical applicability.

Capability enhancement patterns show sophisticated approaches to improving medical AI. Microsoft's Project InnerEye demonstrates how organizations systematically enhance medical imaging capabilities. Their current achievements in maintaining high accuracy while significantly reducing radiotherapy planning time, shows how development focuses on improving efficiency without compromising clinical standards.

Integration methods demonstrate careful attention to system connectivity. Apple's health data integration initiatives show how organizations enhance medical information flow.

Their current development in connecting patient-generated data with clinical systems demonstrates how future systems might achieve more comprehensive health monitoring while maintaining privacy standards.

Application growth reveals interesting patterns in use case expansion. Siemens Healthineers' research into advanced diagnostics shows how organizations explore new medical applications. Their current prototype achieves simultaneous analysis of multiple biomarkers while maintaining diagnostic accuracy, demonstrating how development aims to broaden utility while maintaining performance standards.

Research directions reveal careful attention to emerging capabilities. IBM's quantum computing applications in drug discovery show how organizations prepare for future technological advances. Their current research achieves significantly faster molecular simulation while maintaining accuracy, demonstrating how research aims to address future challenges while maintaining current functionality.

Development trends indicate sophisticated approaches to enhancement. Phillips' work on adaptive intelligence shows how organizations improve healthcare workflows. Their current implementation achieves substantial reduction in routine tasks while maintaining clinical accuracy, demonstrating how development focuses on improving efficiency while maintaining quality standards.

Innovation paths reveal interesting patterns in advancement strategies. Mayo Clinic's Platform initiative shows how organizations approach future healthcare delivery. Their current development in AI-enabled care platforms demonstrates how future systems might achieve more personalized treatment while maintaining scalability.

The synthesis of multiple advancement directions creates comprehensive improvement opportunities. The combination of enhanced diagnostic capabilities with sophisticated treatment planning shows how different innovation streams complement each other. These integrations demonstrate how future development may proceed through careful combination of advances while maintaining clinical utility.

These directional patterns continue influencing healthcare development approaches. Understanding these trends provides crucial context for appreciating future possibilities while maintaining practical perspective. The success of different approaches demonstrates the importance of systematic innovation in advancing healthcare AI capabilities.

Our exploration of healthcare AI breakthroughs reveals the sophisticated evolution of medical technology capabilities. From Google DeepMind's prediction of protein structures at scale to Mayo Clinic's processing of numerous patient interactions annually, we see how systematic innovation enables increasingly advanced healthcare applications while maintaining clinical reliability. For practitioners and organizations working with healthcare AI, these developments provide crucial insights into both current capabilities and implementation approaches.

The advancement patterns we've examined demonstrate multiple paths for engaging with healthcare technology. Whether through Philips' eICU program monitoring numerous ICU patients or Atomwise's screening of molecules at scale daily, organizations can choose approaches that align with their specific requirements and objectives. The success of different approaches shows how various development paths can effectively address distinct clinical challenges while maintaining operational effectiveness.

Implementation considerations continue influencing how organizations approach healthcare AI deployment. Epic Systems' support of extensive patient records and Cleveland Clinic's optimization of hospital beds across their facilities demonstrate how practical requirements shape operational decisions. Understanding these relationships becomes crucial for organizations implementing healthcare AI systems, as deployment choices significantly influence clinical success.

The relationship between innovation and patient care

creates interesting opportunities for advancement. Mount Sinai's quality management across their hospital network and Kaiser Permanente's extensive care delivery network show how thoughtful implementation enables significant improvements. These developments demonstrate the importance of understanding technical trade-offs while suggesting approaches for enhancing healthcare AI capabilities.

As we move forward to examine robotics AI developments in our next chapter, we carry forward understanding of how healthcare applications inform mechanical precision and safety requirements. The advanced approaches to medical systems we've explored provide crucial context for understanding how AI systems manage complex physical interactions. For practitioners and organizations, this understanding becomes increasingly valuable as AI technology continues advancing.

Engage actively with these healthcare AI developments, whether through experimental implementation or systematic evaluation of different approaches. Major healthcare technology providers offer extensive resources for exploring AI capabilities, while specialized platforms provide focused environments for specific applications. These resources offer excellent starting points for practical engagement with healthcare AI advancement.

The field of healthcare AI continues evolving, offering new opportunities for innovation and implementation. By understanding current capabilities and emerging trends, practitioners and organizations can better position themselves to leverage advancing healthcare AI technologies. Explore these opportunities while maintaining awareness of how medical AI capabilities influence practical implementation success.

CHAPTER 12: ROBOTICS AI DEVELOPMENTS

Robotics AI represents a transformative convergence of physical and digital intelligence, building upon the precision and safety principles explored in healthcare applications. Boston Dynamics' latest achievements demonstrate this evolution, with their Atlas robot now performing complex dynamic movements previously thought impossible for machines. Their system processes environmental data through multiple sensor arrays while maintaining balance and adapting to changing conditions in real-time, establishing new benchmarks for robotic agility and control.

The current landscape of robotics AI reveals remarkable progress across multiple dimensions. FANUC's implementation of intelligent robots shows how organizations achieve unprecedented levels of manufacturing precision and adaptability. Their systems currently manage numerous connected robots worldwide, achieving sub-millimeter accuracy while processing complex visual and tactile data streams. These innovations transform how industries approach automation while maintaining operational reliability.

Implementation patterns reveal sophisticated approaches to practical deployment. ABB's YuMi collaborative robots demonstrate how organizations balance advanced capabilities with human safety requirements. Their systems operate alongside human workers in facilities globally, maintaining safety while achieving high uptime. These developments influence how organizations implement robotic systems in real-world environments.

The relationship between perception and control has grown increasingly sophisticated. NVIDIA's Isaac platform demonstrates how organizations optimize robotic decision-making through advanced AI integration. Their system enables real-time processing of multiple sensor streams while managing complex environmental interactions, supporting thousands of deployed robots across diverse applications. This integration of AI with robotics continues establishing new standards for autonomous operation.

Specialized applications continue emerging through focused development. Intuitive Surgical's da Vinci platform shows how robotics AI enables sophisticated medical procedures. Their systems have performed numerous procedures globally, maintaining sub-millimeter precision while processing surgeon inputs and environmental data in real-time. These innovations demonstrate how robotics AI addresses specific operational needs while ensuring safety and reliability.

In this chapter, we explore the sophisticated world of robotics AI, examining how different approaches enable advanced physical automation. From fundamental control systems to complex learning capabilities, we'll investigate how robotics AI continues advancing. This exploration reveals both current achievements and emerging directions in robotic intelligence, providing crucial context for understanding modern capabilities.

For practitioners and organizations implementing robotics AI systems, understanding these developments becomes increasingly important. The advances in robotic capabilities influence every aspect of implementation and deployment. As we proceed, we'll examine how different approaches address various challenges, offering insights valuable for those working with robotics AI technologies.

Core control systems in modern robotics demonstrate sophisticated approaches to managing complex physical interactions. Boston Dynamics' control architecture shows how organizations achieve advanced dynamic movement capabilities. Their Atlas robot processes multiple sensor inputs simultaneously while maintaining balance during complex athletic maneuvers, demonstrating how modern control systems balance sophisticated capability with reliable operation.

Motion control reveals careful attention to dynamic adaptation requirements. KUKA's latest KR QUANTEC series demonstrates how organizations enhance movement precision. Their implementation achieves rapid response times while managing heavy payloads, maintaining high accuracy across complex motion paths. These innovations transform how industrial robots handle sophisticated movement tasks while ensuring operational reliability.

Real-time dynamic balancing shows sophisticated approaches to stability management. Agility Robotics' Digit robot demonstrates how organizations handle complex environmental interactions. Their system processes multiple feedback loops while maintaining balance during package delivery tasks, showing how modern robots adapt to varying surface conditions. These developments influence how organizations approach dynamic robot deployment.

Force control integration reveals interesting patterns in physical interaction. Universal Robots' e-Series cobots show how organizations implement precise force management. Their systems achieve force sensitivity comparable to human touch while maintaining safe operation, processing force feedback to ensure controlled interactions. These advances

227

establish new standards for collaborative robotics.

Multi-joint coordination demonstrates careful attention to complex movement requirements. ABB's IRB series shows how organizations manage sophisticated articulation. Their implementation achieves high precision repeatability while processing real-time environmental data, demonstrating how modern systems handle complex motion planning. These innovations establish new approaches to robotic movement control.

Decision systems reveal sophisticated approaches to autonomous operation. NVIDIA's Jetson AGX Orin demonstrates how organizations enhance robotic decision-making. Their platform enables complex AI decision-making in mobile robots while maintaining efficient power consumption. These developments influence how organizations approach autonomous control.

Risk assessment capabilities show careful attention to operational safety. Fanuc's FIELD system demonstrates how organizations implement comprehensive safety protocols. Their implementation monitors thousands of connected robots while maintaining zero safety incidents, processing risk assessments in real-time. These advances transform how organizations manage robot safety.

Performance optimization reveals interesting patterns in system enhancement. Yaskawa's Motoman HC-series shows how organizations improve operational efficiency. Their systems improved cycle times while reducing energy consumption, demonstrating how modern robots balance performance with efficiency. These innovations influence how organizations approach robot deployment.

The integration of these control capabilities creates comprehensive movement systems. The combination of enhanced motion control with sophisticated decision-making shows how different control approaches complement each other. These integrations demonstrate how control systems advance through careful combination of techniques while maintaining operational reliability.

These control patterns continue influencing robotics development. Understanding these advances provides crucial context for appreciating current capabilities while suggesting future directions. The success of different approaches demonstrates the importance of systematic innovation in advancing robotic control capabilities.

Environmental understanding in robotics AI demonstrates sophisticated approaches to perceiving and interpreting complex operational spaces. Intel's RealSense technology shows how organizations achieve advanced spatial awareness in robotic systems. Their latest D455 sensor processes environmental data with high accuracy and range, demonstrating how modern systems balance detailed perception with real-time processing requirements.

Sensor integration reveals careful attention to comprehensive environmental awareness. Velodyne's Alpha Prime lidar system demonstrates how organizations enhance robotic perception. Their implementation combines multiple laser channels with advanced signal processing, achieving extended range while maintaining accuracy in varying light conditions. These innovations transform how robots understand their operational environment.

Multi-modal fusion shows sophisticated approaches to data integration. NVIDIA's Isaac Sim demonstrates how organizations combine multiple sensor inputs effectively. Their platform processes visual, depth, and tactile data simultaneously while maintaining real-time response rates, enabling robots to build comprehensive environmental models. These developments influence how organizations approach sensor system design.

Scene analysis capabilities demonstrate careful attention to environmental complexity. Microsoft's Azure Percept shows how organizations implement sophisticated visual understanding. Their system processes environmental data with high accuracy in object recognition while maintaining real-time performance across diverse lighting conditions. These advances establish new standards for robotic vision systems.

Dynamic mapping reveals interesting patterns in spatial understanding. Waymo's autonomous systems show how organizations handle complex environmental modeling. Their implementation processes terabytes of sensor data daily while maintaining submeter accuracy in dynamic environments, demonstrating how modern robots build and update spatial models. These innovations establish new approaches to environmental mapping.

Movement prediction capabilities show sophisticated approaches to dynamic scene understanding. Tesla's Autopilot demonstrates how organizations anticipate environmental changes. Their system predicts object trajectories while processing data from multiple cameras simultaneously, enabling proactive response to dynamic situations. These developments influence how robots interact with moving objects.

Context assessment reveals careful attention to situational understanding. Amazon Robotics' warehouse systems show how organizations process complex operational contexts. Their implementation coordinates thousands of robots while maintaining real-time awareness of changing warehouse conditions, demonstrating how modern systems handle dynamic environments. These advances transform how organizations approach robotic deployment.

Pattern recognition demonstrates sophisticated approaches to environmental regularities. Fetch Robotics' autonomous mobile robots show how organizations identify operational patterns. Their systems process environmental data to recognize and adapt to facility traffic patterns achieving highly successful navigation rates while maintaining safe operation. These innovations influence how robots learn from environmental experience.

The integration of these environmental understanding

capabilities creates comprehensive perception systems. The combination of enhanced sensor fusion with sophisticated scene analysis shows how different perception approaches complement each other. These integrations demonstrate how environmental understanding advances through careful combination of techniques while maintaining operational reliability.

These understanding patterns continue influencing robotics development. Understanding these advances provides crucial context for appreciating current capabilities while suggesting future directions. The success of different approaches demonstrates the importance of systematic innovation in advancing robotic perception capabilities.

Interaction systems in robotics AI demonstrate sophisticated approaches to human-machine collaboration and environmental engagement. Universal Robots' e-Series shows how organizations achieve advanced collaborative capabilities. Their latest UR20 cobot processes interaction data while maintaining safety protocols across global installations.

Human-robot collaboration reveals careful attention to safety requirements. FANUC's CRX series demonstrates how organizations enhance cooperative work. Their implementation maintains safety while maintaining productivity across numerous installations, processing multiple safety parameters simultaneously. These innovations transform how industries approach human-robot integration in shared workspaces.

Communication systems show sophisticated approaches to human-machine interaction. ABB's YuMi demonstrates how organizations implement intuitive interfaces. Their system processes human gestures and voice commands with high accuracy while maintaining positioning precision, enabling natural interaction patterns. These developments influence how organizations design collaborative workspaces.

Object manipulation capabilities demonstrate careful

attention to handling requirements. Schunk's intelligent gripping systems show how organizations achieve sophisticated manipulation. Their implementation processes tactile feedback while maintaining precise force control across diverse materials. These advances establish new standards for robotic manipulation.

Grasping strategies reveal interesting patterns in object handling. Soft Robotics' mGrip system shows how organizations approach complex manipulation tasks. Their implementation maintains consistent handling success while adapting to varying object shapes and textures, demonstrating how modern systems handle diverse materials. These innovations establish new approaches to flexible manipulation.

Force management demonstrates sophisticated approaches to delicate operations. KUKA's LBR series shows how organizations implement sensitive handling. Their systems process force feedback with millisecond response times while maintaining safe operation, enabling precise assembly operations. These developments influence how robots handle delicate materials.

Navigation systems reveal careful attention to movement planning. Mobile Industrial Robots' autonomous platforms show how organizations handle complex environments. Their implementation processes environmental data achieving highly successful navigation while managing dynamic obstacles, demonstrating how modern systems handle unpredictable environments. These advances transform how organizations approach mobile robotics.

Path planning capabilities show sophisticated approaches to movement optimization. Omron's LD series demonstrates how organizations implement efficient navigation. Their systems process real-time environmental data while maintaining optimal path selection, achieving significant improvement in movement efficiency. These innovations influence how organizations approach robotic mobility.

The integration of these interaction capabilities creates comprehensive collaboration systems. The combination of enhanced safety protocols with sophisticated manipulation shows how different interaction approaches complement each other. These integrations demonstrate how interaction systems advance through careful combination of techniques while maintaining operational effectiveness.

These interaction patterns continue influencing robotics development. Understanding these advances provides crucial context for appreciating current capabilities while suggesting future directions. The success of different approaches demonstrates the importance of systematic innovation in advancing robotic interaction capabilities.

Learning frameworks in robotics AI demonstrate sophisticated approaches to skill acquisition and capability enhancement. NVIDIA's Isaac Gym shows how organizations achieve advanced learning capabilities in robotic systems. Their platform processes thousands of simultaneous simulations, enabling robots to acquire complex skills significantly faster than real-world training alone, demonstrating how modern systems balance rapid learning with practical application.

Skill acquisition reveals careful attention to task mastery requirements. Google's robotics research demonstrates how organizations enhance learning efficiency. Their implementation achieves high success rates in novel task execution after learning from minimal demonstrations, processing multiple learning streams simultaneously. These innovations transform how robots develop new capabilities through experience.

Task learning shows sophisticated approaches to capability development. OpenAI's robotic learning systems demonstrate how organizations implement efficient skill transfer. Their platform enables robots to learn complex manipulation tasks from human demonstrations while maintaining high success rates in novel situations. These developments influence how organizations approach robot training.

Performance improvement capabilities demonstrate careful attention to optimization. Berkshire Grey's picking systems show how organizations enhance operational efficiency through learning. Their implementation improves pick rates through continuous learning while maintaining high accuracy, demonstrating how modern systems refine capabilities through experience. These advances establish new standards for robotic learning.

Knowledge transfer reveals interesting patterns in skill propagation. Amazon Robotics' fleet learning system shows how organizations scale learned capabilities. Their implementation shares learned behaviors across thousands of robots achieving faster deployment of new skills while maintaining consistent performance. These innovations establish new approaches to distributed learning.

Behavioral adaptation demonstrates sophisticated approaches to situational response. Boston Dynamics' learning frameworks show how organizations implement adaptive behaviors. Their systems process environmental feedback to develop new movement strategies while maintaining stability, enabling robots to handle unprecedented situations. These developments influence how robots adapt to changing conditions.

Pattern recognition capabilities show careful attention to experiential learning. Fetch Robotics' autonomous systems demonstrate how organizations implement learned navigation patterns. Their implementation identifies and adapts to facility traffic patterns while achieving significant improvement in path efficiency through experience. These advances transform how robots optimize their operations.

Strategy optimization reveals sophisticated approaches to performance enhancement. Covariant's AI platform shows how organizations improve robot decision-making. Their system achieves high success rates in complex picking tasks through continuous learning while handling previously unseen items. These innovations influence how organizations approach robotic problem-solving.

The integration of these learning capabilities creates comprehensive development frameworks. The combination of enhanced skill acquisition with sophisticated knowledge transfer shows how different learning approaches complement each other. These integrations demonstrate how learning systems advance through careful combination of techniques while maintaining operational reliability.

These learning patterns continue influencing robotics development. Understanding these advances provides crucial context for appreciating current capabilities while suggesting future directions. The success of different approaches demonstrates the importance of systematic innovation in advancing robotic learning capabilities.

Implementation frameworks in robotics AI demonstrate sophisticated approaches to deploying and managing complex robotic systems. ABB's RobotStudio shows how organizations achieve advanced deployment capabilities across industrial settings. Their platform manages numerous robots globally while maintaining high uptime, demonstrating how modern systems balance sophisticated functionality with reliable operation.

Deployment systems reveal careful attention to integration requirements. FANUC's FIELD system demonstrates how organizations enhance implementation efficiency. Their platform achieves significantly faster deployment times while maintaining comprehensive safety protocols, managing thousands of connected robots across diverse manufacturing environments. These innovations transform how industries approach robotic system deployment.

Setup automation shows sophisticated approaches to system initialization. Yaskawa's Smart Pendant demonstrates how organizations implement rapid deployment. Their system significantly reduces robot programming time while maintaining accuracy standards, enabling efficient setup even for complex applications. These developments influence how organizations approach initial system configuration.

Resource management capabilities demonstrate careful attention to operational efficiency. KUKA's iiQoT platform shows how organizations optimize system resources. Their implementation achieves substantial energy reduction while maintaining peak performance, processing real-time efficiency data across connected robots. These advances establish new standards for sustainable robotics operation.

Energy optimization reveals interesting patterns in resource utilization. Siemens' SIMATIC Robot Integrator shows how organizations enhance power efficiency. Their system reduces energy consumption through intelligent power management while maintaining production targets. These innovations establish new approaches to sustainable robotics.

Maintenance planning demonstrates sophisticated approaches to system longevity. Omron's predictive maintenance platform shows how organizations implement proactive care. Their system predicts potential failures with high accuracy while significantly reducing downtime, enabling strategic maintenance scheduling. These developments influence how organizations approach system reliability.

Performance monitoring capabilities show careful attention to operational oversight. Rockwell Automation's FactoryTalk Analytics demonstrates how organizations implement comprehensive monitoring. Their platform processes millions of data points hourly while providing real-time performance insights, achieving significant improvement in system efficiency. These advances transform how organizations track robotic operations.

Quality control reveals sophisticated approaches to performance validation. Cognex's ViDi deep learning system shows how organizations ensure operational standards. Their implementation achieves high inspection accuracy while processing thousands of items hourly, demonstrating how modern systems maintain quality through AI-enhanced monitoring. These innovations influence how organizations approach quality assurance.

The integration of these implementation frameworks creates comprehensive management systems. The combination of enhanced deployment capabilities with sophisticated monitoring shows how different implementation approaches complement each other. These integrations demonstrate how implementation frameworks advance through careful combination of techniques while maintaining operational effectiveness.

These implementation patterns continue influencing robotics development. Understanding these advances provides crucial context for appreciating current capabilities while suggesting future directions. The success of different approaches demonstrates the importance of systematic innovation in advancing robotic implementation capabilities.

Application domains in robotics AI demonstrate sophisticated approaches to addressing specific industry needs. Tesla's manufacturing systems show how organizations achieve advanced automation in automotive production. Their implementation coordinates numerous robots per facility while maintaining high uptime, demonstrating how modern systems balance complex manufacturing requirements with consistent production quality.

Industrial applications reveal careful attention to manufacturing precision. BMW's AI-enhanced assembly lines demonstrate how organizations optimize production processes. Their implementation achieves significant improvement in assembly efficiency while maintaining zero-defect standards across global facilities. These innovations transform how automotive manufacturers approach complex assembly operations.

Process automation shows sophisticated approaches to continuous operations. BASF's smart manufacturing platform demonstrates how organizations implement advanced chemical processing. Their system manages complex reactions with millisecond precision while monitoring thousands of parameters simultaneously, achieving substantial improvement in process efficiency. These developments influence how organizations approach automated manufacturing.

Quality control capabilities demonstrate careful attention to inspection requirements. Amazon's fulfillment centers show how organizations implement sophisticated verification. Their robotic systems process numerous items daily while maintaining high accuracy in quality assessment, demonstrating how modern systems handle high-volume inspection. These advances establish new standards for automated quality control.

Service robotics reveals interesting patterns in human interaction. Softbank Robotics' Pepper platform shows how organizations approach customer service applications. Their implementation processes natural language interactions while maintaining high customer satisfaction rates, handling numerous daily interactions across retail environments. These innovations establish new approaches to service automation.

Healthcare support demonstrates sophisticated approaches to medical assistance. Intuitive Surgical's da Vinci systems show how organizations implement precise medical robotics. Their platform has performed numerous procedures while maintaining high precision accuracy, enabling complex surgical operations. These developments influence how healthcare providers approach robotic assistance.

Specialized systems reveal careful attention to unique operational requirements. Boston Dynamics' Spot Enterprise demonstrates how organizations address complex inspection needs. Their implementation achieves high coverage in hazardous environment monitoring while maintaining operational safety, showing how robots handle dangerous tasks effectively. These advances transform how organizations approach specialized operations.

Research platforms show sophisticated approaches to

experimental development. OpenAI's robotic learning environments demonstrate how organizations implement advanced research capabilities. Their systems process thousands of simultaneous experiments while enabling rapid prototype development, achieving significant acceleration in robotics research. These innovations influence how organizations approach robotics development.

The integration of these application domains creates comprehensive solution frameworks. The combination of enhanced industrial capabilities with sophisticated service applications shows how different domains complement each other. These integrations demonstrate how application domains advance through careful combination of techniques while maintaining operational effectiveness.

These application patterns continue influencing robotics development. Understanding these advances provides crucial context for appreciating current capabilities while suggesting future directions. The success of different approaches demonstrates the importance of systematic innovation in advancing robotic applications.

The trajectory of robotics AI reveals emerging patterns that suggest promising directions for continued advancement. Boston Dynamics' research into dynamic locomotion demonstrates how organizations approach enhanced mobility capabilities. Their current development achieving significant improvement in energy efficiency while maintaining complex movement capabilities shows how development focuses on balancing sophisticated functionality with practical operation.

Technical evolution reveals careful attention to fundamental improvements. NVIDIA's work on next-generation robotics processors demonstrates how organizations address core processing challenges. Their latest Jetson AGX Orin achieves 275 TOPS of AI performance while consuming only 15-60 watts, showing how development continues advancing basic capabilities while maintaining energy efficiency.

Architecture advancement patterns show sophisticated approaches to system design. Google's research into scalable robotics architectures demonstrates how organizations systematically enhance robot capabilities. Their current achievements in significantly reducing learning time while improving task success rates show how development focuses on improving efficiency without compromising reliability.

Integration methods demonstrate careful attention to system connectivity. ABB's development of enhanced robot coordination shows how organizations improve multi-robot operations. Their current implementation achieves significantly better throughput in coordinated tasks while maintaining safety standards, demonstrating how development aims to broaden utility while maintaining performance.

Application growth reveals interesting patterns in use case expansion. Amazon's research into advanced warehouse automation shows how organizations explore new operational domains. Their current prototype achieves substantially faster item processing speed while reducing error rates, demonstrating how development aims to enhance capability while maintaining accuracy.

Market development patterns reveal sophisticated approaches to industry adoption. Universal Robots' expansion in collaborative robotics shows how organizations improve accessibility. Their current implementation significantly reduces deployment time while maintaining safety standards, demonstrating how development focuses on practical adoption considerations.

Implementation trends indicate careful attention to operational requirements. FANUC's development of enhanced deployment systems shows how organizations improve installation efficiency. Their current achievement of significantly faster setup times while maintaining quality standards demonstrates how development focuses on practical considerations while maintaining capability.

Research focus reveals interesting patterns in innovation direction. Toyota Research Institute's work on advanced manipulation shows how organizations approach complex challenges. Their current development in household robot assistance achieves high success rates in novel tasks while maintaining safety, demonstrating how research aims to address future challenges.

The synthesis of multiple advancement directions creates comprehensive improvement opportunities. The combination of enhanced processing capabilities with sophisticated control systems shows how different innovation streams complement each other. These integrations demonstrate how future development may proceed through careful combination of advances while maintaining practical utility.

These directional patterns continue influencing development approaches. Understanding these trends provides crucial context for appreciating future possibilities while maintaining practical perspective. The success of different approaches demonstrates the importance of systematic innovation in advancing robotics AI capabilities.

Our exploration of robotics AI developments reveals the sophisticated evolution of intelligent physical systems. From Boston Dynamics' achievement of complex dynamic movements to Tesla's coordination of over 1,000 robots per facility, we see how systematic innovation enables increasingly advanced robotic capabilities while maintaining operational reliability. For practitioners and organizations working with robotics AI, these developments provide crucial insights into both current capabilities and implementation approaches.

The advancement patterns we've examined demonstrate multiple paths for engaging with robotics technology. Whether through Universal Robots' collaborative systems processing interaction data at 500Hz or FANUC's FIELD system managing thousands of connected robots, organizations can choose approaches that align with their specific requirements and objectives. The success of different approaches shows how various development paths can effectively address distinct challenges while maintaining operational effectiveness.

Implementation considerations continue influencing how organizations approach robotics AI deployment. ABB's management of 500,000 global robots and Amazon's processing of millions of items daily demonstrate how practical requirements shape operational decisions. Understanding these relationships becomes crucial for organizations implementing robotics AI systems, as deployment choices significantly influence operational success.

The relationship between physical capability and intelligence creates interesting opportunities for innovation. NVIDIA's achievement of 275 TOPS processing power and Intuitive Surgical's sub-millimeter precision show how thoughtful design enables significant improvements. These developments demonstrate the importance of understanding technical trade-offs while suggesting approaches for enhancing robotics AI capabilities.

As we move forward to examine gaming AI innovations in our next chapter, we carry forward understanding of how real-time control and adaptive learning enable sophisticated interactive systems. The advanced approaches to robotics control we've explored provide crucial context for understanding how AI systems manage complex, dynamic interactions. For practitioners and organizations, this understanding becomes increasingly valuable as AI technology continues advancing.

Engage actively with these robotics AI developments, whether through experimental implementation or systematic evaluation of different approaches. Major robotics providers offer extensive resources for exploring automation capabilities, while specialized platforms provide focused environments for specific applications. These resources offer excellent starting points for practical engagement with robotics AI advancement.

The field of robotics AI continues evolving, offering new opportunities for innovation and implementation. By understanding current capabilities and emerging trends, practitioners and organizations can better position themselves to leverage advancing robotics AI technologies. Explore these opportunities while maintaining awareness of how robotic capabilities influence practical implementation success.

CHAPTER 13: GAMING AI INNOVATIONS

Gaming AI represents a sophisticated convergence of real-time decision making and adaptive intelligence, building upon the dynamic control principles we explored in robotics systems. Unity's advancement in ML-Agents demonstrates how organizations achieve unprecedented levels of intelligent behavior in gaming environments. Their framework processes numerous training iterations daily across a large developer community, enabling games to exhibit increasingly sophisticated and natural behaviors while maintaining real-time performance.

The current landscape of gaming AI reveals remarkable progress across multiple dimensions. Epic Games' MetaHuman Creator shows how organizations enhance character intelligence and interaction. Their system enables the creation of photorealistic characters with sophisticated behavioral models, processing emotional and social responses in real-time while maintaining natural interactions. These innovations transform how games approach character behavior and player engagement.

Implementation patterns reveal sophisticated approaches to practical deployment. Electronic Arts' implementation of dynamic difficulty adjustment demonstrates how organizations balance challenge with player engagement. Their systems process player behavior data across millions of gaming sessions while maintaining high player satisfaction rates, showing how gaming AI addresses both performance requirements and user experience optimization.

The relationship between environmental generation and player interaction has grown increasingly sophisticated. No Man's Sky's procedural universe demonstrates how organizations manage vast dynamic worlds. Their system generates vast numbers of unique planets and ecosystems while maintaining consistent physical rules and engaging gameplay, processing environmental variations in real-time as players explore.

Specialized applications continue emerging through focused development. Google DeepMind's AlphaCode demonstrates how gaming principles extend into broader problem-solving domains. Their system achieves competitive-level performance in programming competitions, showing how game-based AI approaches can address complex cognitive challenges while maintaining real-time decision making capabilities.

In this chapter, we explore the sophisticated world of gaming AI, examining how different approaches enable advanced interactive experiences. From fundamental behavior systems to complex environmental generation, we'll investigate how gaming AI continues advancing. This exploration reveals both current achievements and emerging directions in game intelligence, providing crucial context for understanding modern capabilities.

For practitioners and organizations implementing gaming AI systems, understanding these developments becomes increasingly important. The advances in game intelligence capabilities influence every aspect of implementation and deployment. As we proceed, we'll examine how different approaches address various challenges, offering insights valuable for those working with gaming AI technologies.

Core game AI systems demonstrate sophisticated approaches to real-time decision making and behavioral modeling. Unreal Engine 5's AI system shows how organizations achieve advanced strategic planning capabilities. Their implementation processes numerous AI decisions per second while managing complex character behaviors across massive environments, demonstrating how modern systems balance sophisticated intelligence with performance requirements.

Decision architecture reveals careful attention to strategic planning requirements. Creative Assembly's Total War series demonstrates how organizations enhance military strategy AI. Their latest implementation manages thousands of individual units while maintaining coherent army-level tactics, processing battlefield decisions with human-like adaptation to changing conditions. These innovations transform how strategy games approach complex decision making.

Tactical response systems show sophisticated approaches to immediate action planning. Guerrilla Games' Horizon series demonstrates how organizations implement advanced combat AI. Their system processes environmental data and enemy behavior patterns in real-time, enabling creatures to exhibit unique hunting strategies while maintaining natural movement patterns. These developments influence how games approach dynamic combat scenarios.

Resource management capabilities demonstrate careful attention to economic simulation. Paradox Interactive's grand strategy games show how organizations implement complex economic AI. Their systems manage thousands of interconnected resources across global economies, maintaining realistic market behaviors while processing millions of transactions per game session. These advances establish new standards for economic simulation in games.

Behavior systems reveal interesting patterns in character intelligence. CD Projekt Red's implementation in Cyberpunk 2077 shows how organizations approach NPC daily routines. Their system manages numerous unique NPCs with individual schedules and behavioral patterns, maintaining consistent character behavior while adapting to player actions. These innovations establish new approaches to population simulation.

Character interaction demonstrates sophisticated approaches to social simulation. The Sims 4 shows how Maxis implements complex social AI. Their system processes thousands of possible social interactions while maintaining coherent relationship development, enabling emergent storytelling through character relationships. These developments influence how games approach social dynamics.

Emotional modeling reveals careful attention to character depth. Sony's AI systems show how organizations implement sophisticated personality models. Their implementation in games like God of War: Ragnarök enables characters to exhibit complex emotional responses while maintaining narrative consistency. These advances transform how games approach character development.

Game logic enhancement shows sophisticated approaches to rule processing. Civilization VI's AI demonstrates how Firaxis implements complex strategic decision-making. Their system evaluates thousands of possible actions while maintaining consistent AI personality traits, enabling sophisticated diplomatic and military strategies. These innovations influence how strategy games approach AI opponents.

The integration of these core systems creates comprehensive game intelligence. The combination of enhanced strategic planning with sophisticated behavioral modeling shows how different AI approaches complement each other. These integrations demonstrate how game AI advances through careful combination of techniques while maintaining player engagement.

These core system patterns continue influencing game development. Understanding these advances provides crucial context for appreciating current capabilities while suggesting future directions. The success of different approaches demonstrates the importance of systematic innovation in advancing gaming AI capabilities.

Environmental generation in gaming AI demonstrates sophisticated approaches to creating dynamic, responsive worlds. Hello Games' No Man's Sky shows how organizations achieve unprecedented scale in procedural generation. Their system generates vast numbers of unique planets with coherent ecosystems and geological features, processing environmental variations in real-time while maintaining consistent physical rules and biological diversity.

World creation reveals careful attention to environmental coherence. Minecraft's terrain generation demonstrates how Mojang enhances procedural worlds. Their latest implementation creates diverse biomes across numerous unique seeds, maintaining geological consistency while generating a vast number of new worlds daily. These innovations transform how games approach infinite world generation.

Procedural generation shows sophisticated approaches to content scaling. Ubisoft's Watch Dogs: Legion demonstrates how organizations implement dynamic city generation. Their system manages numerous unique character combinations while maintaining consistent architectural and social patterns across London's recreation. These developments influence how open-world games approach population and environmental diversity.

Dynamic systems demonstrate careful attention to environmental response. Red Dead Redemption 2's ecosystem shows how Rockstar implements complex environmental interactions. Their implementation manages hundreds of interacting species with realistic behavioral patterns, maintaining food chains and population dynamics across vast territories. These advances establish new standards for environmental simulation.

Weather simulation reveals interesting patterns in atmospheric modeling. Microsoft Flight Simulator demonstrates how organizations implement global weather systems. Their implementation processes real-world weather data to create accurate atmospheric conditions, managing complex weather patterns while maintaining realistic flight physics. These innovations establish new approaches to environmental realism.

Economic systems show sophisticated approaches to resource flow. EVE Online's market system demonstrates how CCP Games implements complex economic simulation. Their implementation processes millions of player-driven transactions daily, maintaining realistic market behaviors while adapting to player activities. These developments influence how games approach economic modeling.

Content generation reveals careful attention to narrative integration. Bethesda's Radiant AI system shows how organizations implement dynamic quest generation. Their implementation creates contextual missions based on player actions and world state, maintaining narrative coherence while providing endless content variation. These advances transform how games approach content longevity.

Social dynamics demonstrate sophisticated approaches to population behavior. Grand Theft Auto Online shows how Rockstar implements complex crowd dynamics. Their system manages thousands of NPCs with individual routines and responses, maintaining realistic urban behavior while adapting to player actions. These innovations influence how games approach living cities.

The integration of these environmental systems creates comprehensive world simulation. The combination of enhanced procedural generation with sophisticated dynamic systems shows how different environmental approaches complement each other. These integrations demonstrate how environmental generation advances through careful combination of techniques while maintaining player immersion.

These environmental patterns continue influencing game development. Understanding these advances provides crucial context for appreciating current capabilities while suggesting future directions. The success of different approaches demonstrates the importance of systematic innovation in advancing gaming world generation.

Player interaction in gaming AI demonstrates sophisticated approaches to dynamic response and engagement optimization. FromSoftware's Elden Ring shows how organizations achieve advanced combat adaptation. Their system processes player behavior patterns across millions of encounters, adapting enemy strategies in real-time while maintaining challenging but fair gameplay, demonstrated by the large number of players engaging with its dynamic combat system.

Response systems reveal careful attention to player behavior analysis. EA Sports' FIFA series demonstrates how organizations enhance competitive AI. Their latest implementation analyzes a vast number of matches daily, adapting tactical responses while maintaining unique play styles for each of the thousands of players. These innovations transform how sports games approach realistic opponent behavior.

Behavior adaptation shows sophisticated approaches to difficulty management. Insomniac's Spider-Man 2 demonstrates how organizations implement dynamic challenge scaling. Their system processes player performance metrics in real-time, adjusting combat intensity and enemy behavior patterns while maintaining narrative consistency. These developments influence how games approach accessibility and challenge.

Learning patterns demonstrate careful attention to player skill progression. Ninja Theory's Hellblade series shows how organizations implement psychological profiling. Their system tracks player behavior across multiple dimensions, adjusting psychological horror elements while maintaining emotional impact, processing numerous behavioral variables per session. These advances establish new standards for personalized gaming experiences.

Experience optimization reveals interesting patterns in engagement management. Riot Games' League of Legends demonstrates how organizations handle player satisfaction. Their matchmaking system processes millions of matches daily, maintaining balanced win rates while considering hundreds of variables per player. These innovations establish new approaches to competitive balance.

Player profiling shows sophisticated approaches to preference learning. Ubisoft's Assassin's Creed series demonstrates how organizations implement adaptive content delivery. Their system analyzes player behavior across multiple gameplay styles, adjusting mission types and rewards while maintaining narrative flow. These developments influence how games approach content personalization.

Social integration demonstrates careful attention to multiplayer dynamics. Bungie's Destiny 2 shows how organizations implement complex cooperative experiences. Their system manages millions of simultaneous players in shared-world activities, maintaining balanced experiences while processing real-time player interactions. These advances transform how games approach social gameplay.

Team dynamics reveal sophisticated approaches to group behavior. Valve's Dota 2 demonstrates how organizations handle complex team interactions. Their implementation processes team compositions and strategies across millions of matches, maintaining competitive balance while adapting to emerging meta-strategies. These innovations influence how competitive games approach team play.

The integration of these interaction systems creates comprehensive player engagement frameworks. The combination of enhanced behavior adaptation with sophisticated social systems shows how different interaction approaches complement each other. These integrations demonstrate how player interaction advances through careful combination of techniques while maintaining player satisfaction.

These interaction patterns continue influencing game development. Understanding these advances provides crucial context for appreciating current capabilities while suggesting future directions. The success of different approaches demonstrates the importance of systematic innovation in advancing gaming interaction systems.

Performance systems in gaming AI demonstrate sophisticated approaches to optimizing complex real-time operations. Unity's DOTS (Data-Oriented Technology Stack) shows how organizations achieve advanced processing efficiency in AI-driven games. Their system manages millions of AI entities simultaneously while significantly reducing CPU usage, demonstrating how modern engines balance sophisticated AI with performance requirements.

Resource management reveals careful attention to processing efficiency. Epic Games' Unreal Engine 5 demonstrates how organizations enhance AI performance through Nanite virtualized geometry. Their implementation processes vast numbers of polygons while maintaining AI pathfinding and spatial awareness, achieving sub-millisecond performance for thousands of AI agents. These innovations transform how games approach large-scale AI simulation.

Processing efficiency shows sophisticated approaches to computational optimization. Nvidia's DLSS 3 demonstrates how organizations implement AI-enhanced rendering. Their system processes high frame rates while maintaining visual quality, freeing computational resources for more complex AI behaviors. These developments influence how games balance visual fidelity with AI complexity.

Memory utilization demonstrates careful attention to resource constraints. CD Projekt Red's REDengine 4 shows how organizations optimize AI memory management. Their implementation handles complex NPC behaviors across vast cityscapes while maintaining efficient memory footprint, processing thousands of AI routines simultaneously. These advances establish new standards for AI resource efficiency.

Network optimization reveals interesting patterns in multiplayer AI coordination. Battlefield 2042's implementation shows how DICE manages distributed AI processing. Their system manages numerous simultaneous players and AI agents while maintaining stable server rates, demonstrating how modern games handle complex AI in networked environments. These innovations establish new approaches to scalable AI.

Graphics enhancement shows sophisticated approaches to AI-driven visual systems. PlayStation 5's Gran Turismo 7 demonstrates how Polyphony Digital implements AI-enhanced racing simulation. Their system processes complex physics and AI decisions while managing multiple sophisticated AI drivers per race. These developments influence how games approach performance-intensive AI applications.

Quality management reveals careful attention to system reliability. Blizzard's Overwatch 2 demonstrates how organizations implement performance monitoring. Their system processes millions of matches while maintaining consistent AI behavior across different hardware configurations with high server stability. These advances transform how games approach AI reliability.

System integration demonstrates sophisticated approaches to platform compatibility. Xbox Game Studios' Flight Simulator shows how organizations handle complex AI across platforms. Their implementation maintains consistent AI behavior while scaling across PC and console hardware, processing terabytes of real-world data for AI navigation. These innovations influence how games approach cross-platform AI.

The integration of these performance systems creates comprehensive optimization frameworks. The combination of enhanced resource management with sophisticated quality control shows how different performance approaches complement each other. These integrations demonstrate how performance systems advance through careful combination of techniques while maintaining player experience.

These performance patterns continue influencing game development. Understanding these advances provides crucial context for appreciating current capabilities while suggesting future directions. The success of different approaches demonstrates the importance of systematic innovation in advancing gaming AI performance.

Implementation advances in gaming AI demonstrate sophisticated approaches to deploying and managing complex game systems. Unity's Machine Learning Agents toolkit shows how organizations achieve streamlined AI development and deployment. Their framework enables developers to implement advanced AI behaviors while significantly reducing development time maintaining high-quality outcomes across diverse game genres.

Development frameworks reveal careful attention to implementation efficiency. Epic Games' MetaHuman framework demonstrates how organizations enhance character AI implementation. Their system reduces character development time from months to hours while maintaining sophisticated behavioral models, processing complex emotional responses and social interactions. These innovations transform how games approach character AI deployment.

Engine integration shows sophisticated approaches to AI implementation. Valve's Source 2 engine demonstrates how organizations implement advanced AI systems. Their implementation enables rapid deployment of complex behaviors while maintaining consistent performance across Steam's large number of active users. These developments influence how games approach AI integration at scale.

Testing systems demonstrate careful attention to quality assurance. Electronic Arts' SEED division shows how organizations implement AI validation. Their automated testing framework processes millions of gameplay scenarios daily, identifying behavioral edge cases while maintaining high detection rates. These advances establish new standards for AI quality control.

Pipeline optimization reveals interesting patterns in development efficiency. Ubisoft's Anvil engine demonstrates how organizations streamline AI implementation. Their system enables rapid iteration on AI behaviors while maintaining consistent quality across multiple development teams, processing thousands of daily code changes. These innovations establish new approaches to AI development workflows.

Resource management shows sophisticated approaches to asset optimization. Square Enix's Luminous Engine demonstrates how organizations handle complex AI resource allocation. Their implementation manages detailed character behaviors while maintaining efficient memory usage across diverse hardware configurations. These developments influence how games approach AI resource optimization.

Deployment methods reveal careful attention to distribution requirements. Microsoft's Azure PlayFab shows how organizations implement cloud-based AI systems. Their platform manages AI behaviors for hundreds of millions of players while maintaining rapid response times, demonstrating how modern games handle distributed AI processing. These advances transform how games approach AI deployment.

Maintenance protocols demonstrate sophisticated approaches to system updates. Riot Games' implementation shows how organizations manage live service AI. Their system enables continuous AI improvements while maintaining competitive balance across millions of daily matches. These innovations influence how games approach ongoing AI refinement.

The integration of these implementation advances creates comprehensive development frameworks. The combination of enhanced development tools with sophisticated deployment systems shows how different implementation approaches complement each other. These integrations demonstrate how implementation advances through careful combination of techniques while maintaining development efficiency.

These implementation patterns continue influencing game development. Understanding these advances provides crucial context for appreciating current capabilities while suggesting future directions. The success of different approaches demonstrates the importance of systematic innovation in advancing gaming AI implementation.

The trajectory of gaming AI reveals emerging patterns that suggest promising directions for continued advancement. Unity's research into neural rendering demonstrates how organizations approach enhanced visual intelligence. Their current development achieves significantly better performance while reducing resource requirements, showing how development focuses on balancing sophisticated capabilities with practical constraints.

Technical evolution reveals careful attention to fundamental improvements. Nvidia's research into AI-accelerated gaming demonstrates how organizations address core processing challenges. Their latest RTX 4090 architecture achieves high AI performance while maintaining energy efficiency, showing how development continues advancing basic capabilities while considering practical limitations.

Architecture advancement patterns show sophisticated approaches to system design. Epic Games' research into next-generation world systems demonstrates how organizations systematically enhance environmental intelligence. Their current achievements in significantly reducing world generation overhead while improving detail shows how development focuses on efficiency without compromising quality.

Integration methods demonstrate careful attention to system connectivity. PlayStation's research into adaptive AI shows how organizations improve player interaction. Their current implementation achieves improved player engagement while maintaining consistent challenge levels, demonstrating how development aims to broaden utility while maintaining player satisfaction.

Application growth reveals interesting patterns in use case expansion. Microsoft's research into cloud gaming AI shows how organizations explore new operational domains. Their current Azure Gaming development processes reduce latency while handling numerous simultaneous AI calculations, demonstrating how development aims to enhance capability while maintaining scalability.

Market development patterns reveal sophisticated approaches to industry adoption. Electronic Arts' investment in AI research shows how organizations improve accessibility. Their current implementation substantially reduces AI development time while maintaining quality standards, demonstrating how development focuses on practical adoption considerations.

Research focus reveals interesting patterns in innovation direction. Google DeepMind's work on game-based learning shows how organizations approach complex challenges. Their current development in general game playing achieves competitive performance across multiple genres while maintaining learning efficiency, demonstrating how research aims to address future challenges.

Development trends indicate careful attention to operational requirements. Take-Two's research into advanced NPC systems shows how organizations improve character intelligence. Their current achievement of more realistic behavior patterns while maintaining performance demonstrates how development focuses on practical considerations.

The synthesis of multiple advancement directions creates comprehensive improvement opportunities. The combination of enhanced processing capabilities with sophisticated behavioral systems shows how different innovation streams complement each other. These integrations demonstrate how future development may proceed through careful combination of advances while maintaining practical utility.

These directional patterns continue influencing development approaches. Understanding these trends provides crucial context for appreciating future possibilities while maintaining practical perspective. The success of different approaches demonstrates the importance of systematic innovation in advancing gaming AI capabilities.

Our exploration of gaming AI innovations reveals the sophisticated evolution of interactive intelligence systems. From Unity's ML-Agents processing millions of training iterations to Epic Games' MetaHuman creating photorealistic character behaviors, we see how systematic innovation enables increasingly advanced gaming experiences while maintaining real-time performance. For practitioners and organizations working with gaming AI, these developments provide crucial insights into both current capabilities and implementation approaches.

The advancement patterns we've examined demonstrate multiple paths for engaging with gaming technology. Whether through No Man's Sky's generation of countless unique planets or FIFA's analysis of millions of matches, organizations can choose approaches that align with their specific requirements and objectives. The success of different approaches shows how various development paths can effectively address distinct challenges while maintaining player engagement.

Implementation considerations continue influencing how organizations approach gaming AI deployment. Riot Games' management of a large number of simultaneous players and Ubisoft's coordination of complex NPC behaviors demonstrate how practical requirements shape operational decisions. Understanding these relationships becomes crucial for organizations implementing gaming AI systems, as deployment choices significantly influence player experience.

The relationship between performance and intelligence creates interesting opportunities for innovation. Nvidia's achievement of high AI processing and Unity's DOTS substantially reducing CPU usage show how thoughtful design enables significant improvements. These developments demonstrate the importance of understanding technical trade-offs while suggesting approaches for enhancing gaming AI capabilities.

As we move forward to examine cross-domain integration in our next chapter, we carry forward understanding of how real-time decision making and adaptive behavior enable sophisticated interactive systems. The advanced approaches to gaming AI we've explored provide crucial context for understanding how AI systems manage complex, dynamic interactions across different domains. For practitioners and organizations, this understanding becomes increasingly valuable as AI technology continues advancing.

Engage actively with these gaming AI developments, whether through experimental implementation or systematic evaluation of different approaches. Major game engine providers offer extensive resources for exploring AI capabilities, while specialized frameworks provide focused environments for specific applications. These resources offer excellent starting points for practical engagement with gaming AI advancement.

The field of gaming AI continues evolving, offering new opportunities for innovation and implementation. By understanding current capabilities and emerging trends, practitioners and organizations can better position themselves to leverage advancing gaming AI technologies. Explore these opportunities while maintaining awareness of how interactive capabilities influence practical implementation success.

CHAPTER 14: CROSS-DOMAIN INTEGRATION

Cross-domain integration represents a sophisticated convergence of AI capabilities, building upon the real-time processing and adaptive behaviors we explored in gaming systems. OpenAI's GPT-4V demonstrates how organizations achieve advanced integration of vision and language understanding. Their system processes complex visual inputs alongside natural language, enabling sophisticated multimodal interactions while maintaining response coherence across different types of information.

The current landscape of cross-domain integration reveals remarkable progress across multiple dimensions. Google's PaLM 2 shows how organizations enhance capability integration through unified architectures. Their implementation processes multiple input types simultaneously while maintaining contextual understanding, demonstrating how modern systems balance diverse capabilities with coherent output. These innovations transform how organizations approach integrated AI systems.

Implementation patterns reveal sophisticated approaches

263

to practical deployment. Microsoft's Azure Cognitive Services demonstrates how organizations balance multiple AI capabilities in production environments. Their platform processes numerous transactions monthly across vision, language, and speech services while maintaining high availability, showing how integrated systems address both performance requirements and operational reliability.

The relationship between different AI domains has grown increasingly sophisticated. Meta's advancement in multimodal understanding shows how organizations optimize cross-domain processing. Their development of integrated neural networks demonstrates how systems maintain performance while processing diverse input types simultaneously, supporting numerous daily interactions across different modalities.

Specialized applications continue emerging through focused integration. Adobe's Creative Suite demonstrates how organizations combine multiple AI capabilities for creative applications. Their implementation of integrated visual and language processing shows how systems address specific creative needs while maintaining natural workflows, processing a vast number of creative operations daily.

In this chapter, we explore the sophisticated world of cross-domain integration, examining how different AI capabilities combine to enable advanced applications. From fundamental architecture to complex implementation methods, we'll investigate how integration continues advancing. This exploration reveals both current achievements and emerging directions in capability integration, providing crucial context for understanding modern systems.

For practitioners and organizations implementing integrated AI systems, understanding these developments becomes increasingly important. The advances in integration capabilities influence every aspect of implementation and deployment. As we proceed, we'll examine how different approaches address various challenges, offering insights valuable for those working with cross-domain AI technologies.

Integration architecture in cross-domain AI demonstrates sophisticated approaches to combining diverse capabilities. Google Cloud's Vertex AI shows how organizations achieve advanced system integration. Their platform coordinates numerous specialized AI services while processing predictions daily, demonstrating how modern architectures balance complex capability integration with reliable operation.

Core systems design reveals careful attention to component interaction. AWS's SageMaker demonstrates how organizations enhance service coordination. Their implementation manages thousands of model endpoints simultaneously while maintaining low latency, processing data across multiple AI domains. These innovations transform how organizations approach integrated AI architecture.

Service coordination shows sophisticated approaches to system management. Microsoft's Azure AI platform demonstrates how organizations implement cross-service communication. Their system processes numerous API calls daily across language, vision, and speech services while maintaining data consistency. These developments influence how organizations approach multi-capability deployment.

Data flow management demonstrates careful attention to information routing. Snowflake's Data Cloud shows how organizations handle complex data integration. Their implementation processes petabytes of data across multiple AI services while maintaining sub-second query response times. These advances establish new standards for integrated data processing.

Performance optimization reveals interesting patterns in resource utilization. NVIDIA's Triton Inference Server demonstrates how organizations handle multi-model deployment. Their system manages numerous concurrent models while achieving high inference rates per GPU. These innovations establish new approaches to integrated processing.

Scalability patterns show sophisticated approaches to growth management. Databricks' Lakehouse Platform demonstrates how organizations implement extensible architectures. Their system scales to handle exabytes of data while maintaining consistent performance across integrated AI services. These developments influence how organizations approach architectural scaling.

Security implementation reveals careful attention to protection requirements. IBM's Watson platform shows how organizations maintain data safety across domains. Their implementation processes sensitive information across multiple services while maintaining zero-trust security architecture. These advances transform how organizations approach integrated security.

Framework development demonstrates sophisticated approaches to system organization. Apache's Spark ecosystem shows how organizations implement integrated processing frameworks. Their platform coordinates machine learning, graph processing, and streaming analytics while maintaining unified data access. These innovations influence how organizations approach integrated development.

The integration of these architectural elements creates comprehensive system frameworks. The combination of enhanced service coordination with sophisticated security measures shows how different architectural approaches complement each other. These integrations demonstrate how architecture advances through careful combination of techniques while maintaining system reliability.

These architectural patterns continue influencing system development. Understanding these advances provides crucial context for appreciating current capabilities while suggesting future directions. The success of different approaches demonstrates the importance of systematic innovation in advancing cross-domain integration.

Domain convergence in cross-domain AI demonstrates sophisticated approaches to combining specialized capabilities. OpenAI's GPT-4V shows how organizations achieve advanced integration of vision and language processing. Their system simultaneously processes images and text while maintaining contextual understanding across modalities, generating coherent responses that demonstrate deep comprehension of both visual and textual elements.

Language-vision integration reveals careful attention to multimodal understanding. Google's PaLM 2 demonstrates how organizations enhance cross-domain comprehension. Their implementation processes visual and textual information simultaneously while maintaining semantic connections, achieving high accuracy in multimodal tasks. These innovations transform how organizations approach combined understanding systems.

Content understanding shows sophisticated approaches to cross-modal analysis. Meta's multimodal models demonstrate how organizations implement comprehensive interpretation. Their system processes text, images, and video simultaneously while maintaining contextual relationships, analyzing numerous multi-format posts daily. These developments influence how organizations approach integrated content analysis.

Audio-visual systems demonstrate careful attention to temporal coordination. NVIDIA's Maxine platform shows how organizations implement synchronized processing. Their system manages real-time audio-visual streams maintaining accurate lip-sync while processing concurrent video calls. These advances establish new standards for multimodal synchronization.

Signal processing reveals interesting patterns in cross-domain coordination. Adobe's Creative Cloud demonstrates how organizations handle complex media integration. Their implementation processes audio and visual signals simultaneously while maintaining creative quality, enabling sophisticated media manipulation across domains. These innovations establish new approaches to media processing.

Pattern recognition shows sophisticated approaches to cross-modal understanding. Microsoft's Azure Cognitive Services demonstrates how organizations implement integrated analysis. Their system identifies patterns across text, speech, and vision maintaining high accuracy while processing numerous API calls monthly. These developments influence how organizations approach comprehensive pattern detection.

Data-decision systems reveal careful attention to integrated analysis. Palantir's Foundry platform shows how organizations implement cross-domain decision support. Their implementation analyzes multiple data types simultaneously while maintaining decision consistency, enabling complex operational insights. These advances transform how organizations approach integrated decision-making.

Action planning demonstrates sophisticated approaches to multi-domain coordination. IBM's Watson orchestration shows how organizations implement integrated responses. Their system coordinates actions across multiple AI services while maintaining operational coherence, processing millions of integrated workflows daily. These innovations influence how organizations approach complex automation.

The integration of these convergence capabilities creates comprehensive understanding systems. The combination of enhanced multimodal processing with sophisticated decision support shows how different domain approaches complement each other. These integrations demonstrate how domain convergence advances through careful combination of techniques while maintaining practical utility.

These convergence patterns continue influencing system development. Understanding these advances provides crucial context for appreciating current capabilities while suggesting future directions. The success of different approaches demonstrates the importance of systematic innovation in

268

advancing cross-domain integration.

Implementation methods in cross-domain AI demonstrate sophisticated approaches to deploying integrated systems. Google Cloud's Vertex AI shows how organizations achieve advanced deployment capabilities. Their platform manages over 50 different AI services in production while maintaining high reliability, demonstrating how modern systems balance complex integration with operational stability.

Deployment strategies reveal careful attention to system coordination. AWS's SageMaker demonstrates how organizations enhance service implementation. Their platform deploys thousands of integrated endpoints daily while maintaining consistent performance, processing vast numbers of predictions monthly across multiple domains. These innovations transform how organizations approach integrated AI deployment.

Service deployment shows sophisticated approaches to operational management. Microsoft's Azure AI platform demonstrates how organizations implement complex service orchestration. Their system coordinates language, vision, and speech services while maintaining low latency, handling numerous API calls monthly. These developments influence how organizations approach multi-service operations.

Resource allocation demonstrates careful attention to system efficiency. NVIDIA's AI Enterprise platform shows how organizations handle integrated resource management. Their implementation optimizes GPU utilization across multiple AI workloads achieving high resource efficiency, while maintaining performance guarantees. These advances establish new standards for integrated resource management.

Performance management reveals interesting patterns in system optimization. Oracle's Cloud Infrastructure demonstrates how organizations implement comprehensive monitoring. Their system tracks performance across integrated services, processing numerous metrics while maintaining real-time visibility. These innovations establish new approaches to integrated performance control.

Operation management shows sophisticated approaches to service coordination. IBM's Cloud Pak for Data demonstrates how organizations implement integrated operations. Their platform manages hundreds of AI services while maintaining operational coherence, enabling complex workflow automation. These developments influence how organizations approach integrated service management.

Quality assurance reveals careful attention to system validation. Databricks' MLflow shows how organizations implement comprehensive testing. Their platform validates integrated AI workflows while maintaining quality standards, processing thousands of model deployments daily. These advances transform how organizations approach integrated quality control.

Integration validation demonstrates sophisticated approaches to system verification. Red Hat's OpenShift platform shows how organizations implement deployment validation. Their system ensures service compatibility while maintaining security standards, managing thousands of containerized AI services. These innovations influence how organizations approach integrated system validation.

The integration of these implementation methods creates comprehensive deployment frameworks. The combination of enhanced deployment strategies with sophisticated operation management shows how different implementation approaches complement each other. These integrations demonstrate how implementation methods advance through careful combination of techniques while maintaining operational reliability.

These implementation patterns continue influencing system development. Understanding these advances provides crucial context for appreciating current capabilities while suggesting future directions. The success of different approaches demonstrates the importance of systematic innovation in advancing cross-domain implementation.

Performance enhancement in cross-domain AI demonstrates sophisticated approaches to optimizing integrated systems. NVIDIA's AI Enterprise platform shows how organizations achieve advanced processing efficiency. Their implementation processes numerous inferences while coordinating multiple AI domains, demonstrating how modern systems balance complex integration with high performance.

Resource optimization reveals careful attention to processing efficiency. Intel's OpenVINO toolkit demonstrates how organizations enhance computational performance. Their implementation achieves significantly better CPU utilization across integrated AI workloads while maintaining accuracy, processing multiple models simultaneously. These innovations transform how organizations approach integrated resource management.

Memory management shows sophisticated approaches to resource utilization. AMD's ROCm platform demonstrates how organizations implement efficient memory handling. Their system reduces memory overhead while maintaining performance across multiple AI domains, enabling more efficient integrated processing. These developments influence how organizations approach memory optimization.

Network utilization demonstrates careful attention to communication efficiency. Cisco's AI networking solutions show how organizations handle complex data routing. Their implementation achieves improved throughput for integrated AI services while maintaining low latency, processing petabytes of cross-domain data daily. These advances establish new standards for integrated network performance.

Storage optimization reveals interesting patterns in data management. Pure Storage's AI-Ready Infrastructure demonstrates how organizations implement efficient data handling. Their system processes integrated AI workloads achieving faster data access while enabling seamless operation across multiple domains. These innovations establish new approaches to storage optimization.

System coordination shows sophisticated approaches to service integration. Kubernetes' orchestration capabilities demonstrate how organizations implement efficient service management. Their platform coordinates thousands of AI containers maintaining high uptime while enabling complex cross-domain workflows. These developments influence how organizations approach service coordination.

Process synchronization reveals careful attention to timing requirements. Apache Kafka's event streaming platform shows how organizations implement coordinated processing. Their system handles millions of events per second while maintaining message ordering across integrated services. These advances transform how organizations approach event coordination.

Error recovery demonstrates sophisticated approaches to system reliability. HashiCorp's Consul demonstrates how organizations implement robust service discovery. Their platform manages service health across integrated AI systems while enabling rapid recovery, maintaining high availability for complex deployments. These innovations influence how organizations approach system resilience.

The integration of these performance enhancements creates comprehensive optimization frameworks. The combination of enhanced resource management with sophisticated system coordination shows how different optimization approaches complement each other. These integrations demonstrate how performance enhancement advances through careful combination of techniques while maintaining system reliability.

These performance patterns continue influencing system development. Understanding these advances provides crucial context for appreciating current capabilities while suggesting future directions. The success of different approaches demonstrates the importance of systematic innovation in advancing cross-domain performance.

Application domains in cross-domain AI demonstrate sophisticated approaches to real-world implementation. Salesforce's Einstein platform shows how organizations achieve advanced business integration. Their system processes numerous AI predictions daily across sales, service, and marketing domains while maintaining accuracy, demonstrating how modern systems balance diverse business requirements with reliable operation.

Enterprise integration reveals careful attention to business requirements. SAP's Business AI demonstrates how organizations enhance operational intelligence. Their implementation coordinates multiple AI capabilities across finance, supply chain, and human resources while maintaining real-time processing capabilities, serving customers globally. These innovations transform how organizations approach integrated business operations.

Process automation shows sophisticated approaches to workflow integration. UiPath's enterprise platform demonstrates how organizations implement comprehensive automation. Their system orchestrates AI-driven processes across multiple departments achieving significant reduction in processing time while handling numerous automated tasks daily. These developments influence how organizations approach integrated automation.

Decision support demonstrates careful attention to analytical integration. Palantir's Foundry platform shows how organizations implement complex decision systems. Their implementation analyzes diverse data streams while maintaining contextual understanding, enabling sophisticated decision-making across multiple domains. These advances establish new standards for integrated analytics.

Scientific applications reveal interesting patterns in research integration. Google DeepMind's AlphaFold system demonstrates how organizations implement cross-domain scientific computing. Their platform combines multiple AI approaches while maintaining atomic-level accuracy, processing complex protein structures for millions of researchers. These innovations establish new approaches to scientific discovery.

Data analysis shows sophisticated approaches to research computation. CERN's AI infrastructure demonstrates how organizations implement integrated analysis. Their system processes petabytes of particle physics data while coordinating multiple AI models, enabling complex scientific discoveries. These developments influence how organizations approach research computing.

Consumer systems reveal careful attention to user experience integration. Apple's iOS platform shows how organizations implement integrated AI services. Their implementation coordinates multiple AI capabilities while maintaining privacy, processing numerous on-device AI operations daily. These advances transform how organizations approach consumer AI integration.

Service integration demonstrates sophisticated approaches to feature coordination. Google's Android platform shows how organizations implement comprehensive AI services. Their system manages multiple AI capabilities while maintaining consistent user experience, serving billions of daily interactions. These innovations influence how organizations approach integrated mobile services.

The integration of these application domains creates comprehensive solution frameworks. The combination of enhanced enterprise capabilities with sophisticated scientific applications shows how different domain approaches complement each other. These integrations demonstrate how application domains advance through careful combination of techniques while maintaining practical utility.

These application patterns continue influencing system development. Understanding these advances provides crucial context for appreciating current capabilities while suggesting future directions. The success of different approaches demonstrates the importance of systematic innovation in advancing cross-domain applications.

The trajectory of cross-domain integration reveals emerging patterns that suggest promising directions for continued advancement. Google's research into next-generation multimodal systems demonstrates how organizations approach enhanced integration capabilities. Their development of PaLM 3 architecture shows significant improvement in cross-domain understanding while reducing computational requirements, demonstrating how development focuses on balancing sophisticated integration with practical efficiency.

Technical evolution reveals careful attention to fundamental improvements. NVIDIA's research into unified AI architectures demonstrates how organizations address core processing challenges. Their latest Hopper architecture achieves substantially better performance in multi-domain workloads while maintaining energy efficiency, showing how development continues advancing basic capabilities while considering operational constraints.

Architecture enhancement patterns show sophisticated approaches to system design. Microsoft's research into advanced cognitive services demonstrates how organizations systematically enhance integration capabilities. Their current achievements in reducing API latency while improving cross-service coordination shows how development focuses on efficiency without compromising functionality.

Capability integration demonstrates careful attention to system coordination. Meta's research into universal AI models shows how organizations improve cross-domain processing. Their current implementation achieves improved performance in combined vision-language tasks while maintaining real-time response, demonstrating how development aims to broaden utility while maintaining performance.

Application growth reveals interesting patterns in use case expansion. AWS's research into integrated cloud services shows how organizations explore new operational domains. Their current development processes reduce cross-service latency while handling numerous simultaneous operations, demonstrating how development aims to enhance capability while maintaining scalability.

Service evolution patterns reveal sophisticated approaches to feature enhancement. IBM's research into quantum-ready AI integration shows how organizations improve future readiness. Their current implementation achieves significant improvements in hybrid classical-quantum workflows while maintaining compatibility with existing systems.

Development trends indicate careful attention to operational requirements. Oracle's research into autonomous integration shows how organizations improve service coordination. Their current achievement of significant automation in cross-domain workflows while maintaining accuracy demonstrates how development focuses on practical considerations.

Research focus reveals interesting patterns in innovation direction. Apple's work on integrated on-device AI shows how organizations approach privacy-preserving integration. Their current development achieves competitive performance across multiple domains while maintaining data privacy, demonstrating how research aims to address future challenges.

The synthesis of multiple advancement directions creates comprehensive improvement opportunities. The combination of enhanced processing capabilities with sophisticated integration methods shows how different innovation streams complement each other. These integrations demonstrate how future development may proceed through careful combination of advances while maintaining practical utility.

These directional patterns continue influencing development approaches. Understanding these trends provides crucial context for appreciating future possibilities while maintaining practical perspective. The success of different approaches demonstrates the importance of systematic innovation in advancing cross-domain integration capabilities.

Our exploration of cross-domain integration reveals the sophisticated evolution of combined AI capabilities. From Google's PaLM processing billions of multimodal predictions to NVIDIA's Hopper architecture achieving significant performance improvements in multi-domain workloads, we see how systematic innovation enables increasingly advanced integrated systems while maintaining operational reliability. For practitioners and organizations working with cross-domain AI, these developments provide crucial insights into both current capabilities and implementation approaches.

The advancement patterns we've examined demonstrate multiple paths for engaging with integrated technology. Whether through Salesforce's Einstein platform processing numerous daily AI predictions or Google DeepMind's AlphaFold combining multiple AI approaches for scientific discovery, organizations can choose approaches that align with their specific requirements and objectives. The success of different approaches shows how various development paths can effectively address distinct challenges while maintaining system coherence.

Implementation considerations continue influencing how organizations approach cross-domain integration. Microsoft's coordination of multiple AI services and SAP's integration across business operations demonstrate how practical requirements shape operational decisions. Understanding these relationships becomes crucial for organizations implementing integrated AI systems, as deployment choices significantly influence operational success.

The relationship between performance and integration creates interesting opportunities for innovation. Intel's achievement of significantly better CPU utilization and Apache Kafka's processing of numerous events per second show how thoughtful design enables significant improvements. These developments demonstrate the importance of understanding technical trade-offs while suggesting approaches for enhancing cross-domain capabilities.

As we move forward to examine AI ethics and responsibility in our next chapter, we carry forward understanding of how integrated systems influence broader societal impacts. The advanced approaches to cross-domain integration we've explored provide crucial context for understanding how AI systems affect various aspects of society and business. For practitioners and organizations, this understanding becomes increasingly valuable as AI technology continues advancing.

Engage actively with these cross-domain integration developments, whether through experimental implementation or systematic evaluation of different approaches. Major cloud providers offer extensive resources for exploring integrated AI capabilities, while specialized platforms provide focused environments for specific applications. These resources offer excellent starting points for practical engagement with cross-domain AI advancement.

The field of cross-domain integration continues evolving, offering new opportunities for innovation and implementation. By understanding current capabilities and emerging trends, practitioners and organizations can better position themselves to leverage advancing integrated AI technologies. Explore these opportunities while maintaining awareness of how integration capabilities influence practical implementation success.

CHAPTER 15: AI ETHICS AT THE FRONTIER

AI ethics at the frontier represents a crucial dimension of advanced artificial intelligence, building upon the integrated capabilities we explored in cross-domain systems. Anthropic's development of constitutional AI demonstrates how organizations achieve sophisticated ethical implementations. Their system processes numerous interactions while maintaining explicit ethical constraints, showing how modern AI can balance advanced capabilities with responsible operation.

The current landscape of AI ethics reveals remarkable progress across multiple dimensions. Google's AI Principles implementation shows how organizations enhance ethical oversight of complex systems. Their framework governs development across numerous AI projects while maintaining consistent ethical standards, demonstrating how modern organizations balance innovation with responsibility. These approaches transform how companies implement ethical AI development.

Implementation patterns reveal sophisticated approaches

to practical ethics. Microsoft's Office of Responsible AI demonstrates how organizations structure ethical governance. Their implementation oversees AI development across global operations while maintaining comprehensive ethical standards, processing substantial numbers of ethical reviews annually. These developments show how organizations address both ethical requirements and operational needs.

The relationship between capability and responsibility has grown increasingly sophisticated. OpenAI's approach to staged model release demonstrates how organizations balance advancement with safety. Their development process includes extensive testing and graduated deployment, showing how systems maintain ethical constraints while pushing technical boundaries. These practices establish new standards for responsible AI development.

Specialized applications continue emerging through focused ethical development. IBM's AI Ethics Board shows how organizations implement comprehensive oversight. Their implementation of ethical review processes demonstrates how systems address specific ethical challenges while maintaining innovation momentum, regularly processing project reviews. These innovations transform how organizations approach ethical AI deployment.

In this chapter, we explore the sophisticated world of AI ethics, examining how different approaches enable responsible advancement. From fundamental frameworks to complex implementation methods, we'll investigate how ethical considerations continue evolving. This exploration reveals both current achievements and emerging directions in responsible AI, providing crucial context for understanding modern approaches.

For practitioners and organizations implementing AI systems, understanding these ethical developments becomes increasingly important. The advances in ethical frameworks influence every aspect of implementation and deployment. As we proceed, we'll examine how different approaches address various challenges, offering insights valuable for those working with advanced AI technologies.

Advanced ethical frameworks in AI demonstrate sophisticated approaches to responsible development and deployment. Google DeepMind's ethical review system shows how organizations achieve comprehensive oversight of advanced AI systems. Their framework processes research projects through multiple ethical review stages while maintaining development momentum, demonstrating how modern organizations balance innovation with ethical rigor.

Responsibility models reveal careful attention to accountability requirements. Microsoft's Responsible AI Standards demonstrate how organizations structure ethical governance. Their implementation guides AI projects globally while maintaining consistent ethical standards across diverse applications. These innovations transform how organizations approach ethical AI development, achieving significant compliance rates across their development ecosystem.

Governance structures show sophisticated approaches to ethical oversight. Google's AI Ethics Board demonstrates how organizations implement comprehensive review systems. Their framework evaluates AI initiatives annually while maintaining transparent decision-making processes, documenting significant ethical decisions. These developments influence how organizations approach ethical governance at scale.

Decision frameworks demonstrate careful attention to ethical choice-making. IBM's AI Ethics Board shows how organizations structure ethical decision-making. Their system processes project reviews regularly while maintaining consistent ethical standards, achieving substantial alignment with established principles. These advances establish new standards for ethical decision-making in AI development.

Impact assessment reveals interesting patterns in ethical evaluation. Salesforce's Office of Ethical and Humane Use demonstrates how organizations analyze AI impacts. Their implementation assesses features annually while maintaining comprehensive documentation, effectively identifying potential ethical issues. These innovations establish new approaches to impact analysis.

Compliance integration shows sophisticated approaches to regulatory alignment. Amazon's AI governance framework demonstrates how organizations implement regulatory requirements. Their system processes compliance checks across global operations while maintaining adherence to diverse regional standards. These developments influence how organizations approach ethical compliance.

Training programs reveal careful attention to ethical awareness. Meta's responsible AI training demonstrates how organizations develop ethical competency. Their implementation has trained substantial numbers of developers while maintaining high engagement rates and strong knowledge retention. These advances transform how organizations approach ethical education.

Monitoring systems demonstrate sophisticated approaches to ongoing oversight. OpenAI's deployment monitoring shows how organizations maintain ethical standards post-release. Their system tracks model interactions continuously while identifying potential ethical issues in real-time. These innovations influence how organizations approach continuous ethical oversight.

The integration of these ethical frameworks creates comprehensive governance systems. The combination of enhanced responsibility models with sophisticated monitoring shows how different ethical approaches complement each other. These integrations demonstrate how ethical frameworks advance through careful combination of techniques while maintaining practical effectiveness.

These ethical patterns continue influencing AI development. Understanding these advances provides crucial context for appreciating current capabilities while suggesting future directions. The success of different approaches demonstrates the importance of systematic innovation in advancing AI ethics.

Responsible innovation in AI demonstrates sophisticated approaches to ethical advancement. Anthropic's constitutional AI development shows how organizations achieve principled progress in advanced capabilities. Their system incorporates ethical constraints directly into model architecture while maintaining state-of-the-art performance, processing significant numbers of ethical decisions daily with consistent adherence to established principles.

Development practices reveal careful attention to ethical design requirements. OpenAI's staged release approach demonstrates how organizations enhance safety in deployment. Their implementation includes extensive red-team testing across multiple release stages while maintaining transparency, documenting comprehensive safety evaluations before each major release. These innovations transform how organizations approach responsible AI development.

Testing protocols show sophisticated approaches to ethical validation. Google's AI Red Team demonstrates how organizations implement comprehensive safety testing. Their framework conducts regular adversarial tests while maintaining detailed documentation, effectively identifying potential ethical issues. These developments influence how organizations approach safety validation.

Validation methods demonstrate careful attention to ethical verification. Microsoft's AI testing framework shows how organizations ensure ethical compliance. Their system processes numerous test cases while maintaining rigorous ethical standards, achieving substantial coverage of identified ethical concerns. These advances establish new standards for ethical validation.

Safety measures reveal interesting patterns in risk management. Google DeepMind's safety protocols demonstrate how organizations implement protective measures. Their implementation includes multiple layers of safety checks while maintaining development efficiency, processing regular safety evaluations. These innovations establish new approaches to AI safety.

Scale considerations show sophisticated approaches to growth management. Meta's responsible scaling framework demonstrates how organizations handle ethical challenges at scale. Their system maintains ethical standards across numerous interactions while adapting to emerging challenges. These developments influence how organizations approach ethical scaling.

Implementation ethics reveal careful attention to deployment requirements. IBM's ethical deployment framework shows how organizations structure responsible rollout. Their implementation guides AI deployments regularly while maintaining strict ethical standards, achieving strong compliance with established guidelines. These advances transform how organizations approach ethical implementation.

Control mechanisms demonstrate sophisticated approaches to ongoing oversight. Amazon's AI governance system shows how organizations maintain ethical standards in production. Their framework monitors AI decisions continuously while identifying potential ethical violations in real-time. These innovations influence how organizations approach operational ethics.

The integration of these responsible innovation practices creates comprehensive development frameworks. The combination of enhanced safety measures with sophisticated validation methods shows how different approaches complement each other. These integrations demonstrate how responsible innovation advances through careful combination of techniques while maintaining practical effectiveness.

These innovation patterns continue influencing AI development. Understanding these advances provides crucial context for appreciating current capabilities while suggesting future directions. The success of different approaches demonstrates the importance of systematic innovation in advancing responsible AI development.

Privacy systems in AI demonstrate sophisticated approaches to data protection and user rights. Apple's implementation of on-device AI shows how organizations achieve advanced capabilities while maintaining privacy. Their system processes billions of AI operations daily entirely on local devices, demonstrating how modern systems balance sophisticated functionality with robust privacy protection, achieving privacy preservation while maintaining rapid response times.

Data protection reveals careful attention to security requirements. Google's federated learning implementation demonstrates how organizations enhance privacy in AI training. Their system enables model improvement across millions of devices while keeping personal data local, processing numerous training instances monthly without centralizing sensitive information. These innovations transform how organizations approach private AI development.

Security frameworks show sophisticated approaches to data safeguarding. Microsoft's Azure Confidential Computing demonstrates how organizations implement secure AI processing. Their platform processes sensitive AI workloads in encrypted environments while maintaining performance, protecting data even during computation. These developments influence how organizations approach secure AI operations.

Access control demonstrates careful attention to data governance. Salesforce's Shield Platform shows how organizations structure data protection. Their implementation manages AI access across numerous customer records while maintaining granular control, achieving zero reported privacy breaches across major deployments. These advances establish new standards for AI data protection.

Encryption standards reveal interesting patterns in privacy

protection. IBM's homomorphic encryption implementation demonstrates how organizations enable secure AI computation. Their system processes encrypted data without decryption while maintaining accuracy, enabling privacy-preserving analysis across sensitive datasets. These innovations establish new approaches to private computation.

Privacy enhancement shows sophisticated approaches to data minimization. Meta's privacy-preserving AI demonstrates how organizations implement data protection at scale. Their system processes numreous interactions while minimizing personal data exposure, achieving privacy compliance across global operations. These developments influence how organizations approach privacy-aware AI.

Consent management reveals careful attention to user rights. Amazon's privacy controls show how organizations implement user choice in AI systems. Their framework manages privacy preferences for users while maintaining transparent operation. These advances transform how organizations approach user privacy.

Compliance management demonstrates sophisticated approaches to regulatory requirements. Oracle's privacy framework shows how organizations maintain regulatory alignment. Their system ensures compliance across diverse jurisdictions while managing AI operations, achieving high compliance rates across global deployments. These innovations influence how organizations approach privacy regulation.

The integration of these privacy systems creates comprehensive protection frameworks. The combination of enhanced security measures with sophisticated consent management shows how different privacy approaches complement each other. These integrations demonstrate how privacy systems advance through careful combination of techniques while maintaining practical effectiveness.

These privacy patterns continue influencing AI development. Understanding these advances provides crucial context for appreciating current capabilities while suggesting future directions. The success of different approaches demonstrates the importance of systematic innovation in advancing AI privacy protection.

Fairness management in AI demonstrates sophisticated approaches to ensuring equitable system behavior. Google's ML Fairness initiatives show how organizations achieve comprehensive bias detection and mitigation. Their framework analyzes numerous model characteristics for potential bias while maintaining performance, demonstrating how modern systems balance sophisticated capabilities with fairness requirements.

Bias detection reveals careful attention to fairness requirements. IBM's AI Fairness 360 toolkit demonstrates how organizations enhance fairness testing. Their implementation processes substantial data points while identifying potential biases across multiple metrics, enabling teams to detect subtle fairness issues effectively. These innovations transform how organizations approach fairness validation.

Analysis systems show sophisticated approaches to fairness evaluation. Microsoft's Fairlearn demonstrates how organizations implement comprehensive fairness assessment. Their platform evaluates models across multiple fairness criteria while maintaining performance objectives, processing regular fairness checks. These developments influence how organizations approach bias detection.

Testing methods demonstrate careful attention to validation requirements. Salesforce's ethical AI testing shows how organizations structure fairness validation. Their system processes model evaluations across diverse demographic groups while maintaining detailed documentation, achieving comprehensive coverage in fairness testing. These advances establish new standards for fairness validation.

Mitigation strategies reveal interesting patterns in bias correction. Amazon's fairness-aware ML platform demonstrates how organizations implement bias mitigation. Their system applies automated corrections while maintaining model performance, substantially reducing detected bias. These innovations establish new approaches to fairness enhancement.

Prevention methods show sophisticated approaches to proactive fairness. Meta's fairness by design framework demonstrates how organizations implement preventive measures. Their system incorporates fairness considerations throughout the development lifecycle while maintaining development efficiency, significantly reducing post-deployment bias issues. These developments influence how organizations approach fairness design.

Monitoring tools reveal careful attention to ongoing assessment. LinkedIn's fairness monitoring demonstrates how organizations maintain equitable operation. Their implementation tracks fairness metrics across numerous recommendations while enabling real-time intervention, achieving consistent fairness scores across user segments. These advances transform how organizations approach continuous fairness.

Implementation methods demonstrate sophisticated approaches to fairness integration. PyTorch's fairness libraries show how organizations enable systematic bias mitigation. Their framework supports developers in implementing fairness measures while maintaining development flexibility. These innovations influence how organizations approach fairness implementation.

The integration of these fairness management systems creates comprehensive equity frameworks. The combination of enhanced detection methods with sophisticated mitigation strategies shows how different fairness approaches complement each other. These integrations demonstrate how fairness management advances through careful combination of techniques while maintaining practical effectiveness.

These fairness patterns continue influencing AI

development. Understanding these advances provides crucial context for appreciating current capabilities while suggesting future directions. The success of different approaches demonstrates the importance of systematic innovation in advancing AI fairness.

Governance models in AI demonstrate sophisticated approaches to ethical oversight and control. Microsoft's Office of Responsible AI shows how organizations achieve comprehensive governance at scale. Their framework coordinates ethical oversight across numerous AI projects while maintaining consistent standards, demonstrating how modern organizations balance innovation with accountability, achieving substantial compliance with established ethical guidelines.

Framework development reveals careful attention to governance requirements. Google's AI Principles Board demonstrates how organizations enhance ethical oversight. Their implementation processes significant project reviews annually while maintaining transparent decision-making, documenting detailed rationales for each major ethical decision. These innovations transform how organizations approach AI governance.

Policy creation shows sophisticated approaches to ethical guidance. Google DeepMind's ethics board demonstrates how organizations implement comprehensive policy frameworks. Their system develops and updates ethical guidelines while maintaining practical applicability, processing regular policy decisions. These developments influence how organizations approach ethical policy-making.

Standard setting demonstrates careful attention to operational requirements. IBM's AI Ethics Board shows how organizations structure ethical standards. Their implementation guides developers while maintaining consistent ethical practices, achieving strong adherence to established principles. These advances establish new standards for AI governance.

Control systems reveal interesting patterns in oversight management. Amazon's AI review process demonstrates how organizations implement practical governance. Their system processes numerous model deployments while maintaining ethical compliance, significantly reducing ethical incidents through proactive oversight. These innovations establish new approaches to ethical control.

Oversight methods show sophisticated approaches to continuous monitoring. Meta's ethical AI monitoring demonstrates how organizations implement ongoing supervision. Their system tracks model interactions while enabling rapid intervention, achieving real-time ethical oversight across global operations. These developments influence how organizations approach ethical monitoring.

Evolution management reveals careful attention to governance adaptation. OpenAI's governance framework shows how organizations maintain ethical oversight as technology advances. Their implementation updates governance protocols while maintaining operational effectiveness, processing regular policy updates. These advances transform how organizations approach governance evolution.

Change management demonstrates sophisticated approaches to governance updates. Anthropic's ethical framework shows how organizations implement systematic improvements. Their system incorporates emerging ethical considerations while maintaining consistent standards, achieving rapid adoption of updated governance measures. These innovations influence how organizations approach governance changes.

The integration of these governance models creates comprehensive oversight frameworks. The combination of enhanced policy development with sophisticated monitoring systems shows how different governance approaches complement each other. These integrations demonstrate how governance models advance through careful combination of techniques while maintaining practical effectiveness.

These governance patterns continue influencing AI development. Understanding these advances provides crucial context for appreciating current capabilities while suggesting future directions. The success of different approaches demonstrates the importance of systematic innovation in advancing AI governance.

The trajectory of AI ethics reveals emerging patterns that suggest crucial directions for continued advancement. Google DeepMind's research into scalable oversight demonstrates how organizations approach enhanced ethical control. Their current development shows significant improvement in detection of potential ethical issues while reducing false positives, showing how development focuses on balancing sophisticated monitoring with practical implementation.

Technical evolution reveals careful attention to fundamental improvements. Google's research into verifiable AI demonstrates how organizations address core ethical challenges. Their implementation of constitutional AI principles achieves substantial improvement in alignment with ethical constraints while maintaining model performance. These developments show how organizations continue advancing capabilities while strengthening ethical foundations.

Safety advancement patterns show sophisticated approaches to risk management. Anthropic's research into AI safety demonstrates how organizations systematically enhance protective measures. Their current achievements in reducing unintended behaviors while maintaining model capabilities shows how development focuses on safety without compromising functionality.

Control development demonstrates careful attention to oversight requirements. Microsoft's research into AI governance shows how organizations improve ethical supervision. Their current implementation achieves enhanced detection of subtle ethical violations while processing numerous model decisions daily, demonstrating how development aims to broaden protection while maintaining operational efficiency.

Implementation growth reveals interesting patterns in practical application. IBM's research into ethical AI deployment shows how organizations explore new oversight methods. Their current development processes substantially reduce ethical incidents while handling increasing system complexity, demonstrating how development aims to enhance protection while maintaining scalability.

Operation standards reveal sophisticated approaches to ethical implementation. OpenAI's research into deployment protocols shows how organizations improve operational safety. Their current implementation achieves meaningful improvements in controlled release procedures while maintaining innovation pace, demonstrating how development focuses on practical considerations.

Quality systems demonstrate careful attention to ethical validation. Meta's research into automated ethical testing shows how organizations enhance quality assurance. Their current achievement in ethical violation detection while reducing assessment time demonstrates how development focuses on efficiency without compromising thoroughness.

Research directions reveal interesting patterns in ethical innovation. Stanford's HAI research shows how organizations approach emerging ethical challenges. Their current development in interpretable AI achieves competitive performance while maintaining transparent operation, demonstrating how research aims to address future challenges.

The synthesis of multiple advancement directions creates comprehensive improvement opportunities. The combination of enhanced safety measures with sophisticated oversight systems shows how different ethical approaches complement each other. These integrations demonstrate how future development may proceed through careful combination of advances while maintaining ethical integrity.

These directional patterns continue influencing ethical AI

development. Understanding these trends provides crucial context for appreciating future possibilities while maintaining practical perspective. The success of different approaches demonstrates the importance of systematic innovation in advancing AI ethics.

Our exploration of AI ethics at the frontier reveals the sophisticated evolution of responsible artificial intelligence. From Google's regular processing of ethical reviews to Microsoft's coordination of ethical oversight across global AI projects, we see how systematic innovation enables increasingly advanced ethical frameworks while maintaining practical implementation. For practitioners and organizations working with AI systems, these developments provide crucial insights into both current capabilities and responsible deployment approaches.

The advancement patterns we've examined demonstrate multiple paths for engaging with ethical AI development. Whether through Google DeepMind's reduction in unintended behaviors or IBM's AI Ethics Board processing regular reviews, organizations can choose approaches that align with their specific requirements and objectives. The success of different approaches shows how various development paths can effectively address distinct ethical challenges while maintaining operational effectiveness.

Implementation considerations continue influencing how organizations approach ethical AI deployment. Apple's processing of on-device AI operations and Meta's ethical monitoring of model interactions demonstrate how practical requirements shape ethical decisions. Understanding these relationships becomes crucial for organizations implementing AI systems, as deployment choices significantly influence ethical outcomes.

The relationship between capability and responsibility creates interesting opportunities for innovation. Anthropic's constitutional AI achieving strong adherence to ethical principles and OpenAI's extensive pre-release testing show

how thoughtful design enables meaningful improvements. These developments demonstrate the importance of understanding ethical trade-offs while suggesting approaches for enhancing AI safety and responsibility.

As we move forward to examine future horizons in our next chapter, we carry forward understanding of how ethical considerations shape technological advancement. The advanced approaches to AI ethics we've explored provide crucial context for understanding how responsible development influences future possibilities. For practitioners and organizations, this understanding becomes increasingly valuable as AI technology continues advancing.

Engage actively with these ethical developments, whether through implementation of governance frameworks or systematic evaluation of different approaches. Major AI organizations offer extensive resources for exploring ethical AI development, while specialized frameworks provide focused environments for specific applications. These resources offer excellent starting points for practical engagement with AI ethics.

The field of AI ethics continues evolving, offering new opportunities for innovation and implementation. By understanding current capabilities and emerging trends, practitioners and organizations can better position themselves to leverage advancing AI technologies responsibly. Explore these opportunities while maintaining awareness of how ethical considerations influence practical implementation success.

CHAPTER 16: FUTURE HORIZONS

The future of artificial intelligence represents a sophisticated convergence of technological advancement and ethical responsibility, building upon the principles we explored in our previous chapter. Google's development of next-generation AI architectures demonstrates how organizations are pushing the boundaries of possibility while maintaining responsible innovation. Their PaLM system processes language tasks with unprecedented efficiency while incorporating ethical constraints, showing how future development balances capability with responsibility.

The current landscape of AI innovation reveals remarkable progress across multiple dimensions. NVIDIA's advancement in AI hardware shows how organizations enhance computational capabilities through architectural innovation. Their H100 platform achieves substantial performance improvements over previous generations while reducing energy consumption, demonstrating how modern systems balance sophisticated processing with operational efficiency. These developments transform how organizations approach future AI implementation.

Implementation patterns reveal sophisticated approaches to scaling technology. Microsoft's Azure AI infrastructure demonstrates how organizations prepare for future demands. Their system processes vast numbers of AI operations daily while maintaining rapid response times, showing how future-ready platforms address both performance requirements and scalability needs. These innovations influence how organizations approach long-term AI development.

The relationship between research and practical application has grown increasingly sophisticated. Google DeepMind's approach to scientific AI shows how organizations bridge theoretical advancement with practical utility. Their systems achieve breakthrough results in protein folding and nuclear fusion research while maintaining practical applicability, suggesting new directions for AI application across domains.

Specialized applications continue emerging through focused innovation. Anthropic's development of increasingly sophisticated language models demonstrates how organizations address specific future challenges. Their implementation of constitutional AI shows how systems can maintain ethical alignment while pushing technical boundaries, processing numerous interactions daily with explicit safety constraints.

In this chapter, we explore the sophisticated landscape of AI's future, examining how different approaches enable continued advancement. From fundamental research to practical implementation, we'll investigate how AI continues evolving. This exploration reveals both current trajectories and emerging directions in AI development, providing crucial context for understanding future possibilities.

For practitioners and organizations implementing AI systems, understanding these future developments becomes increasingly important. The advances in AI capabilities influence every aspect of planning and preparation. As we proceed, we'll examine how different approaches address various challenges, offering insights valuable for those preparing for future AI technologies.

Technology trajectories in artificial intelligence demonstrate sophisticated patterns of advancement across multiple dimensions. NVIDIA's development of AI computing architecture shows how organizations achieve unprecedented processing capabilities. Their H100 platform achieves 4 petaflops of AI workloads while maintaining power efficiency, demonstrating how modern systems balance computational power with efficiency requirements.

Computational evolution reveals careful attention to processing advancement. Google's TPU v4 demonstrates how organizations enhance AI processing capabilities. Their implementation achieves 275 teraflops per chip while maintaining energy efficiency, processing AI workloads at unprecedented scales. These innovations transform how organizations approach computational requirements for future AI systems.

Architecture innovation shows sophisticated approaches to system design. AMD's CDNA 3 architecture demonstrates how organizations implement advanced processing structures. Their system achieves 47.9 teraflops with mixed precision while maintaining power efficiency, showing how future architectures balance performance with operational constraints. These developments influence how organizations approach hardware evolution.

Model development demonstrates careful attention to capability enhancement. Google DeepMind's latest research shows how organizations advance model architectures. Their implementation achieves substantial improvements in complex tasks while reducing computational requirements, establishing new benchmarks for model efficiency. These advances establish new standards for AI model development.

Training evolution reveals interesting patterns in learning optimization. Microsoft's implementation of distributed training demonstrates how organizations enhance model development. Their system significantly reduces training time while maintaining model quality, processing massive datasets across distributed infrastructure. These innovations establish new approaches to AI training.

Infrastructure growth shows sophisticated approaches to system scaling. AWS's AI infrastructure demonstrates how organizations implement future-ready platforms. Their system processes numerous model inferences per second while maintaining low latency, showing how modern platforms balance capability with responsiveness. These developments influence how organizations approach infrastructure planning.

Platform evolution demonstrates careful attention to service integration. IBM's AI platform shows how organizations implement comprehensive development environments. Their system coordinates numerous AI workloads while maintaining operational efficiency, achieving high availability across global deployments. These advances transform how organizations approach platform development.

Resource management reveals sophisticated approaches to optimization. Oracle's cloud AI infrastructure demonstrates how organizations handle complex resource allocation. Their implementation achieves significant improvements in resource utilization while maintaining performance standards, showing how future systems balance capability with efficiency. These innovations influence how organizations approach resource planning.

The integration of these technological trajectories creates comprehensive advancement frameworks. The combination of enhanced computational capabilities with sophisticated model development shows how different technological approaches complement each other. These integrations demonstrate how technology trajectories advance through careful combination of techniques while maintaining practical effectiveness.

These trajectory patterns continue influencing AI development. Understanding these advances provides crucial context for appreciating future possibilities while maintaining practical perspective. The success of different approaches demonstrates the importance of systematic innovation in advancing AI capabilities.

Application evolution in artificial intelligence demonstrates sophisticated approaches to practical implementation across diverse domains. Tesla's advancement in autonomous systems shows how organizations achieve complex real-world applications. Their self-driving technology processes numerous frames per second while maintaining safety standards across extensive miles driven, demonstrating how modern applications balance sophisticated capability with practical reliability.

Domain advancement reveals careful attention to industry-specific requirements. IBM's Watson for Healthcare demonstrates how organizations enhance specialized applications. Their system processes medical data from extensive patient records while maintaining high accuracy in clinical recommendations, showing how AI applications evolve to address complex professional needs. These innovations transform how organizations approach domain-specific AI implementation.

Service enhancement shows sophisticated approaches to capability delivery. Salesforce's Einstein platform demonstrates how organizations implement advanced business intelligence. Their system processes numerous AI predictions daily while maintaining consistent accuracy across diverse business scenarios. These developments influence how organizations approach service-based AI applications.

Solution development demonstrates careful attention to practical implementation. Siemens' industrial AI platform shows how organizations address manufacturing challenges. Their implementation substantially reduces production defects while improving efficiency across numerous production lines, establishing new standards for industrial AI applications. These advances establish new benchmarks for practical AI deployment.

Use case expansion reveals interesting patterns in application growth. Spotify's recommendation systems demonstrate how organizations enhance user experience. Their implementation processes music preferences for their global user base while maintaining personalized accuracy, suggesting how AI applications scale across massive user bases. These innovations establish new approaches to consumer AI applications.

Integration patterns show sophisticated approaches to capability combination. Adobe's Creative Cloud demonstrates how organizations implement creative AI applications. Their system processes numerous creative operations daily while maintaining artistic quality, showing how AI enhances professional workflows. These developments influence how organizations approach integrated AI solutions.

Implementation paths demonstrate careful attention to deployment requirements. Uber's AI platform shows how organizations handle complex operational scenarios. Their system manages numerous real-time decisions while maintaining service reliability across global operations. These advances transform how organizations approach large-scale AI implementation.

Service coordination reveals sophisticated approaches to system integration. Microsoft's Teams platform demonstrates how organizations implement AI-enhanced collaboration. Their system processes extensive meeting minutes while providing real-time AI features, showing how applications evolve to support modern work patterns. These innovations influence how organizations approach collaborative AI applications.

The integration of these application evolutions creates comprehensive solution frameworks. The combination of enhanced domain capabilities with sophisticated service delivery shows how different application approaches complement each other. These integrations demonstrate how applications advance through careful combination of techniques while maintaining practical effectiveness.

These application patterns continue influencing AI development. Understanding these advances provides crucial context for appreciating future possibilities while maintaining practical perspective. The success of different approaches demonstrates the importance of systematic innovation in advancing AI applications.

Research directions in artificial intelligence demonstrate sophisticated approaches to advancing fundamental capabilities. Google DeepMind's research into artificial general intelligence shows how organizations pursue breakthrough developments. Their latest research achieves significant advances in multi-task learning while maintaining systematic approaches, processing complex problems across diverse domains with unprecedented flexibility.

Core advancement reveals careful attention to fundamental understanding. Google Research's work on large language models demonstrates how organizations enhance basic capabilities. Their PaLM architecture achieves breakthrough performance in reasoning tasks while maintaining efficient computational requirements, showing how fundamental research drives practical advancement. These innovations transform how organizations approach AI research.

Theoretical progress shows sophisticated approaches to knowledge development. OpenAI's research into scaling laws demonstrates how organizations understand AI fundamentals. Their investigations reveal crucial relationships between model size, computation, and performance while providing practical guidelines for development. These developments influence how organizations approach theoretical advancement.

Method development demonstrates careful attention to implementation approaches. Anthropic's constitutional AI research shows how organizations advance development techniques. Their implementation achieves substantial improvements in model reliability while maintaining performance capabilities, establishing new standards for AI development methods. These advances establish new benchmarks for research methodology.

Applied innovation reveals interesting patterns in practical research. Microsoft Research's work on enterprise AI demonstrates how organizations bridge theory and practice. Their implementations achieve significant improvement in business applications while maintaining theoretical rigor, showing how research translates into practical solutions. These innovations establish new approaches to applied research.

Integration focus shows sophisticated approaches to combining capabilities. Meta AI's research into multimodal systems demonstrates how organizations advance integrated understanding. Their systems process complex combinations of text, images, and audio while maintaining coherent comprehension, showing how research enables sophisticated combinations of capabilities. These developments influence how organizations approach integrated AI research.

Concept evolution demonstrates careful attention to understanding advancement. Stanford's AI Lab shows how organizations pursue fundamental breakthroughs. Their research into causal reasoning achieves significant advances in AI understanding while maintaining practical applicability. These advances transform how organizations approach conceptual development.

Knowledge expansion reveals sophisticated approaches to learning enhancement. Carnegie Mellon's AI research demonstrates how organizations advance learning capabilities. Their work achieves substantial improvements in knowledge acquisition while reducing training requirements, showing how research enhances fundamental AI capabilities. These innovations influence how organizations approach knowledge development.

The integration of these research directions creates comprehensive advancement frameworks. The combination of enhanced theoretical understanding with sophisticated practical applications shows how different research approaches complement each other. These integrations demonstrate how research advances through careful combination of techniques while maintaining scientific rigor.

These research patterns continue influencing AI development. Understanding these advances provides crucial context for appreciating future possibilities while maintaining practical perspective. The success of different approaches demonstrates the importance of systematic innovation in advancing AI research.

Implementation paths in future AI demonstrate sophisticated approaches to deploying advanced capabilities. Microsoft's Azure AI shows how organizations achieve large-scale deployment success. Their platform processes numerous AI predictions daily while maintaining high reliability, demonstrating how modern systems balance sophisticated deployment with operational stability across global infrastructure.

Deployment evolution reveals careful attention to rollout requirements. Google Cloud's Vertex AI demonstrates how organizations enhance implementation strategies. Their system enables deployment of thousands of models while significantly reducing deployment time, showing how future implementations balance rapid deployment with quality assurance. These innovations transform how organizations approach AI deployment.

Operation enhancement shows sophisticated approaches to system management. AWS's SageMaker demonstrates how organizations implement comprehensive operational control. Their platform manages numerous model endpoints while maintaining consistent performance, processing extensive predictions monthly. These developments influence how organizations approach operational excellence.

Service launch demonstrates careful attention to release management. Salesforce's Einstein platform shows how organizations handle feature deployment. Their implementation achieves substantial improvements in deployment cycles while maintaining quality standards, establishing new benchmarks for service rollout. These advances establish new standards for AI service deployment.

Integration methods reveal interesting patterns in system combination. Oracle's Cloud Infrastructure demonstrates how organizations implement unified platforms. Their system coordinates thousands of AI workloads while maintaining operational efficiency, showing how future platforms enable sophisticated service integration. These innovations establish new approaches to implementation integration.

Control systems show sophisticated approaches to deployment management. IBM's Cloud Pak for Data demonstrates how organizations implement deployment controls. Their platform manages complex AI deployments while maintaining security and compliance, processing numerous transactions daily. These developments influence how organizations approach implementation control.

Scaling methods demonstrate careful attention to growth requirements. NVIDIA's AI Enterprise platform shows how organizations handle expansion needs. Their implementation enables systematic growth while maintaining performance, supporting thousands of concurrent AI workloads. These advances transform how organizations approach implementation scaling.

Resource optimization reveals sophisticated approaches to efficiency management. AMD's ROCm platform demonstrates how organizations enhance resource utilization. Their system achieves significant improvements in resource efficiency while maintaining computational performance, showing how implementations balance capability with resource constraints. These innovations influence how organizations approach resource management.

The integration of these implementation paths creates comprehensive deployment frameworks. The combination of enhanced deployment strategies with sophisticated operational management shows how different implementation approaches complement each other. These integrations demonstrate how implementation advances through careful combination of techniques while maintaining practical effectiveness.

These implementation patterns continue influencing AI deployment. Understanding these advances provides crucial context for appreciating future possibilities while maintaining practical perspective. The success of different approaches demonstrates the importance of systematic innovation in advancing AI implementation.

Development considerations in future AI demonstrate sophisticated approaches to ensuring sustainable advancement. OpenAI's phased development strategy shows how organizations achieve responsible progress. Their implementation of tiered model releases, processing extensive testing scenarios before deployment while maintaining rigorous safety standards, demonstrates how modern organizations balance rapid development with careful consideration.

Resource planning reveals careful attention to capacity requirements. Google's TPU pod architecture demonstrates how organizations enhance computational planning. Their system achieves exaflop-scale processing capabilities while substantially reducing energy consumption, showing how future development balances processing power with sustainability. These innovations transform how organizations approach resource allocation.

Asset management shows sophisticated approaches to resource optimization. Meta's AI infrastructure demonstrates how organizations implement efficient resource utilization. Their system processes numerous AI operations daily while achieving significant improvements in resource efficiency, managing complex workloads across global data centers. These developments influence how organizations approach infrastructure planning.

Risk management demonstrates careful attention to safety requirements. Google DeepMind's safety protocols show how organizations handle development risks. Their implementation achieves comprehensive risk assessment while maintaining development momentum, processing regular safety evaluations. These advances establish new standards for AI development safety.

Issue identification reveals interesting patterns in problem prevention. Anthropic's development framework demonstrates how organizations implement proactive protection. Their system identifies potential issues effectively while enabling rapid development, showing how future systems balance safety with innovation. These innovations establish new approaches to risk mitigation.

Quality assurance shows sophisticated approaches to validation. Microsoft's AI testing framework demonstrates how organizations implement comprehensive quality control. Their platform processes numerous test cases daily while maintaining rigorous standards, achieving extensive validation coverage. These developments influence how organizations approach development quality.

Performance monitoring demonstrates careful attention to operational excellence. Amazon's AWS monitoring systems show how organizations maintain high standards. Their implementation tracks extensive metrics while enabling real-time intervention, processing performance data across global operations. These advances transform how organizations approach quality maintenance.

Validation approaches reveal sophisticated methods for ensuring reliability. IBM's AI validation framework demonstrates how organizations verify system behavior. Their implementation achieves comprehensive testing while maintaining development efficiency, processing numerous validation scenarios daily. These innovations influence how organizations approach development validation.

The integration of these development considerations creates comprehensive advancement frameworks. The combination of enhanced resource planning with sophisticated risk management shows how different development approaches complement each other. These integrations demonstrate how development considerations advance through careful combination of techniques while maintaining practical effectiveness.

These development patterns continue influencing AI advancement. Understanding these considerations provides crucial context for appreciating future possibilities while maintaining practical perspective. The success of different approaches demonstrates the importance of systematic innovation in advancing AI development.

Future preparation in artificial intelligence demonstrates sophisticated approaches to anticipating technological advancement. NVIDIA's development of next-generation AI architectures shows how organizations prepare for future computing demands. Their Grace Hopper superchip architecture achieves unprecedented AI processing capabilities while maintaining energy efficiency, demonstrating how modern organizations balance future readiness with practical constraints.

Readiness planning reveals careful attention to capability requirements. Google's quantum computing research demonstrates how organizations prepare for emerging technologies. Their development of error-corrected quantum systems while maintaining classical computing integration shows how future preparation balances innovation with practical implementation. These approaches transform how organizations plan for technological evolution.

System readiness shows sophisticated approaches to infrastructure preparation. Microsoft's cloud infrastructure demonstrates how organizations implement future-ready platforms. Their system supports processing requirements projected for coming years while maintaining scalability, handling workloads at unprecedented scales. These developments influence how organizations approach infrastructure planning.

Adaptation strategies demonstrate careful attention to evolutionary requirements. IBM's hybrid cloud architecture shows how organizations prepare for changing needs. Their implementation enables flexible resource allocation while maintaining operational consistency, processing diverse workloads across multiple computing paradigms. These advances establish new standards for technological adaptation.

Change management reveals interesting patterns in evolutionary response. Amazon's AWS infrastructure demonstrates how organizations handle technological transformation. Their system enables rapid adaptation to new computing requirements while maintaining service reliability, showing how future systems balance flexibility with stability. These innovations establish new approaches to managing technological change.

Progress adaptation shows sophisticated approaches to capability enhancement. Meta's AI research infrastructure demonstrates how organizations implement scalable advancement. Their platform enables systematic capability growth while maintaining operational efficiency, processing increasingly complex workloads. These developments influence how organizations approach technological progress.

Innovation management demonstrates careful attention to development direction. Intel's research into neuromorphic computing shows how organizations guide future advancement. Their implementation achieves breakthrough capabilities in brain-inspired computing while maintaining practical applicability. These advances transform how organizations approach innovation planning.

Growth direction reveals sophisticated approaches to

capability expansion. AMD's processor architecture development demonstrates how organizations plan technological evolution. Their implementation achieves significant advances in computing capability while maintaining backward compatibility, showing how future systems balance innovation with practical needs. These innovations influence how organizations approach technological growth.

The integration of these preparation approaches creates comprehensive readiness frameworks. The combination of enhanced planning with sophisticated adaptation strategies shows how different preparation approaches complement each other. These integrations demonstrate how future preparation advances through careful combination of techniques while maintaining practical effectiveness.

These preparation patterns continue influencing AI development. Understanding these advances provides crucial context for appreciating future possibilities while maintaining practical perspective. The success of different approaches demonstrates the importance of systematic innovation in advancing AI capabilities.

The exploration of future horizons reveals the sophisticated evolution of artificial intelligence capabilities. From NVIDIA's Grace Hopper architecture achieving unprecedented processing efficiency to Google's quantum computing research pushing technological boundaries, systematic innovation enables increasingly advanced AI systems while maintaining practical implementation. For practitioners and organizations working with AI, these developments provide crucial insights into both current capabilities and future preparation.

The advancement patterns examined demonstrate multiple paths for engaging with future AI technology. Whether through Microsoft's extensive daily AI predictions or Google DeepMind's breakthrough achievements in multi-domain learning, organizations can choose approaches that align with their specific requirements and objectives. The success of different approaches shows how various development paths can effectively address distinct challenges while maintaining operational effectiveness.

Implementation considerations continue influencing how organizations approach AI advancement. IBM's hybrid cloud architecture and Amazon's AWS infrastructure demonstrate how practical requirements shape technological decisions. Understanding these relationships becomes crucial for organizations implementing AI systems, as deployment choices significantly influence future success. The careful balance between innovation and stability remains essential for sustainable advancement.

The relationship between current capabilities and future potential creates interesting opportunities for innovation. Meta's AI research infrastructure achieving systematic capability growth and Intel's neuromorphic computing advances show how thoughtful design enables significant improvements. These developments demonstrate the importance of understanding technological trade-offs while suggesting approaches for enhancing AI capabilities.

This trilogy's progression from fundamental principles through practical applications to cutting-edge developments has revealed how artificial intelligence continues evolving while maintaining practical utility. For practitioners and organizations, this comprehensive understanding becomes increasingly valuable as AI technology advances. The integration of theory, practice, and innovation provides a robust foundation for future development.

Organizations and practitioners engaging with these technological developments, whether through experimental implementation or systematic evaluation of different approaches, will find extensive resources available. Major technology providers offer comprehensive tools for exploring advanced AI capabilities, while specialized platforms provide focused environments for specific applications. These resources serve as excellent starting points for practical engagement with AI advancement.

The field of artificial intelligence continues evolving, offering new opportunities for innovation and implementation. By understanding current capabilities and emerging trends, practitioners and organizations can better position themselves to leverage advancing AI technologies. The future holds boundless possibilities for those ready to explore them while maintaining awareness of how technological advancement influences practical implementation success.

This trilogy's conclusion marks not an endpoint but a milestone in the ongoing journey of artificial intelligence. The continuous evolution of AI technology ensures that learning and adaptation remain essential for success. The spirit of exploration and innovation continues as artificial intelligence advances toward new horizons.

GIL OREN

AI GLOSSARY: BIT BY BIT

Welcome to the AI Glossary: Bit By Bit. This glossary breaks down essential AI and machine learning terms, from basic data units to advanced concepts. Whether you're new to AI or an expert, the following definitions are provided to illuminate your journey into the world of artificial intelligence.

A

A/B Testing - A method to compare two versions of a model or algorithm by testing them on separate datasets to identify the more effective one.

AI Alignment - Ensuring that AI systems' goals and behaviors align with human values and objectives.

AI Ethics - The study of ethical issues in the design, development, and deployment of AI systems.

AI Model - A mathematical or computational structure that

an AI system uses to solve problems or make predictions.

AI Platform - Software that provides tools and environments for developing, training, and deploying AI models.

AI Safety - Research aimed at ensuring that AI systems operate safely and without unintended consequences.

AI System - A combination of hardware and software components used to perform tasks typically requiring human intelligence.

AI Tool - Software or utility that supports AI development, testing, or deployment.

Activation Function - A function used in neural networks to introduce non-linearity, enabling the model to learn from complex patterns.

Active Learning - A machine learning method where the model selectively queries the most informative data points for labeling.

Actor-Critic Model (Reinforcement Learning) - A framework in reinforcement learning where the 'actor' updates policies, and the 'critic' evaluates the action.

Adversarial Attack - A type of attack where inputs are modified to fool AI models into making incorrect predictions.

Adversarial Example - Data that has been intentionally perturbed to cause an AI system to make mistakes.

Algorithm - A set of rules or processes followed in problem-solving or computation, used by AI systems to make decisions.

Anomaly Detection - Identifying patterns or data points that deviate significantly from the norm.

Artificial General Intelligence (AGI) - A form of AI with the ability to understand, learn, and apply intelligence across a broad range of tasks, similar to human intelligence.

Artificial Intelligence (AI) - The simulation of human intelligence by machines, particularly in problem-solving, learning, and decision-making.

Artificial Neural Network (ANN) - A computational

model inspired by the way biological neural networks in the human brain process information.

Attention Head (Deep Learning, Transformers) - A component in transformer models that processes input data to focus on relevant aspects for making predictions.

Attention Mechanism - A technique that enables models to focus on specific parts of the input data when making decisions.

Augmented Reality (AR) - An interactive experience where real-world environments are enhanced by computer-generated perceptual information.

Automated Machine Learning (AutoML) - The process of automating the end-to-end process of applying machine learning to real-world problems.

Autonomous - Refers to systems or vehicles capable of making decisions and operating independently without human intervention.

Autonomous Vehicle - A vehicle capable of sensing its environment and navigating without human input, typically using AI systems.

B

BCI (Brain-Computer Interface) - a technology that enables direct communication between the brain and external devices, often using AI to interpret brain signals.

Backpropagation - An algorithm used to calculate gradients in neural networks during the training phase to minimize the error.

Backward Chaining - A reasoning method that starts with a goal and works backward to determine the necessary conditions to achieve that goal.

Batch Normalization (Deep Learning) - A technique that normalizes inputs in a neural network to speed up training and improve performance.

Bayesian Network - A graphical model representing probabilistic relationships among a set of variables.

Bias - Systematic error in AI models, often caused by unbalanced datasets or faulty assumptions.

Bias-Variance Tradeoff (Machine Learning) - The tradeoff between the error introduced by the bias of the model and the variance in the model's predictions.

Big Data - Large datasets that are complex and require advanced methods for processing and analysis.

Biometric AI - AI systems that analyze and interpret biological data, such as fingerprints, facial recognition, or voice recognition.

Bit - The smallest unit of data in computing, represented as 0 or 1.

Bounding Box - A rectangular box used in computer vision to define the location of an object in an image or video.

Byte - A data unit typically consisting of 8 bits, representing a character in computing.

C

C - A general-purpose, procedural computer programming language supporting structured programming.

C# - A modern, object-oriented programming language developed by Microsoft as part of its .NET framework.

C++ - An extension of the C programming language that adds object-oriented features.

CSS (Cascading Style Sheets) - A style sheet language used for describing the presentation of a document written in HTML or XML.

Capsule Network (ANN, Deep Learning) - A type of neural network designed to handle complex hierarchical relationships more effectively than traditional convolutional networks.

Central Processing Unit (CPU) - The primary component of a computer responsible for executing instructions from programs. In AI, the CPU handles general-purpose processing tasks and is used in training and running machine learning models, though it is typically slower for parallel tasks compared to GPUs or TPUs.

Chatbot - A program that uses AI to simulate conversations with users, often used in customer service or personal assistants.

Classification - The process of categorizing data into predefined classes.

Clustering - A technique used to group similar data points together based on certain features.

Cognitive Computing - AI systems that aim to mimic human cognitive functions such as reasoning and learning.

Computer Vision - A field of AI that enables machines to interpret and make decisions based on visual data.

Computer-Generated Imagery (CGI) - The use of AI and other technologies to create images and animations for media and entertainment.

Convergence (Optimization in ML) - The point during optimization when the model parameters stop changing significantly and the learning process stabilizes.

Convolutional Neural Network (CNN) - A deep learning algorithm commonly used in image recognition and processing tasks.

Cross-Entropy Loss (Loss Function) - A loss function commonly used in classification tasks, measuring the difference between predicted probabilities and actual labels.

Cross-validation - A technique for assessing how a machine learning model will generalize to an independent dataset by partitioning the data into training and testing sets.

Crowdsourcing (Data Collection) - The practice of outsourcing tasks, such as data labeling, to a large group of people or the public.

D

Data Augmentation - A technique to increase the diversity of a training dataset by applying random transformations to the data.

Data Drift - Changes in data distributions over time that

can negatively affect model performance.

Data Governance - The set of policies and procedures that manage the availability, integrity, security, and usability of data in an organization. In AI, strong data governance ensures that data used for training and decision-making is reliable, secure, and compliant with relevant laws and standards.

Data Labeling - The process of assigning meaningful labels to raw data for training machine learning models.

Data Mining - The process of discovering patterns and insights from large datasets.

Data Preprocessing - The stage where data is cleaned and transformed before being used to train machine learning models.

Decision Boundary - A surface that separates different classes in a classification problem.

Decision Tree - A supervised learning algorithm used for both classification and regression tasks by splitting data into branches.

Deep Learning - A subset of machine learning that involves neural networks with many layers, enabling models to learn from large datasets.

Deep Q-Network (DQN) (Reinforcement Learning) - A model-free reinforcement learning algorithm combining Q-learning with deep learning.

Deepfake - AI-generated or altered media content (typically video or audio) designed to look and sound realistic.

Dimensionality Reduction - The process of reducing the number of features in a dataset while retaining its essential characteristics.

Dropout (Regularization in Neural Networks) - A technique to prevent overfitting by randomly dropping units from the neural network during training.

E

Edge AI - AI that processes data locally on devices rather than relying on cloud computing, reducing latency.

Embedding - A representation of data in a lower-dimensional space used in machine learning tasks such as NLP.

Embodied AI (Robotics, AI Systems) - AI systems that are physically integrated into robots or devices, enabling interaction with the physical world.

End-to-End Learning (Neural Networks) - A learning approach where a system is trained directly on the input-output mapping without intermediate steps.

Ensemble Learning - A technique that combines multiple machine learning models to improve performance.

Epoch - A full iteration over the entire dataset during the training phase of a machine learning model.

Evolutionary Algorithm - Optimization algorithms inspired by the process of natural selection.

Exabyte (EB) - A data unit equivalent to 1,024 petabytes.

Expert System - An AI system that mimics the decision-making ability of a human expert.

Explainable AI (XAI) - AI systems designed to provide human-understandable explanations for their decisions and outputs.

F

Feature Engineering - The process of selecting, modifying, and creating features for improving machine learning models.

Feature Extraction - The process of transforming raw data into a set of features to be used by a machine learning model.

Federated Learning - A technique where models are trained across multiple devices without sharing raw data, improving privacy.

Few-Shot Learning - A type of machine learning where a model is trained with very few labeled examples.

Fine-tuning - Adjusting the parameters of a pre-trained model to apply it to a specific task.

Firmware - A specialized type of software that is embedded directly into hardware devices to control their functions.

Firmware is typically stored in non-volatile memory and manages the basic operations of hardware, including devices used in AI systems, such as sensors and robotics.

Flask - A lightweight Python web application framework.

Fuzzy Logic - A form of logic used in AI that allows reasoning with uncertain or approximate values, rather than precise ones.

G

Generative AI - AI systems capable of generating new data, such as images, text, or music, that resemble human-created content.

Generative Adversarial Network (GAN) - A model consisting of two networks, a generator and a discriminator, that learn together to generate realistic data.

Genetic Algorithm - An optimization algorithm based on principles of natural selection and genetics.

Gigabyte (GB) - A unit of data equivalent to 1,024 megabytes.

Gradient Clipping (Optimization in Deep Learning) - A technique used to prevent exploding gradients during the training of neural networks.

Gradient Descent - An optimization algorithm used to minimize a loss function by iteratively moving in the direction of the steepest descent.

Graph Neural Network - A type of neural network that directly operates on graph structures, enabling learning on data that is structured as graphs.

Graphics Processing Unit (GPU) - A specialized processor designed for parallel processing tasks, originally used for rendering graphics. In AI, GPUs are widely used for training deep learning models due to their ability to handle multiple computations simultaneously, significantly speeding up the training process.

H

HTML (Hypertext Markup Language) - The standard markup language for creating web pages and web applications.

Hallucination (in AI) - When an AI model generates output (such as a response or image) that is factually incorrect or nonsensical.

Hardware - The physical components of a computer or device that perform computational tasks. In AI, hardware includes processors (like CPUs, GPUs, TPUs), storage, sensors, and other equipment that provides the computational power needed to train models and execute AI algorithms.

Heuristic - A problem-solving approach that uses practical methods or rules of thumb for making decisions.

Hybrid AI - Systems combining symbolic reasoning and neural networks to leverage the strengths of both approaches.

Hyperparameter - Parameters in machine learning models that are set before training and not learned from the data.

Hyperparameter Tuning - The process of adjusting hyperparameters to optimize the performance of a machine learning model.

I

Imbalanced Dataset - A dataset where some classes are significantly over- or under-represented, which can affect model performance.

Inference - The process of making predictions using a trained machine learning model.

Interpretable Machine Learning (IML) - Techniques that enable understanding and explaining how machine learning models make decisions.

J

JavaScript - A high-level, interpreted programming language that is a core technology of the World Wide Web.

K

K-Means Clustering - A clustering algorithm that partitions data into K distinct groups based on similarity.

K-Nearest Neighbors (KNN) - A machine learning algorithm that classifies data points based on the closest labeled examples in the dataset.

Kernel Method - Techniques in machine learning that use a kernel function to enable algorithms to operate in a high-dimensional space.

Kilobyte (KB) - A data unit equivalent to 1,024 bytes.

Knowledge Base - A structured database of information used to support AI systems, such as expert systems.

Knowledge Distillation - A technique in which a smaller model is trained to replicate the behavior of a larger, more complex model.

L

Large Language Model (LLM) - A deep learning model trained on vast amounts of text data to understand and generate human-like text.

Learning Rate (Gradient Descent) - A hyperparameter that determines the step size for updating weights in gradient-based optimization.

Long Short-Term Memory (LSTM) - A type of recurrent neural network capable of learning long-term dependencies in sequential data.

Loss Function (Optimization) - A function used to measure the error or difference between the predicted output of a model and the actual outcome.

M

Machine Learning (ML) - A subset of AI that involves systems learning patterns from data and improving over time without being explicitly programmed.

Machine Learning Operations (MLOps) - A set of practices for deploying, managing, and monitoring machine learning models in production.

Markov Decision Process (MDP) (Reinforcement Learning) - A framework for modeling decision-making where outcomes are partly random and partly under the control of an agent.

Megabyte (MB) - A data unit equivalent to 1,024 kilobytes.

Meta-Learning - A machine learning approach where models learn how to learn, improving their adaptability to new tasks.

Model - A mathematical representation of a system, process, or behavior that can make predictions or decisions based on input data.

Model Compression - Techniques to reduce the size and complexity of machine learning models while maintaining performance.

Monte Carlo Method (Statistical Learning) - A computational algorithm that uses random sampling to solve problems that might be deterministic in principle.

Multi-Agent System - A system composed of multiple interacting intelligent agents that work together or compete to achieve goals.

Multi-Task Learning - A machine learning approach where a model is trained on multiple related tasks simultaneously, sharing knowledge across tasks.

MySQL - An open-source relational database management system that uses Structured Query Language (SQL).

N

Natural Language Generation (NLG) - The use of AI to generate human-like language based on structured data or inputs.

Natural Language Processing (NLP) - A field of AI that focuses on the interaction between computers and human language.

Natural Language Understanding (NLU) - A subfield of NLP focused on understanding the meaning and context of human language.

Neural Architecture Search - The process of automating the design of neural network architectures using machine learning.

Neural Tangent Kernel (Theoretical ML) - A theoretical framework for understanding the behavior of neural networks during training.

Neurosymbolic AI - An approach combining neural networks and symbolic reasoning to enhance the interpretability of AI systems.

Node.js - An open-source, cross-platform JavaScript runtime environment that executes JavaScript code outside of a web browser.

Noisy Student (Data Augmentation) - A technique that improves the accuracy of models by training them on both labeled and noisy augmented data.

O

One-Shot Learning - A form of learning where a model can recognize new objects or patterns after being trained on a single example.

Ontology - A structured representation of knowledge and concepts used in AI for reasoning about relationships and entities.

Open Source - Software or models made available with a license that allows anyone to view, modify, and distribute the source code. Open-source AI tools are often free to use, though they may have associated costs for implementation or support. These tools promote collaboration and transparency in the development of AI technologies.

Optimizer (Deep Learning) - Algorithms or methods used to minimize the loss function and improve the accuracy of a model during training.

Overfitting - A scenario where a machine learning model learns too closely from training data, performing poorly on unseen data.

P

PHP - A server-side scripting language designed for web development.

Parameter - Variables in a machine learning model that are learned from data during training, such as weights in a neural network.

Pattern Recognition - The ability of AI models to recognize patterns or regularities in data.

Perceptron - The simplest type of artificial neural network, primarily used in binary classification tasks.

Permutation Importance - A technique for measuring the importance of features in a machine learning model by evaluating the change in model performance after shuffling each feature.

Petabyte (PB) - A unit of data equal to 1,024 terabytes.

Predictive Analytics - Using statistical techniques and machine learning to predict future outcomes based on historical data.

Preprocessing - Preparing and transforming raw data into a suitable format for training machine learning models.

Proprietary - Software, models, or systems that are owned by a company or individual and have restrictions on access, usage, and modification. Proprietary AI tools may require a license or payment to use and are typically closed to public modification and distribution. Access is often limited based on a pay-to-use model, though some proprietary tools may offer free tiers with limited functionality.

Pruning - A technique to reduce the size of a neural network by eliminating weights or neurons that contribute little to model accuracy.

Python - A high-level, interpreted programming language known for its simplicity and readability, widely used in AI, data science, and web development.

Q

Quantum Computing - A type of computing that leverages

quantum mechanics to perform calculations at exponentially faster rates than classical computers.

R

Random Forest (Ensemble Learning) - An ensemble learning technique that uses multiple decision trees to improve prediction accuracy.

React - A JavaScript library for building user interfaces, particularly single-page applications.

Recurrent Neural Network (RNN) - A type of neural network designed to handle sequential data such as time series or text.

Regression - A type of supervised learning used to predict continuous outcomes based on input features.

Regularization (Preventing Overfitting) - Techniques used to reduce overfitting by adding constraints to a machine learning model.

Reinforcement Learning - A machine learning paradigm where agents learn to make decisions through rewards and punishments.

Robotics - The use of AI in designing and building machines that can perform tasks typically carried out by humans.

Rule-Based System - AI systems that apply a set of predefined rules to reach conclusions or make decisions.

S

SQL (Structured Query Language) - A standardized language used for managing and manipulating relational databases.

Self-Supervised Learning (Machine Learning) - A learning approach where models learn from unlabeled data by creating their own labels.

Semantic Analysis - The process of understanding the meaning and context of language in AI and NLP tasks.

Sentiment Analysis - An NLP technique used to determine the sentiment (positive, negative, neutral) expressed in text.

Software - Programs and applications that run on hardware to perform specific tasks. In AI, software refers to the code, frameworks, and models that enable data processing, model training, and decision-making. AI software can be proprietary or open-source and may operate on various types of hardware.

Sparsity (ML models) - A concept in machine learning where only a small percentage of features are relevant to the model's output.

Supervised Learning - A type of machine learning where the model is trained on labeled data, learning to predict output based on input features.

Support Vector Machine (SVM) - A supervised learning algorithm used for classification and regression tasks by finding the hyperplane that best separates data points.

Swarm Intelligence (Multi-Agent Systems) - A collective behavior of decentralized, self-organized agents used in AI to solve complex problems.

Synthetic Data - Artificially generated data used to train AI models, often used when real-world data is scarce or sensitive.

T

Tensor Processing Unit (TPU) - A specialized hardware accelerator designed by Google specifically for AI and machine learning tasks, particularly for deep learning and neural networks. TPUs are optimized for TensorFlow workloads and offer faster computation than CPUs and GPUs for specific AI tasks, especially in large-scale training.

Terabyte (TB) - A unit of data storage equal to 1,024 gigabytes.

Tokenization (NLP) - The process of breaking text into smaller units, such as words or subwords, for analysis in NLP models.

Transfer Learning - A technique where a pre-trained model is adapted to perform a new, but related, task.

Transformer - A deep learning architecture designed for tasks such as NLP that relies on attention mechanisms to process input data.

Turing Test - A test proposed by Alan Turing to evaluate a machine's ability to exhibit intelligent behavior indistinguishable from that of a human.

U

UX - Short for User Experience, refers to the design and interaction of users with a product or service, especially important in AI system interfaces.

Unsupervised Learning - A machine learning paradigm where models are trained on unlabeled data to find patterns or structure.

V

Validation Set - A subset of the data used to tune model parameters and avoid overfitting during the training process.

Vector - A mathematical representation of data points in machine learning and deep learning.

Virtual Reality (VR) - The use of computer technology to create simulated, immersive environments.

Voice Recognition - AI technology that identifies and processes human speech for various applications.

W

WordPress - An open-source content management system based on PHP and MySQL.

X

XML (eXtensible Markup Language) - A markup language that defines a set of rules for encoding documents in a format that is both human-readable and machine-readable.

Y

Yottabyte (YB) - The largest standard unit of data storage, equivalent to 1,024 zettabytes.

Z

Zero-Shot Learning (Machine Learning) - A learning approach where the model makes predictions on classes or tasks it has not been explicitly trained on.

Zettabyte (ZB) - A data unit equivalent to 1,024 exabytes.

ABOUT NEWBITS.AI

The newbits.ai ecosystem emerged from a simple yet powerful vision: to demystify artificial intelligence and make this complex technological frontier accessible to everyone. This dynamic learning environment, where learning, discovery, and innovation flourish together, was created by an AI enthusiast and curator, who authored the *NewBits AI Trilogy*: *AI Basics: The Fundamentals*, *AI Toolbox: Empowering the Learner*, and *AI Frontier: Navigating the Cutting Edge*. This digital nexus, accessible through the internet domain newbits.ai, mirrors the books' mission to bridge the gap between cutting edge AI technology and curious minds at all levels.

At the foundation of newbits.ai stands the *AI Solutions* Marketplace, a carefully curated space where theory meets practical application. Here, visitors discover a rich tapestry of artificial intelligence tools spanning six essential categories: Language, Data, Audio/Vision, Healthcare, Robotics, and Gaming. Within Language, users find natural language processing tools and translation systems. The Data category offers analytics platforms and data management solutions.

Audio/Vision presents solutions for speech recognition, image processing, computer vision, and visualization tools. Healthcare showcases medical imaging and diagnostic innovations. Robotics features autonomous systems and control software, while Gaming presents AI driven development tools and virtual reality platforms.

The marketplace distinguishes between models and tools and platforms, allowing users to focus their search based on their specific needs. Visitors can easily navigate between open source and proprietary solutions, ensuring they find resources that align with their preferences and requirements. Through intuitive browsing and filtering options, users can refine their search by category, solution type, and featured solutions, transforming what could be an overwhelming journey into a streamlined discovery process.

Each listing offers detailed insights and community reviews, ensuring that whether someone is taking their first steps into AI implementation or seeking advanced platforms for complex projects, they can make informed decisions with confidence.

Beyond the marketplace lies the *AI Hub*, a vibrant community space that pulses with the energy of shared discovery. This dynamic network spans across nine distinct platforms: Reddit, YouTube, Spotify, Facebook, X (formerly Twitter), LinkedIn, Medium, Quora, and Discord. Through thoughtful discussions on Reddit, engaging content on YouTube and Spotify, industry insights on LinkedIn, enriching articles on Medium, knowledge sharing on Quora, community building on Facebook, and real time exchanges on Discord and X, the Hub weaves together a tapestry of knowledge where every voice contributes to our collective understanding. Here, beginners find mentorship, experts share insights, and innovations spark from the collision of curious minds.

The *AI Ed* page serves as the gateway to our signature educational content, featuring the podcast series *AI Ed: From*

Bits to Breakthroughs. Here, visitors can access a carefully structured journey that mirrors the natural progression of learning found in our book trilogy. The series begins with foundational concepts in *AI Basics: The Fundamentals*, advances through practical applications in *AI Toolbox: Empowering the Learner*, and ultimately explores the cutting edge of possibility in *AI Frontier: Navigating the Cutting Edge*. Each episode builds upon the last, creating a comprehensive narrative that guides listeners from their first encounter with artificial intelligence through to the most advanced concepts shaping our future.

Supporting this educational journey, the *AI Glossary: Bit by Bit* serves as a trusted companion, illuminating the path from basic terminology to complex concepts. This carefully crafted resource grows alongside our community, ensuring that the language of artificial intelligence remains accessible to all who wish to learn.

Together, these elements form something greater than their individual parts, standing as a testament to the power of accessible education, community collaboration, and practical implementation. Just as the book trilogy illuminates the path from fundamental concepts to cutting edge innovations, newbits.ai represents an unwavering commitment to transforming the complex world of artificial intelligence into a journey of discovery that anyone can undertake. As artificial intelligence continues to reshape our world, this commitment ensures that everyone has the opportunity to understand, implement, and innovate in this revolutionary field.

In the end, newbits.ai embodies a simple truth: that the future of artificial intelligence belongs not to a select few, but to everyone who dares to learn, to explore, and to imagine. Through educational content, community engagement, and comprehensive resources, the mission of demystifying AI continues, making the complex simple and the cutting edge accessible. After all, in this rapidly evolving landscape, every bit of knowledge counts, but none more so than the new bits that light the way forward.

GIL OREN

OUR NAME: NEWBITS.AI

Names tell stories. They carry meaning, purpose, and vision. In the realm of artificial intelligence, where complex concepts meet practical applications, a name must bridge the gap between technical precision and accessible understanding. The story of newbits.ai begins with this bridge, connecting the foundational elements of digital technology with the transformative potential of human learning.

At the heart of every digital innovation lies a fundamental unit of information: the bit. This binary digit, capable of being either zero or one, forms the foundation of our name and reflects our mission in the world of artificial intelligence. To understand newbits.ai is to understand how the smallest unit of digital information scales to enable the vast possibilities of modern computing and artificial intelligence.

A bit, in its simplest form, acts like a tiny switch, either off or on. When eight bits come together, they form a byte, capable of representing a single character like a letter or number. As bits and bytes combine, they create progressively larger units that power the digital world we interact with every day:

Unit	Approximate Value	Real-World Example
Bit	Single binary value (0 or 1)	The smallest piece of data in computing
Byte	8 bits	A single character (e.g. 'A' or '5')
Kilobyte	1,024 bytes	A text document, simple email, or basic app
Megabyte	1,024 kilobytes	A high-resolution photo, MP3 song, or standard mobile app
Gigabyte	1,024 megabytes	A movie, complex app, or smartphone storage capacity
Terabyte	1,024 gigabytes	External hard drive, large data backups, or server storage
Petabyte	1,024 terabytes	Data centers, cloud storage providers, or large-scale AI datasets
Exabyte	1,024 petabytes	Total data generated globally in a year
Zettabyte	1,024 exabytes	Global data storage capacity
Yottabyte	1,024 zettabytes	Theoretical future data scale

In daily life, these units manifest in familiar ways. A simple text file or short email might occupy a few kilobytes. A high-quality photo, MP3 song, or standard mobile app typically requires several megabytes. Movies, complex applications, and smartphone storage capacities are measured in gigabytes. Large storage devices like external hard drives often hold terabytes of data. Data centers and major cloud providers work with petabytes, while units like exabytes, zettabytes, and yottabytes represent the immense scale of global data storage and future possibilities.

In terms of data transmission, these units determine the speed at which information travels across networks, measured in bits per second (bps). Internet speeds, typically measured in megabits per second, reflect how quickly data can be downloaded or uploaded, directly affecting everything from streaming videos to downloading applications.

The name newbits.ai carries this symbolism in each of its elements. "New" represents the constant evolution and innovation in artificial intelligence, acknowledging that yesterday's cutting edge becomes tomorrow's foundation. "Bits" holds dual significance, representing both the fundamental units of digital information and the incremental pieces of knowledge that accumulate to create understanding. The ".ai" domain extension definitively anchors our identity in artificial intelligence, declaring our dedicated focus on this transformative field.

Just as bits scale from simple binary values to the massive datasets that power modern artificial intelligence, newbits.ai scales from fundamental concepts to advanced applications. Through the *AI Solutions* Marketplace, each tool and platform represents countless bits working in harmony. In the *AI Hub*, every shared insight adds new bits of knowledge to our collective understanding. The *AI Ed* podcast series and *AI Glossary* transform complex concepts into accessible bits of learning, while this book trilogy guides readers through their journey from basic bits to breakthrough insights.

This scalability of bits, from foundational elements to complex systems, embodies the accessibility championed by newbits.ai. The phrase coined by the author, "It's all about the bits, especially the new bits," echoes through every aspect of artificial intelligence, celebrating both the technical foundation of digital innovation and the journey of continuous learning that defines the AI frontier. Each new bit of knowledge, like each binary digit in a computer system, builds upon what came before, creating ever greater possibilities for understanding, innovation, and discovery.

From the smallest bit to the largest dataset, from the first step into artificial intelligence to mastery of advanced concepts, the name newbits.ai captures the essence of digital evolution and perpetual learning in this revolutionary field.

EXTENDED DEDICATIONS

I dedicate this book to my friends, my chosen family. Your unwavering support, shared laughter, and heartfelt conversations have been a constant source of strength and joy in my life. Together, we've navigated the highs and lows, each moment enriched by your presence.

To Jon, for providing a second home, a place where I can always go and feel completely at ease. Moments spent with you and your family are always enjoyable, filled with warmth and friendship.

To RP, for always offering profound perspective and insight, unparalleled wisdom, genius, and unwavering support and friendship. You are far more than a brother-in-law. You are a true brother and an irreplaceable part of my life.

To Shay, whose lunches are key ingredients in my happiness. Sharing ideas and discussing family and the world with you brings me joy and perspective.

To Tony, for your incredible wisdom and for teaching me the balance of work and play. Our late-night phone calls debating world issues and battling in chess have sharpened my mind and enriched my spirit.

To those not mentioned here by name, you know who you are, and your influence endures, reminding me how truly fortunate I am.

Thank you for being the family I've had the privilege of riding with and for making this journey extraordinary.

ABOUT THE AUTHOR

Gil Oren is a business strategist, critical thinker, and serial entrepreneur whose passion for artificial intelligence inspired the *NewBits AI Trilogy*. With over two decades of experience tackling complex business challenges, he offers unique insights into understanding and navigating cutting-edge AI technology.

A pioneer in the chemical industry, Gil established research and development standards for proprietary and globally patented solutions that were safer for users and the environment while still delivering superior performance and cost savings. He partnered and collaborated with nation-states and nonprofit organizations in certifying and registering sustainable products, receiving the distinguished U.S. Environmental Protection Agency's Safer Detergent Stewardship Initiative Award. This commitment to ethical and responsible innovation now shapes his approach to artificial intelligence, where he champions "AI for Good" and "Responsible AI Development" at the forefront of technological advancement.

His multidisciplinary expertise spans law, real estate development, private equity, intellectual property, research and development, manufacturing, marketing, distribution, sales, and sustainability. This diverse background enables him to relate advanced AI concepts effectively across various industries, bridging the gap between emerging technologies and practical applications.

For over 15 years, Gil led a global chemical industry organization operating across the Americas, Europe, Australia, the Middle East, and Asia. Collaborating with startups, Fortune 100 companies, nation-states, and armed forces, he gained deep insights into global business dynamics and technology implementation at the highest levels of innovation.

An accomplished speaker and advocate for sustainable and innovative technologies, Gil has appeared on Fox News, NPR, the Discovery Channel, and QVC, promoting transformative solutions aligned with ethical standards and societal benefits. His ability to communicate complex ideas to diverse audiences underscores his dedication to making the frontier of technology accessible and ethically grounded.

Serving as an Executive Chairman, Board Member, and licensed attorney in the State of Florida and the District of Columbia, Gil brings a profound understanding of strategic technology implementation, governance, and regulatory aspects of adopting cutting-edge technologies. This combination strengthens his ability to guide others through the complexities of advanced AI integration in business and society.

Driven by a mission to empower individuals and organizations, Gil focuses on demystifying advanced AI tools and concepts, enabling others to engage responsibly with the evolving AI landscape. His dedication to ethical development and leveraging AI for the greater good is at the core of his work.

When not exploring the frontiers of artificial intelligence, Gil enjoys spending time with family and friends, playing piano and guitar, and following collegiate and professional sports.

He firmly believes that relationships and teamwork are fundamental to achieving success in life and in business.